The Christian Writer's Handbook

The Christian Writer's Handbook

New Revised Edition

MARGARET J. ANDERSON

1817

HARPER & ROW, PUBLISHERS, San Francisco
Cambridge, Hagerstown, New York, Philadelphia
London, Mexico City, São Paulo, Sydney

ACKNOWLEDGMENTS

Grateful acknowledgment is made to the following for permission to include various materials in this book:

Ruth Cox Anderson, for her poem "Puddles"; Bethany Fellowship, Inc., for extracts from *Happy Moments with God*, by Margaret Anderson, copyright © 1962 by Margaret Anderson, published by Bethany Fellowship, Inc., Minneapolis, Minnesota 55438; Carol Gift Page, for suggestions of novels; David C. Cook Publishing Co., for *The Quiet Hour* devotionals of January 13, 1969, and January 14, 1969, reprinted from *Sunday Digest*, copyright © 1969 by the David C. Cook Publishing Co., Elgin, Illinois, and used by permission; Covenant Press, for "The Home-going" by Helga Skogsbergh, from *Songs of Pilgrimage*, copyright © 1962 by Covenant Press and used by permission; The Billy Graham Evangelistic Association for "Film Take," by Morris Anderson, copyright © 1970 by the Billy Graham Evangelistic Association, and for "Give Me a Drum," by Charles A. Waugaman, copyright © 1967 by the Billy Graham Evangelistic Association; Jerry Jenkins, for suggestions of novels; Lois Leurgans, for her poem "Haiku"; the *Moody Monthly*, for extracts from "The Voice of the Arctic"; *Presbyterian Life*, for "The Prodigal's Father" by Joan Truitt, copyright © 1962 by *Presbyterian Life*, used by permission; Tyndale House Publishers and Joseph Bayly, for extracts from "A Psalm on the death of an 18-year-old son," from *Psalms of My Life* by Joseph Bayly, copyright © 1969 by Tyndale House Publishers; *Writer's Digest* and Judson Jerome for extracts from "Poetry, How and Why," by Judson Jerome, copyright © by *Writer's Digest*; "The Love Chapter Revised" originally appeared in *Christian Herald* magazine; John Knapp II, for background information about *Pillar of Pepper and Other Nursery Rhymes*.

Library of Congress Cataloging in Publication Data

Anderson, Margaret J.
THE CHRISTIAN WRITER'S HANDBOOK

Bibliography: p.
Includes index.
1. Christian literature—Authorship—Handbooks, manuals, etc.
I. Title.
BR44.A5   1983   808.02   82-48917
ISBN 0-06-060195-7

Contents

Contents

Part 5: Curriculum

Part 6: Church Outreach

Part 7: Short Stories

Part 8: Books

Part 9: Drama

Part 10: The Business End of Writing

Part 11: The Challenge

Preface

The average person is a curious soul. He reads as subconsciously as he breathes. And because he does, politicians, educators, philosophers, revolutionaries—whoever—vie with each other striving to capture his reading time.

How does a writer who is a Christian fit into this picture? Surely he should have some of that time. Where many writers admonish, "Look at life from my perspective," the Christian writer challenges, "Look at life from God's perspective." Anyone can express concern about the pollution of our world. The Christian goes a step further. He writes about the pollution of man's heart and mind as well. He's concerned about Christian sensitivity, commitment, and spiritual growth, too.

And strange as it may seem, people are ready and willing to listen. Alongside of ecology, war, Women's Liberation, and the gross national product, religion has wide appeal. Jesus is news! Who would have believed a few decades ago that a Christian conversion story such as Adela Rogers St. Johns' *Tell No Man* would make the best-seller list and stay there for so many months? Consider, too, the world-wide circulation of books by Norman Vincent Peale, E. Stanley Jones, Francis A. Schaeffer, Billy Graham, Catherine Marshall, and Ken Taylor, whose *Living Bible* now outsells all other books of its kind.

That these people have learned to extend their witness through writing should be a challenge to all Christians who want to write. Such success didn't just happen, however. Somewhere, at some time, these individuals learned how to write.

Can writing be learned? I believe it can. But people who

believe they are special recipients of God-given inspirations, yet ignore study and a writing apprenticeship, do exist. It is they who clutter editorial offices with hopelessly amateurish manuscripts that demean Christian journalism.

On the other hand certain individuals utilize tools and techniques more ably than others and in that sense may be said to own a gift for writing. For them talent seems an inherent part of their makeup.

Nevertheless, good craftsmanship coupled with a great deal of perspiration is more likely to assure publication. Though this is true of all forms of writing, this book deals only with the varied short forms prepared for publication. I think of its premise as wrapped up in Psalm 45:1: "My heart is inditing a good matter: I speak of the things which I have made touching the king: My tongue is the pen of a ready writer."* I take the liberty to paraphrase: "My typewriter is the tongue of a ready writer."

Ready? Yes, availably ready.

Willing? Of course.

But *prepared* as well.

*Scripture quotations in this volume are from the King James Version.

1

The Preliminaries

1. On Your Mark

When a certain young man assumed his duties as editor of a Christian publication he learned that a first responsibility involved employing a secretary, preferably a Christian. A young woman applied for the position. He hired her.

Too late, he realized he had a problem. If this girl knew the meaning of the words *typing speed* and *accuracy*, she didn't let it be known. Filing assumed hide-and-seek connotations. One can readily understand her employer's relief when she moved out of state a few months later. In searching for a replacement for her, he immediately shuffled his list of job qualifications. Skill topped the list.

A good secretary, a good writer—it all adds up to the same thing. For just as there are no skills designated as Christian shorthand, typing, and filing, so there are no writing skills known as Christian techniques. Rules don't vary with beliefs.

Furthermore, Christians do not become proficient simply because they pray for inspiration and enlightenment. Just as a baker uses different methods to create pie, cake, cookies, or bread, a writer uses varied procedures to create different forms of literature. The finished product will vary in appeal according to the creative genius of the creator. Regardless, each writer needs to go through an apprenticeship, learning rules which through years of trial-and-error testing have so often proved successful that competent writers do not ignore them.

Some people scoff at rule restrictions. I recall hearing a successful author say she had never studied writing. In the next breath she advised her listeners to analyze the work of professional writers to discover reasons for their success. She might as well have said, "to discover the techniques they use."

I learned the value of writing rules one day in a short-story class I attended. "You have to work harder," the instructor told me.

"How?" I wanted to shout. A competent writer herself, she seemed unable to communicate the rules she had learned. Nevertheless her comment challenged me to search for and master pertinent writing techniques, a continuing adventure for me.

In sharing my own and others' experiences I hope to help those of you who wish to travel the road to publication. Here are some general suggestions to aid you in launching your writing career.

1. *Don't let age deter you.* Young people, remember the Apostle Paul told Timothy not to let anyone belittle his youth. It's true you do not possess the maturity and wisdom experience provides, yet you do understand and empathize with your peers. I know a young man who, after mastering the techniques of good fiction writing, earned his way through college and seminary by writing stories for the church-school papers. Benjamin Franklin wrote *Poor Richard's Almanac* when he was twenty-six years old. Charles Dickens was twenty-four when he began his *Pickwick Papers.* A year later *Oliver Twist* began to appear in serial form; others rapidly followed.

On the other hand, maturity does have decided advantages. Life bestows all kinds of joy, disappointment, and sorrow. And because a person has lived, listened, and learned for a longer period of time, concepts and ideas about which he writes may be significantly more meaningful. At eighty, Tennyson wrote "Crossing the Bar." Justice Holmes wrote brilliant opinions at ninety.

2. *Cherish personal relationships.* Don't be a person who merely lives in a house by the side of the road; be also the man who joins life's parade. In contacts with other people be a sponge, constantly soaking up impressions, reactions, and new ideas. Observe settings; listen to people's conversations; mentally file observations for future use. And constantly broaden acquaintanceships. Learn to know people from many fields of

work, from other countries and other cultures.

Before long you will want the fellowship of other writers with whom you can talk writing shop. If there isn't a writers' fellowship in your community, start one.

In Minneapolis, Minnesota, a Christian writers' organization was born when two Minnesota authors met at a writers' conference in Chicago. "There must be other Christian writers in our area," they said. "Let's find them." They did, and organized what is now known as the Minnesota Christian Writers' Guild because of the area it covers. In the intervening years members of this fellowship have moved to other parts of the country, where they have helped organize similar Christian writers' organizations.

Besides holding monthly meetings, some groups break up into smaller critique units of five or six members who get together to read and appraise each other's manuscripts. None is a self-admiration society. Criticism is directed toward meaningful, straight-from-the-shoulder writing appraisal and encouragement.

3. *Read*. Read current as well as classic literature. Read for content as well as technique. Read the Bible. This book must not remain closed if you expect to proclaim its message and profit from its strong, spare language. Read the news, too. Read a wide variety of books and periodicals. You need to know what is going on in the world.

4. *Keep some kind of notebook or idea file*. Memory is a tricky thing. To be sure you keep intact what you see, hear, or read, jot down ideas, facts, bits of dialogue; quotes, titles, descriptions of people, settings. Then when you hit a dry spell in your writing you will have the perfect tool with which to prime your creative pump.

Phyllis Whitney, who is primarily a fiction writer, says she keeps four different kinds of notebooks. One is a plot book in which she sets down sentence plot ideas. The second contains significant quotes; the third, random thoughts—observations, conversations, and characterizations. The fourth records alphabetical lists of first and last names, American and foreign, male and female.

5. *Be alert to publishing trends.* This means trends in the choice of subject matter as well as in technique. An editor expects a manuscript to be currently relevant.

As is true of secular publications, religious periodicals sometimes cease publication. Some of them merge to cut publication costs. You must know which do which.

Increasingly, work is done on assignment. Writers who have proved their worth are asked to write to meet editorial deadlines. Do not let this policy perturb you. Beginners can get assignments, too. They can research an idea, write a query, and —depending on appeal—receive an editor's green light for an on-speculation submission.

Though most adult religious publications use little fiction, the church-school papers constantly need skillfully written short stories.

For the most part payment is better than it has been. While this is true, it is also true that editors demand better writing. And right on the heels of greater excellence comes increased competition.

In writing remember that, though facts never go out of style, feelings make the best-seller lists. It's all a matter of "spiritual take-away," one editor says. "Press harder, go deeper, feel!" is the cry. Toscanini knew this. When he wanted something special from his orchestra he held his baton still and crooked his finger over his heart. "Feel!" he was saying.

6. *Raise your sensory antenna.* .The difference between the artist and the amateur is in part the ability of the former to project meaningful imagery in writing that appeals to the senses. To achieve such skill you must experience your environment. You must be conscious always of how things look, sound, taste, smell, and feel. Store impressions you receive in your subconscious. Better, record them in your resource notebook.

Even realtors have become aware of sensory impressions. They advise clients to schedule appointments so that buyers are met at the door by soft music and the aroma of baking bread.

7. *Know and empathize with your reader*. A clergyman friend told me of an experience he had when beginning a new ministry in a certain church. He preached, he said, yet he felt he did not reach his parish as he ought. So one weekday he went to the church alone. Instead of stepping into the pulpit he moved around, sitting first in one pew and then in another. Each change of location represented a change of personality. Empathetically he became the man or woman who customarily sat where he sat. Then he asked himself, "What would I want to hear from my pastor? What needs do I want him to meet?"

This fits the assessment of "the man of the cloth being caught up in the burlap of experience." A writer has no less obligation to his readers.

The head does not hear unless the heart listens. So, visualize your reader, get under his skin. Ask yourself, "If I were he, would I need to hear this? Would it entice my interest or would it bore me?"

8. *Discipline your life*. Writing is a matter of planned neglect. You choose to bypass certain tasks so you can spend time at your typewriter. To learn to write you must write, write, then re-write. Write something every day. Set deadlines for yourself. Learn to use remnants of time. You will be surprised how quickly they add up to written words on a page.

Widowed during depression years, a Minnesota author knew she would have to make a living for herself and her children. Not wanting to leave the children in someone else's care, she decided to learn how to write. As proficiency increased she set deadlines for herself. The first week of every month she wrote five children's stories, 500 to 800 words in length. The second week, two junior stories, 1800 words in length. The third week she wrote two articles. A love story for young people occupied her time the fourth week. Is it any wonder that this woman was still writing professionally when she was in her eighties?

Discipline also means that you strive for excellence. One day I chided a student about a carelessly written newspaper column. "You aren't practicing what I teach," I told him.

"I know," the boy answered. "I dash those things off in a matter of minutes."

I countered by quoting Christ: "He who is faithful in that which is least. . . ." (Luke 16:10)

I know there will be times when you will come up with such a significant idea or expression you'll be tempted to hoard it, to save it for that masterpiece you are going to write some day. Don't do it. Here's where discipline raises its head again. "Give and you shall receive," seems to be a mysterious law of the universe. It's like the cruse of oil that belonged to the widow of Zarephath. The oil was replenished as long as she gave.

And as soon as you have finished and mailed your manuscript to a suitable market, forget it. Begin immediately to work on something else. Before long you will have several pieces in the mail. If rejections come, study them carefully. A criticism which appears repeatedly may mean you should revise your script.

9. *Weigh specialization against versatility*. Most teachers of writing say, "Specialize." And for some people this is advisable. One person may become a proficient fiction writer; someone else may write nothing but articles. Others will select a particular area of interest, say health, and write in that field continually.

Personally I believe that one who writes for the religious press should be as versatile as possible. If you learn to write many types of articles as well as fiction about a wide variety of subjects, you will broaden your market horizons.

10. *Write simply*. Write in what is called "talk language." Avoid the long impressive word that does little more than puff your ego. Hunt instead for the word that is precisely apt. Even though you use a thesaurus or a synonym-finder, check your dictionary for exact meanings of words. Many words which have similar meanings are not interchangeable.

Refrain from using stilted scholarly language which scans poorly and shrouds meanings. Let simplicity be your cue. An introduction to this book could say, "A disposition toward insistence upon the exercise of proficiency in craftsmanship and clarity of expression prompted the personal compilation of this book." In effect I wrote, "This book is written to help you learn to write effectively."

Recently I heard an editor say, "The more simply you write, the more people you will reach."

11. *Learn how to prepare a professional-looking manuscript.* Always use a typewriter and write on only one side of the paper. Double-space. Leave wide margins. Use good bond paper; no. 16 weight saves postage. Type your name and address in the upper left-hand corner of the first page. Directly below list your social security number. Type approximate word count, to the nearest hundred, in the upper right-hand corner. If you use pica type you will type approximately 250 words per page; if elite, 300 words. Place and center the title, which is capitalized, one third down from the top of the page. Skip a space and type the name which you wish the editor to use as your by-line.

At the top of the second and each successive page type the title of your manuscript, your name, and the page number. You need not write the word *More* at the bottom of each page or *End* when you conclude your typescript.

Always retain a carbon copy of your work and an accurate record of your marketing attempts. Enclose a stamped, self-addressed envelope for the manuscript's return should it be rejected.

12. *Don't be afraid to let your bias show.* Pamela Frankau, a Catholic and a writer, asks, "Does an Englishman hesitate to write freely about his countrymen? Or a loyal American? Or a loyal Frenchman?" A Catholic writer, she says, sets out with his faith as much a part of him as his nose—"it is impossible to hide altogether the part of my nature that is my belief."[1]

In showing your bias, guard against personal prejudice. You will not want to offend readers who do not share your faith.

Above all, stay prayerfully tuned to God. A good writer renews himself spiritually every day.

CHALLENGE ASSIGNMENT

1. Make a list of subjects you think young people could handle effectively.

2. Make a list of subjects a more mature individual should write about.

3. Choose the types of notebooks you believe would be most useful to you. Begin now to use them.

4. List titles of recent articles and short stories which you feel gave you a "spiritual lift." Identify periodical, publication date, and page number.

5. Decide now what time you will set aside for writing each day.

6. Prepare the first page of a pretend manuscript. You might include the details of preparing a manuscript as your first-page information.

7. Describe the inside of a cave, a haunted house, a bakery, or a dilapidated automobile. Include sensory detail.

2. Finders, Keepers

A Minnesota farmer bought a farm which had been owned by bachelor brothers, one of them deceased. While renovating the house, the new owner came upon jar after jar filled with hundred, five-hundred and thousand-dollar bills—thirty-six thousand dollars in all. The deceased brother, who did not believe in banks, had secretly stashed the money between walls and under the eaves of the home.

"What a haul!" people exclaimed when they heard the news. A haul? For the bachelor who outlived his brother, yes, according to law. The purchaser received only a minimal reward.

The exact opposite is true of writing ideas. Stashed everywhere they belong to you, the finder, if you want to keep them. I emphasize *want*, because once an idea has been discovered it must be carefully evaluated. It is retained or discarded depending on its development potential.

Where should you look for idea gold? In your own life, first of all. Ask:

1. What are my educational qualifications?
2. In what areas do I have special knowledge?
3. What am I most vitally interested in?
4. What roles has life imposed on me?
5. What skills do I have?
6. What settings do I know and like well enough to write about?
7. What problems have I faced or am I likely to face?

Profitable idea mining depends on how deeply you probe. So take your time. Constantly remind yourself that surface gold may be fool's gold. To illustrate this introspective probing I refer you to some subsurface digging done by students enrolled in a class geared to writing for the religious press.

A retired minister-missionary said he was interested in

religion	cooking
Bible customs	chess
archeology	travel
gifts of the Spirit	reading
Christ's return	missionary trends
mechanics	social responsibility
gardening	the aged
music	hunting and fishing

This man's interests led him to write an article explaining the seeming discrepancies in Matthew and John's timing of Jesus' crucifixion. He also wrote a devotional article using a dramatic experience connected with his escape from Chinese Communists to point up God's miraculous intervention in his life.

A young pharmacist said she either is or has been a

daughter	chorister	chemistry tutor
"little sister"	violinist	intern pharmacist
single woman	secretary	pharmacist
clerk	youth counselor	Girl Scout

She could write about sibling rivalry. Having been a chemistry tutor qualifies her for writing an article which would show how chemistry students could tutor their way through college. Further, she might write an article defending her single status.

A church youth coordinator said her skills involved

acting	programing
dramatic reading	storytelling
singing	writing

public speaking	interior decorating
sewing	antiques

She has written a number of religious plays. She plans a book detailing party and program plans and procedures. Many of the monologues she has written could be published as chapters in a book.

A middle-aged man said he has held jobs as a

baby-sitter	bill collector
hospital employee	secretary
bookkeeper	camp counselor
chauffeur	office manager

He might consider writing a teenage adventure story in which the lead character solves a mystery because he, the baby-sitter, knew clues no one else knew.

A young mother confessed to the following problems:

a mentally unstable parent	family discord
racial prejudice	divorce
dyslexia (a mental-visual disability)	job security
	loneliness
miscarriage	death

She could write any number of articles about family problems: how to resolve family discord; what to do if your husband leaves you; how to prepare children to cope with death.

Many of the students who included spiritual concerns in their list of problems could write realistically about doubt, fear of death, release from guilt, envy, prejudice.

A nurse indicated familiarity with the following settings, any one of which she could utilize in her writing:

cattle ranch	Switzerland
mother-lode country	medium-sized town
San Francisco	airplane
ocean liner	train
peach country	redwood country
Paris	Lake Tahoe

Now look beyond yourself. Appraise encounters with

fellow workmen	missionaries
clergymen	neighbors
doctors	editors
nurses	businessmen
teachers	children
relatives	teenagers
politicians	handicapped persons

Note their problems, interests, and skills. Suppose a neighbor invents a new mechanical device of some kind. Interview the man, take some pictures, and write a story about the invention.

A St. Paul, Minnesota, writer taught an adult Bible class in the main sanctuary of her church. Her husband noticed that she had difficulty handling her Bible and teaching notes. Because an ordinary stand would not fit between the pews, the man designed a fold-away lectern which, when opened, fastened securely to the back of the pew—an excellent idea for a sure-sale "how-to" article.

Ideas you may wish to pursue can be found by studying the characteristics of individuals in various age groups. A psychologist's analysis chart which details these characteristics is included in the Appendix.

As you study particular characteristics you will become aware of the problems and needs of both old and young. At a national writers' conference a woman who worked with the aged spoke about their problems, interests, and needs. At the close of her lecture she distributed mimeographed sheets on which she had listed a couple of dozen article ideas which she believed editors were looking for.

In another session Lawrence E. Nelson, former Redlands University professor, alerted his listeners to the vast number of articles ripe and ready to be picked from the Sears, Roebuck and Co. catalog, from books about boats and ships, from volumes which detail the history of coins and stamps. His speech, which he called "Acres of Articles," is recorded in the book,

Techniques of Christian Writing, published by The Judson Press.[1]

Newspapers and magazines are good sources of ideas, too. Read them with scissors in your hand. Then file items you clip, always indicating the source and date of the material, remembering they are not to be plagiarized but to be used as idea stimulaters.

Listen to the radio, watch television, take notes when your minister speaks. Investigate library resources. One author says he would never be able to meet the monthly deadline for the column he writes if he didn't spend at least one afternoon a week in the public library. There he scans technical and scholarly journals as well as newspapers and mass-circulation magazines for ideas he can use.

A Midwest author who read a news item about a high-school senior who had spent a summer as a carpenter's helper on a mission station in the Malagasy Republic decided to interview the boy. After securing additional information about the venture, she wrote an article and sold it to the youth's denominational church-school paper.

A television interview alerted another author to a quit-smoking device which she investigated and wrote about in an article for an adult publication.

A news release informed me of a forthcoming appearance in Chicago by Annie Vallotton, illustrator for *Good News for Modern Man.* I wrote the woman's sponsor, the American Bible Society, who published this New Testament, and asked if an interview could be arranged so I could meet the artist either before or after the scheduled meeting. The interview was arranged and the article written and placed, on a simultaneous-submission basis, with several publications whose editors wanted their readers to know Miss Vallotton.

In testing ideas be sure you evaluate your interest in them. If you are completely captivated by a particular subject you can be relatively sure your reader will be. If the idea doesn't grab you, forget it. Your bias will show. And since there are so many ideas about which you can write, why waste time on one which doesn't interest you or lacks a spiritual impact? With each year that passes I realize more fully that I must be more discriminating about what I write.

One writer explained how she was awakened to this challenge. "I'm a new Christian," she told me. "And I'm having a problem. I've been writing Gothic murder mysteries with considerable success. Recently I hit a snag in my plot. I called a friend and asked for help. When she wasn't able to come up with a solution, I said, 'Well, I can always kill off the secretary!'

"At that precise moment my daughter walked into the room. Shocked, she stopped in her tracks. Her eyes saucered. When I hung up she said, 'Mother, shouldn't you be writing about God?' "

When you find an idea you want to pursue, test its market value. Will anyone else be interested in it? Does it have universal appeal? Check the *Reader's Guide to Periodical Literature* in your public library to see if the subject has been used before. If it has, can you come up with a fresh approach, an entirely new angle? Ask yourself, too, if it is timely. Subjects currently in the news can and should be explored in a Christian context.

An article of mine titled "If Senility Strikes"[2] apparently has universal appeal. Published first in *Together* magazine, it reached a million subscribers and many additional readers. After reprint rights were assigned to me, I placed it in several other publications. This enlarged readership easily matched the original.

Determine, further, whether or not the idea is within your range of knowledge or research ability. Though it is advisable to write from experience, don't be afraid to tackle a subject about which you have little knowledge. Just be sure you know where to secure the information you need to handle the idea adequately.

Once one of my favorite authors, Elizabeth Yates, was asked to write a story about UNICEF (the United Nations International Children's Emergency Fund).[3] At the time, she said, she knew very little about UNICEF or the countries to which it gives help. To make matters worse, her writing deadline allowed no time for travel. She did not refuse the assignment, however. In a matter of days she had secured travel films of these countries. She viewed the films until she felt she had actually visited them. She also read everything she could find about UNICEF.

Her story involved a boy who traveled with an aunt visiting areas assisted by UNICEF, and when it was published she was delighted with its ring of authenticity. She had still more reason to be pleased when a neighbor accosted her in a grocery store a few weeks after the book came off the press.

"I see you've been traveling again," the woman said. "I don't suppose you had time for any lengthy correspondence but you could have sent me a postcard from one of those countries you visited."

In a further appraisal of your idea's potential, you will check it for seasonal value. Material appropriate to holidays and special anniversaries is always in demand: Thanksgiving, Easter, Advent, Christmas; birthdays of public leaders, anniversaries of world events. Your library has books which list dates of the latter.

Check also to see whether your idea might be used in a series of articles. An interest in reading led to the writing of a series about how to choose a book, how to care for a book, maximum book enjoyment, books as gifts.

At one time I interviewed a clergyman-ventriloquist and wrote an article about the man and his work. I also wrote a short story about a teenager who found direction in a personal problem when he listened to one of the skits used by the ventriloquist and his dummy. Then I came up with a personal experience article from the dummy's viewpoint. Later I did further research and did a piece telling young people how they could become ventriloquists.

In other instances you may get maximum mileage by using a single idea in a poem, a play, and/or a quiz as well as in an article or short story.

I properly rebuked myself for neglecting these considerations the day an editor sent me a children's skit based on a story

I had written and sold to her. Had I practiced what I teach, I would have written and submitted the skit together with the story.

So you see it's really up to you. Finders are keepers when it comes to mining writing gold.

CHALLENGE ASSIGNMENT

1. Probe your own life. Make a detailed list of each of the following:

educational qualifications	jobs held
life roles	settings you know
skills	problems you face
interests	or are likely to face

2. Make a list of ten ideas the above information suggests.

3. Read your daily newspaper. Clip items you feel you would like to research and write about.

4. Study the letters to the editor in one of your favorite publications. Indicate a recurrent subject readers express an interest in.

5. Read all the articles and short stories in a current mass-circulation magazine. Which do you think grabbed the author?

6. Choose the three articles you liked best. Try to imagine where each idea originated.

3. *Sales Incentive*

A young businessman set out to sell a product his partner had invented. A willing, persistent individual, he put all he had into the venture. Yet when he checked in at home base at the end of the week he had little to show for his efforts.

Sympathetic, his partner tried to cushion the blow.

"Don't feel so badly," he said. "Maybe you aren't cut out to sell."

"Now, wait a minute!" the man countered. "I was selling—folks just weren't buying."

Though we may regret the man's lack of sales, we can commend him for his marketing attempts. Many authors aren't as diligent. They forget their work is only half-finished when a manuscript is completed.

Lesley Conger, columnist for *The Writer* magazine, informs writers that she knows no editor who goes around prowling through would-be writers' desk drawers looking for unpublished manuscripts. If a person possesses talent and a couple of finished manuscripts, she says, the first step toward success may be in the direction of the post office.

No one can dispute the validity of this statement. Yet there is a step you must take before you make that trip to the post office. It involves finding a suitable market for the manuscript—a consideration which should be taken into account even before the manuscript is written.

Failure on the part of the young businessman to locate suitable markets before he hit the road may have been the reason for his lack of selling success. It need not be yours. Religious periodicals provide varied sales opportunities. Increasingly, too, other publications welcome religiously oriented material, especially if it relates to special anniversaries and holidays.

Profiles of important churchmen and stories about oratorios and anthems, composers of religious music, the Christmas crèche, and church decorations have appeared in mass-circulation holiday issues. One of the large women's magazines once described family expenditures of a Christian family of five who made provision for church giving and entertaining in their annual budget.

To locate names and addresses of suitable religious markets, you should begin by checking your own denominational publications. Ask your pastor for a list of periodicals that come to your church. These will include church-school papers for each age level and an official church organ, as well as special administration, instruction, devotional, and guidance publications. If you check with Christian education personnel you may locate surplus copies you can study. Now visit other churches in your community. Ask for sample copies from their surplus stock of publications.

Study also the two most popular writers' magazines: *The Writer* (8 Arlington Street, Boston, Mass., 02116) and *Writer's Digest* (9933 Alliance Road, Cincinnati, Oh., 45242). Periodically they give attention to religious markets, including names and addresses of nondenominational as well as denominational periodicals.

Check, too, books that detail religious market needs. *Writer's Market* and its paperback supplement, the *Writer's Yearbook* are helpful (9933 Alliance Road, Cincinnati, Ohio, 45242). More specific, though not annually updated, is the *Christian Writer's Handbook and Market Guide* (Christian Writer's Institute, Gundersen Drive and Schmale Road, Wheaton, Ill., 60187).

From these market lists you may choose other publications that interest you. Write for sample copies and for brochures which spell out specific editorial requirements. You will, of course, enclose money to cover handling and mailing charges —fifty cents should suffice.

A simple request will do: "Please send me a sample copy (or

copies) of your publication(s) together with whatever writing-instruction brochures you may have. Thank you."

As soon as you have accumulated a number of periodicals, determine which appeal to you most. To do this, study the table of contents first. Ask: Could I have written any of these pieces? Could I produce similar articles or short stories? If you believe you could, take a second look at the periodical. Read a number of past issues from cover to cover. Note what is said in the editorials. They will give you a fairly good idea of the editor's opinion on a number of subjects. If any is different from yours, you may surmise he will not be interested in receiving an article from your point of view. Yet if he is editing a controversial magazine, he may welcome what you write.

Study the magazine also to learn what type of material is published. The articles, short stories, and fillers used indicate its range of interests; the relevance of its contents to current problems; whether or not controversial subjects are considered; the needs and interests of readers; and editorial taboos.

In the "Letters to the Editor" section you will discover reader reaction to what has been published. Some readers may suggest topics they would like to read about, a good cue for you.

Advertisements reveal the age as well as the economic and educational status of the reader.

No study of a publication is complete, however, until you determine the length of material used. You can estimate length by counting two or three 100-word sections. Note the space each takes. Now place a check after each corresponding 100-word-unit space. Count units and multiply by 100.

To illustrate the effectiveness of such thorough study of periodicals I refer you to an acquaintance who attended a writing class while serving a prison sentence. After reading the Bible several times, as well as some 120 religious volumes in the prison chaplain's library, he sent for samples of every publication he could locate. Before long he was submitting and selling a wide range of material. He pursued a writing career when he was released.

"He's one of the most prolific writers in the field," an editor said. "He knows the religious markets better than I do."

So that you may become as familiar with markets as this man, I refer you to the market analysis chart on page 22.

Complete a separate analysis sheet for each publication. Then arrange them alphabetically in a loose-leaf notebook, adding additional information you glean when you begin writing for the publication—or, if you wish, transfer this knowledge to a card market file.

A personal contact with editors can also assist you in learning publication needs. Where do you meet these people? Try attending writers' conferences where editors are scheduled to speak; occasionally visit editorial offices. I say occasionally, because an editor has little time for chitchat with beginners. Once you have achieved a reputation as a competent writer, however, the editor will welcome you, particularly if you bring with you a list of usable article or short story ideas.

I have learned to know many editors through letters we have exchanged and through rejections on which they have made specific comments. On the whole, editors of religious publications are exceedingly helpful. Occasionally they suggest specific revisions or an alternate market. In some instances they point out faults writers should strive to overcome.

Don't bypass writer friends in your search for market sources and market trends. Good rapport with other writers means you share marketing news. At times when I have been unable to take a particular assignment I have referred an editor to a friend who could. As often I have been the recipient of such consideration.

You may be wondering if all this attention to marketing is really necessary. But how else will you learn whether what you write fits a particular market? And fit it must. For example, *Decision* magazine, which strives to influence readers to make personal commitments to Jesus Christ, wouldn't be interested in a how-to article about Sunday-school procedures.

Some publications—*Eternity* magazine for one—publish controversial material. *Christianity Today* and *The Christian Century* use theological material of a scholarly nature.

Periodical Analysis Chart

Name of publication _____

Denominational or nondenominational _____

Publication frequency _____

Editor's name _____

Address _____

Type of periodical _____

Purpose of periodical_____

_____

Reader's age, economic and educational status _____

_____

	Type	*Subject Matter*	*Length*
Articles			
Fillers			
Fiction			
Columns			

Rights purchased_____ Payment _____

Taboos _____

Comments _____

_____

The *Leader Guidebook*, the *Adult Bible Teacher*, *Success*, and *Learning With* look for articles of help to Sunday-school teachers and church administrators.

Other publications (*Scope*, the American Lutheran women's magazine, is one) work on a monthly theme basis. Everything that appears in a given month is centered around the theme assigned to that month. In slanting your material to this market it's important that you know what themes are used when.

Taboos must also be considered. Every periodical has its own list of taboo policies. You are aware, I am sure, that most religious publications do not permit the use of profane language. Nor do they want prissy, goody-goody, unrealistic submissions.

Dancing, smoking, drinking, the movies, and gambling are taboos with many editors. Some refuse to print anything about church leaders and organizations whose doctrines differ from theirs.

As a rule, editors try not to offend their advertisers. They are careful, too, not to demean a particular region, segment of society, or race of people.

Be aware, however, that taboos change. Today many editors encourage authors to write about subjects they used to shun: divorce, homosexuality, promiscuity, abortion, rape, intermarriage. Each would, of course, have to be handled in a Christian context. Study specific publications and author-guidance brochures so that you can keep abreast of current editorial policies.

Time must also be considered in a manuscript's submission. Many periodicals work as much as a year ahead of publication; others no less than six months. All seasonal material should be submitted nine months to a year prior to publication.

Once you hit upon an idea you believe is marketable in a particular magazine, you have two options. You may write the article and send it in, or you may contact the editor by mail asking if he is interested in the subject. This is called a query letter.

In such a letter you strive to present your idea in so favorable a light that the editor will urge, "Do write it." At least you hope he will.

You do have a problem if you are a beginning writer, however. Most editors are reluctant to make a writing assignment without a knowledge of your writing ability. "That's like buying a car from a sales brochure," one editor says. This is understandable. A completed manuscript best proves your writing ability.

Yet we often hear professional writers say, "I never submit a manuscript without first having queried an editor about it." The time will come when you, too, will feel a query letter is a necessary marketing step. If for no other reason, it will save you a lot of preliminary work. You should consider a query letter when

1. The market is limited.
2. A proposed manuscript requires a great deal of research you do not want to do unless some editor expresses an interest.
3. An idea is so timely that you can expect competition in pursuing it.
4. You need specific writing direction.
5. Expense is an important factor.

Ordinarily you will not query an editor about

1. Fiction (an editor prefers seeing a completed short story).
2. Short pieces which take no more time to read than a query letter.
3. Material you believe intuitively several editors would appreciate seeing.

In affirming his magazine's preference for query letters, a *Reader's Digest* editor provided this direction:

Do bone up on the *Digest* before sending us an article suggestion. You'd be surprised at the number of manuscripts we receive which do nothing more than prove the author hasn't read the *Digest* for years.

If, after checking the *Reader's Guide to Periodical Literature*, you are sure we haven't handled the subject before, by all means send us a letter of two or three pages. We'll check it out for content appeal.

We'll also make sure that one of our editors hasn't assigned the subject to some other writer. Then if we like the idea, and this is your first submission to us, we may ask you to give it a speculative try.

But, if you have already written a piece you feel we would like, send it in. Or if you are going to write it anyway, let us see it. There have been instances where first submission won publication when a query letter about the article may have failed to raise any response.[1]

A query letter should be short (some editors say seldom over a page in length). Briefly give the gist of your article. Tell why you feel capable of handling your subject, what kinds of anecdotes and documentation you plan to use. Include your lead if you feel it is especially significant. If research is important, indicate source. Also indicate whether you can supply pictures.

State your willingness to submit the manuscript on speculation, and always enclose a stamped, self-addressed envelope for the editor's reply.

Below you will find sample query letters, two of which won approval the first time out. If possible, always address the editor by name.

Dear Mr. Baldwin:

Do you know that a unique athletic competition, referred to in *Runner's World Magazine* as "The Other Olympics," was held in West Germany at the same time as the International Olympic competitions?

Called the "World Veteran's Meet," it utilized some of the same judging officials the international competitions used.

I am personally acquainted with a man, 44 years old, who is a member of what is known as the *United States Master's Team,* a group that has held track championship events for men over forty for the past five years.

He participated in the "World Veteran's Meet" (track and field events) and won a bronze medal in pole vaulting.

A Christian, my subject has found his interest in sports has led to innumerable opportunities to share his experiences with youth. I believe I can handle this material in about 1500 words. Would you like to see an article about this man? Enclosed is a stamped, self-addressed envelope for your reply.

Sincerely,

Dear Mr. Wilson:

Would you be interested in a 2000-word article titled, "God's Horoscope," which would stress the fallacy of reliance on astrology for personal guidance, then shift to proving the reliability of God's guidance in a person's life? I would share incidents where God intervened in as well as directed my life.

I plan to begin the article telling how a friend, who wears a gold-chain pendant shaped like a fish, is often stopped and asked if she was born under the sign of Pisces. This gives her an opportunity to reply, "Yes, I was. But that's not why I wear this pendant. I don't live by man's horoscope. I live by God's horoscope. Like the early Christians, who adopted the fish as a symbol of their faith, I wear this pendant to show that God is sovereign in my life, too."

I've enclosed a stamped, self-addressed envelope for your reply.

Sincerely,

Dear Mr. Morrow:

One of the most unforgettable women I have met is a pretty, wrinkled, over-seventy granny who finds steady employment as an advertising model.

Always in demand, she has accumulated all sorts of paraphernalia from the past—old-fashioned shoes, button gloves, shawls, sailor hats, innumerable rimless glasses—which heighten the Americana image she portrays in so many ads.

Working through the Eleanor Moore model agency, she is one of the most sought-after models in the area. Dressed in a granny nightie and nightcap she did a series of TV comedy advertisements for a hospital equipment firm. She appears frequently in bank ads. One ad shows her maneuvering a motorcycle. She also models for an artist who does religious calendars.

My subject has made her own living since she was a teenager. She has taught speech, worked in radio, and now when most people her age prefer the rocking chair, she's achieving success in a new venture. Would you be interested in an article about her? On speculation, of course.

I would title this article "This Could Be You" to show how opportunities for this type of work are available to anyone, regardless of color, age, or beauty.

I am enclosing a stamped, self-addressed envelope for the convenience of your reply.

Sincerely,

"If it's that much work, why bother?" a man once asked. "Why don't some of you more knowledgeable people try selling our manuscripts for us? For a fee, of course."

I still recall the laughter with which this comment was greeted. An agent, for the religious markets? Not likely, unless marketing involves book placement. An agent sells manuscripts on a commission basis, usually 10 percent of sales. If an article sells for $15, $25, or $75 after several trips out, the agent would receive $1.50, $2.50, or $7.50, depending on the sale—less than a pittance for the time and postage involved. And what if the manuscript isn't salable? What if it needs revision? Then the agent becomes a teacher of writing.

This does not mean a writer cannot attain the stature that qualifies him for an agent. It's well to remember, however, that an agent seeks a client because he has proven his writing ability in consistent market performance. He must regularly produce top-notch material to make it worth any agent's time to handle his work.

Except for subsidiary rights, a writer can usually do as well as an agent. Elizabeth Yates, who has produced quality work consistently through many years, has never felt she needed an agent.

Don't be lured by agents who charge for their services, or by the so-called "vanity" book publishers who offer to publish your book for a price, usually several thousand dollars. They promise much—promotion, instant popularity, the works—but deliver little.

I recall hearing such a publisher defend his tactics. "Why shouldn't we publish a book, no matter how poor, if the author can afford to pay for it?" the man asked. "We give this man a chance at immortality."

Yet in spite of what I have said, there are times when an author may be justified in paying someone else to print his work. Such instances involve specialized information which can hope to attract only a limited number of readers. When a book of such nature is at stake, the author should arrange for the printing. A well-established printing firm can do the same job as well as a subsidy publisher, and far less expensively.

No matter where you offer your work, be sure it is as neat and free from errors as possible. Harry Emerson Fosdick's book editor praised him for his immaculate submissions. "His manuscripts came to me in such letter-perfect condition they went directly to the printer."

Besides being personally rewarding, such excellence pays dividends in personal esteem as well as in sales.

CHALLENGE ASSIGNMENT

1. Visit local churches. Ask for samples of their church-school papers. Or ask relatives and friends for religious magazines they have discarded. Study several issues of a particular paper or magazine.

2. Using the periodical analysis chart, evaluate five different publications.

3. Choose an interesting article from one of the magazines. Pretend you are the author. Write a query letter asking the editor if he would be interested in the article you plan to write.

4. Proof Texts

When revival fires swept across Scandinavia in the middle of the nineteenth century, people began to study the Bible in their search for truth. If questions arose, they challenged each other by asking, "Where is it written?" In other words, "What is your proof text?"

A similar challenge ought to confront all of us who write. We should be able, through research, to verify whatever message we proclaim.

We have already learned that locating writing ideas requires research. This is essential, too, in checking the accuracy of data, in updating our knowledge of subjects that interest us, and in locating proof texts—human interest stories, statistics, dates, and quotes—which will enhance and authenticate our writing. Occasionally we understand a subject so well that we can write about it without further research. These instances are the exception rather than the rule, however. Even the most familiar subject can be updated and enlivened by further study.

Dr. Roland E. Wolseley, for many years a Syracuse University professor of journalism, constantly urged writers to research systematically and thoroughly. "Don't rely on the accuracy of another writer's research," he said. "Whenever possible go to the original source of information."

The longer you write, the more convinced you will be that such advice has merit. You will find innumerable inaccuracies and contradictions which continue to be perpetuated because writers do not go to the original source to validate information.

In speaking of the amount of research needed for a particular project, Dr. Wolseley advised, "Research until data begins to repeat itself."

You may record research notes on 3" × 5" cards. Or you may use any ordinary piece of paper. Then you can transfer the notes you wish to preserve to cards or to a notebook file at some later date. Again I emphasize the need to record the date and source of every proof text you locate.

After your article has been accepted, be sure you retain your research notes. Keep them intact for several months after publication. A reader may wish to know where you secured your information, or he may challenge something you have said. This is why a record of date and source is so important.

A reader once wrote me asking for proof that the man I had quoted in a particular article actually made the statement. Because I had kept my research notes, I could, by referring to date and page of a particular publication, prove the accuracy of the quotation.

At another time an editor wrote saying she recalled having seen an article I had written about a certain man. "We'd like to introduce him to our readers," she said. "Could you come up with a different angle we could use?" With research notes intact I gladly accepted this assignment.

It's well to remember, too, that you need not copy research material verbatim unless you want to quote a precise statement. Whenever possible rewrite in your own words the information you need. Since facts cannot be copyrighted, you may use them freely provided you do not plagiarize another person's explicit wording or comments about them.

The easiest sort of article to assemble is usually shunned by discriminating periodicals. I refer to the "library job": the dull, lifeless collection of facts that lacks human interest appeal.

Most writers produce such a piece at one time or another. When they do, they earn a rejection that says, "Sounds like an encyclopedia version of the subject. Strive for human interest appeal."

You can acquire material of human interest appeal through

research in a variety of sources—books, newspapers, magazines, journals, government documents, public relations personnel, and personal interviews. Again, research until information begins to repeat itself.

If you are serious about producing meaningful, well-documented writing, you should begin to assemble a home library so that information you need frequently can be located quickly. Since no one can choose for another, I merely suggest materials which I have found helpful in my writing.

The first selection provides Biblical information which you, a Christian, will want to have immediately available.

The Bible
A Bible dictionary
Bible commentaries
A Bible concordance
A Bible atlas
Books dealing with Bible customs

Manners and Customs in Bible Lands
by Fred H. Wight
Everyday Life in Old Testament Times
by E. W. Heaton
Everyday Life in New Testament Times
by A. C. Bouquet
Daily Life in the Time of Jesus
by Henri Daniel-Rops

Religious periodicals
Poetry anthologies
Religious biographies
Books about Bible doctrine
Religious books by favorite authors

C. S. Lewis
E. Stanley Jones
Paul S. Rees
Paul Tournier
Norman Vincent Peale

Francis Schaeffer
Hannah Smith
Elizabeth O'Connor
Charles Allen, clergyman and author
Sherwood E. Wirt

Another list might include writing aids.

A good dictionary

> *Webster's New Collegiate Dictionary,* Eighth Edition
> *Webster's New International Dictionary*
> Funk and Wagnall's *New Collegiate Standard Dictionary*
> Also *Roget's Thesaurus*

A good elementary grammar
A rhyming dictionary

> *The Complete Rhyming Dictionary and Poet's
> Craft Book* edited by Clement Wood

A set of encyclopedias

> *Britannica*
> *Americana*
> *World Book*
> *Collier's*

A world almanac (inexpensive paperback editions are published annually)

Style manuals

> *The Elements of Style* by William Strunk, Jr. and E. B. White
> *A Dictionary of Modern English Usage* by Henry Watson Fowler
> *The Careful Writer* by Theodore M. Bernstein
> *The Art of Readable Writing* by Rudolph Flesch
> *United States Government Printing Office Style Manual* (Abridged)
> *A Manual of Style,* published by University of Chicago Press
> *The Technique of Clear Writing* by Robert Gunning
> *A Dictionary of Contemporary American Usage* by Bergen Evans and Cornelia Evans

Writing magazines

> *The Writer*
> *Writer's Digest*

Market aids

Writer's Market
Writer's Yearbook
Christian Writer's Handbook and Market Guide

Books about writing. (It's well to read each book carefully, to test its value to you personally before you make your purchase.) Investigate books by

George L. Bird	Foster-Harris
Walter S. Campbell	Phyllis A. Whitney
Roland E. Wolseley	Lee Wyndham
Harry Neal	Jane Fitz-Randolph
Paul W. Kearney	Robert C. Meredith and
Lajos Egri	John D. Fitzgerald
Laurence Perrine	Writer-conference anthologies
Richard Armour	from The Judson Press
Duane Newcomb	

As a writer you will depend on the public library for most of your resource material. Because this is true you will need to learn where different types of material can be found in the library. Why not tour the premises some day soon? It's advisable, too, to cultivate the friendship of specific librarians who take pride in helping you locate information you need.

Most libraries permit a limited amount of research to be dispensed by telephone. You may resort to this service when time is at a premium. Do not abuse the privilege, however.

I am continually amazed at the willingness of research personnel who go a third and fourth mile in assisting where they can. I recall an instance when a young man became so interested in a particular project that he hunted until after midnight one night for the source of a quotation both he and the writer believed should be credited to Alexander Pope.

The public library's reference department contains material which cannot be taken from the library. The circulation department, on the other hand, permits books to be taken home for a specific period of time. In many of the great university and seminary libraries borrowing may involve temporary membership arrangements and a substantial fee.

In addition to general works, many libraries also provide information of local interest. This resource is called a "vertical file." It contains clippings from newspapers and magazines, reports from local government agencies, pamphlets, city and state laws, which are filed upright in folders, by subject, in appropriate drawers.

The *Reader's Guide to Periodical Literature* indexes by title, author, and subject the articles that appear in major magazines each year.

The *New York Times' Index* alerts researchers to newspaper articles which have appeared in *Times*.

If you have difficulty finding a book about a particular subject you may check the *Cumulative Book Index* or the *Book Review Digest*, which contains brief descriptions and excerpts of new books.

For biographical research you may look in any one of the many *Who's Who* books and biographical dictionaries in the library.

The library also contains several sets of encyclopedias, books about famous firsts, and books that detail important anniversaries and holidays.

When you wish to locate a particular book go to the library's card catalog, which contains 3″ × 5″ cards filed alphabetically in tiered drawers by author, title, and subject matter. Most libraries use the Dewey decimal system of shelf placement. The general divisions, which are minutely subdivided, are:

000 Generalities (encyclopedias, newspapers, etc.)
100 Philosophy and related disciplines
200 Religion
300 The social sciences
400 Language
500 Pure science
600 Technology (applied sciences)
700 The arts
800 Literature
900 General geography and history (including travel and biography)

A veritable gold mine of pertinent subject matter may be obtained by writing to the Superintendent of Documents, U.S. Government Printing Office, Washington, D.C., 20404, for a monthly catalog of valuable documents.

In handling a specific assignment you may need to contact individuals in various departments of the government, also state travel and information bureaus as well as public relations personnel, most of whom generously share information in their field of knowledge.

You will also want to approach denominational leaders as well as missionary boards to obtain specific information you need.

Let's be realistic about locating proof texts which enhance and authenticate our writing. Since we can't possibly know everything, it's important that we know where specific information can be found. Because this is true you may wish to refer to this chapter frequently.

CHALLENGE ASSIGNMENT

1. Check your home library. Make a list of books you feel you will someday want to own.

2. Visit your public library. Draw a floor plan indicating the location of various types of material it holds.

3. Choose a subject you think you would like to write about. Check the *Reader's Guide to Periodical Literature* to see what articles have been written on the subject in the last two years. How would you approach the subject differently?

4. Examine the 800 (Dewey decimal) section of your library. What are the numbers and subject matter covered in the subdivisions of this particular division?

5. Disciplines of Style

Most beginning writers think of style as something elusive which they must consciously pursue. Not so. Style as it pertains to writing expresses personality. It assumes its individual distinctiveness as you, the writer, mature.

Style is patience, too. A good writer brakes initial flow when necessary. He stops and waits until he can sort out a precise message and decide how to express it most meaningfully, with clarity, vigor, and ease. Then he may shift into high gear and write as spontaneously and rapidly as possible.

Such facility doesn't just happen, however. It comes with *knowledgeable* practice. Practice alone won't do. True, no one can learn to write without writing, but blind repetition of weak, colorless words, monotonous sentence structure, and inept transitions serves only to perpetuate, not eliminate, these faults.

To achieve clear, vigorous writing one begins by understanding there are certain *do* and *don't* directions that govern word, sentence, and transition choice.

Verbs

Select verbs carefully. Be miserly in use of the various forms of the verb "to be" (is, was, are, were, etc.). This is not always possible; sometimes this verb must be employed simply because nothing else sounds right. It is used, too, when you wish to create a reflective mood.

The Lord is my shepherd . . . (Ps. 23:1)
A good name is rather to be chosen . . . (Prov. 22:1)

The longest journey is the journey inwards. . . .—Dag Hammarskjöld
God is and all is well.—John Greenleaf Whittier

When you grope for a substitute for a "to be" verb, try replacing it with one of the following assertion verbs:

appears	implies
becomes	instills
consists	involves
constitutes	resembles
embraces	shapes
enhances	simulates
establishes	substitutes
exists	supports
fulfills	upholds
gives	undergirds
holds	

For greater intensity and force, however, depend chiefly on vibrant, dynamic verbs which Rudolph Flesch calls "kicking" verbs.

> face *eroded* by years
> gray eyes *smoldered*
> Daniel *purposed* in his heart
> He *grouched* around.
> She *stormed* out of the room.
> He *stabbed* at his typewriter keys.

Sports writers are especially adept in choosing such verbs.

> Indians *scalp* their opponents . . .
> Oakland *mauls* Atlanta.
> The ballpark *rocked* as he circled the bases.
> A good player does not only rise to the occasion, he *soars*.

Figures of Speech

Know when and how to use figures of speech effectively. Sparingly employed, they add spice to a piece of writing if they are creatively conceived.

A *simile* is a figure of speech by which one thing is likened or compared to another. It is identified by use of the words *as* and *like*. The overuse of certain similes have made them cliché taboos which should be avoided.

> sly as a fox
> alike as peas in a pod
> like taking milk from a baby
> slow as molasses in January

Try to create fresh, original expressions.

> freeway like huge concrete pretzels
> as crammed with answers as a computer
> Like a rabbit's, her lips nervously nibbled each other.
> as spontaneous as your heat bill
> chic as a hippie

A *metaphor* is a word or phrase which literally identifies one idea or object as another to suggest likeness or analogy between them. It says one thing *is* another, not *like* or *as*.

> A mountain of strength, he . . .
> God's promises are everlasting anchorages.
> The Christian faith is not so much life insurance for the future as it is an annuity for the present.

Shun mixed connotations. Note the coherence of the figures in the second paragraph of this chapter: *"brakes, stops, and waits; shifts into high gear."* These are related, congruent metaphors. Not so, "A storm of protest nipped in the bud."

Personification is a figure of speech which attributes human qualities to inanimate objects or abstract ideas.

> October *danced* barefoot . . .
> The fog spread *dripping fingers* across our valley.

Appeal to the Senses

Onomatopoeia is a figure of speech which involves the use of words which imitate natural sounds:

tinkle of a bell	motorcycle *sputtered*
buzz of a saw	signal *beeped*
hiss of a serpent	car *honked* through traffic
snowmobile *snarled*	sparrows *chirp*

In appealing to the senses use words that paint pictures:

eyebrows *yo-yo* angrily	fewer *missiles,* more *mistletoe*
a *sweater*-cool morning	a *snowballing* rumor
courts *handcuff* the policeman	

You also paint pictures (of characters, setting, and action) through careful selection of intimate detail as told from a specific point of view. Note the detail in this excerpt from a story set in the early 1900s.

Apprehensively Kris moved closer to the large, sunbonneted woman driving the dappled mare. . . .

Warily he headed for the big farm kitchen. The smell of fresh-baked bread met him at the door.

It was a square, log-paneled room. A black over-sized range stood against one wall. The heavy oak table, covered with a red and white checkered tablecloth, filled the center of the room. Beneath one of the two high rectangular windows stood a washstand and pump.

Kris smiled as he looked at the rough board floor that had been scrubbed bone-white. A nice house, he thought.[1]

Anachronisms

Avoid falling into anachronisms. This is writing which attributes to one time or period of history something that belongs in another. One author did this when she had a story character dial a number before the invention of the dial telephone.

Tautology

Shun tautology, redundancy involving needless repetition of words that have the same meaning:

biography of his life	audible to the ear
new beginners	universally by all

new innovation   shattered to pieces

important essentials   fellow playmates

Specific Meanings

Choose nouns, adverbs, and adjectives which identify the specific meaning you wish to convey. Note the difference in vividness in the following alternatives.

food/pancakes   few/five

meat/country-style short ribs   many/five thousand

operation/appendectomy   long ago/last fall

sky/flaming sunset   fall/September

someday/Christmas Day   child/boy in blue suit

In this same context, let's consider words which have similar meanings but are not interchangeable.

eager – anxious   arbitrate – mediate

anticipate – expect   denote – connote

climax – culmination   excuse – pardon

imply – infer   less – fewer

allusion – illusion   famous – notorious

affect – effect   common – familiar

farther – further   pleasure – joy

incapable – unable   similar – analogous

defective – deficient

For further assistance in choice of words, I recommend that you study the style manuals cited in chapter 4.

Word Divisions

If you have room at the end of a line for one or more syllables, but not for the entire word, then separate words

1. According to pronunciation:

democ-racy   cur-few

be-little   dooms-day

re-pent   indict-ment

center-piece   abortion-ist

   (or cen-terpiece)   (or abor-tionist)

lazy-bones	lock-smith
knowl-edge	arith-metic

2. After a vowel unless the rule regarding pronunciation applies:

ceme-tery	liga-ment
pre-cept	Christi-anity
reli-gious	diso-bey

3. Between double letters, unless the line ends with such simple words as pulling, puffy, buggy:

aber-ration	refer-ring
cor-rode	dif-fuse

Other rules for word division may be seen in the Chicago *Manual of Style*, pp. 132–38, derived mainly from the third unabridged Webster. But latest authority (according to Merriam-Webster editors) lies with the *Eighth Collegiate* edition.

Never divide so that a single letter stands alone. Some words cannot be divided:

able	enough	ocean
again	idea	omit
elect	irony	usurp

Specialized Terms or Jargon

If common religious terms are unfamiliar to your reader you may need to explain or rephrase them.

I recall the time when a woman was asked if she had been saved. "Let's see," she answered. "Yes, I remember being in an automobile accident once. The car overturned, but I was saved." Thus a reference to conversion might conceivably prompt an ecologist to spell out procedures involved in the recycling of glass containers.

There may be times when you want your readers to understand such words as *justification, Communion, conversion, redemption, Second Coming, eschatology.* Their introduction parallels the use of unfamiliar scientific and technical terms one wants a reader to understand. In his book, *Writing Non-Fiction*, Walter Campbell suggests presenting an unfamiliar term in such a way that its meaning is clear in the context in which it is used, or by explaining the meaning. He also advises using the word again two or three times in the next few paragraphs, so that it is clearly understood and easily identifiable. Be careful, however, lest you substitute some other jargon in your attempt to make meanings clear.

Aware of the new emphasis in the Catholic Church on the need for a personal encounter with Jesus Christ, I was pleased recently to read some Catholic literature in which the author, assuming reader ignorance, explained such an experience. Though he didn't use "Protestant" terminology, I understood that he was writing about a conversion experience.

Sentence Length

As a rule subject matter determines sentence length and complexity. Technical, reportorial, and contemplative writing demands longer sentences than other material. When action is involved, remember that long sentences slow pace; short sentences speed pace. Nevertheless, variation is recommended. Too many short sentences make staccato reading. Sentences in *Time* and *Reader's Digest* are varied, yet they average eighteen words.

Sentence Structure

Be sure you understand basic grammar. Dip into style manuals (and a grammar if necessary) to hone down your awareness of what is correct, but don't be overawed by rules. It's much better just to keep deepening your *feel* of the language.

Such books may not always agree in details of style, but there are basic rules regarding what one either *must* or *can't* do. Get hold of these, gradually, as firmly as possible.

Most of us make recurrent small grammatical errors. Catch these, as if they were trash fish, by spreading a net for them. Since such faults belong to us alone, we may not be aware of them. Pay careful attention, therefore, to any small habits of incorrectness that may turn up when your work is offered for criticism, for these haunt even competent writers. Pursue them until you understand what's involved, then carefully comb and groom your writing to be sure you don't leave such errors in it. Above all, don't let them frighten you. Good writing isn't guided only by rules. Language is a living thing, and you must spin it out of your own sense of life.

On the whole, sentences should be expressed positively instead of negatively. Wrong: He did not believe we should avoid the study of the book of *Revelation*. Right: He believed we should study of the book of *Revelation*.

For clarity and reading ease be consistent in the way you arrange parallelisms. Wrong: He was in charge of purchasing, supervision, and he was expected to expand sales coverage. Right: He was in charge of purchasing, supervision, and expansion of sales. Or: She was concerned about her home, her church, and her community.

Blessed is the man that walketh not in the counsel of the ungodly, nor standeth in the way of sinners, nor sitteth in the seat of the scornful. (Ps. 1:1)

The law of the Lord is perfect, converting the soul; the testimony of the Lord is sure, making wise the simple. The statutes of the Lord are right . . . . (Ps. 19:7–8)

Feel—Act—Speak

Prepare your reader for dialogue by prefacing it with the emotion and action of the speaker.

Suzie trembled with rage. She moved toward him. "You have no right to imply such a thing," she flung at him.

Horrified she watched his stealthy approach. She stifled a scream. "Mr. McGreggor," she cried, "what are you doing here?"

Jay shrugged. He appreciated John's old-fashioned ideas about loyalty, but what could he do? His hands were tied. "She's not expendable, John," he said.

Transitions

Learn to use transitions skillfully.

Whenever I deplane at San Francisco International Airport I must travel across the San Mateo Bridge to reach my home. The bridge makes smooth logical transfer from peninsula to mainland possible.

In writing we need bridges, too—transitions to carry the reader from one train of thought, one period of time, one place, one emotion, one viewpoint to another. A good writer aims to make these gear changes as smooth as the automatic transmission on his car.

Editors agree that the absence of good transitions constitutes one of the most glaring faults of the novice. Underscoring this conviction, one editor compared a good article to a chain where each paragraph so significantly links with the one that follows that removal would ruin the unity of the piece. In praising an article's unity another editor said, "It tracks."

In studying transitions, learn professional techniques which simplify your choice. You can

1. Make use of common connectives which as a rule indicate an immediate change or note a repetition linking up some earlier element. The following, listed with initial capital, are often used to open a sentence, but may also be found between commas (with lower-case) in the midst of one:

Meanwhile	Again
To repeat	Nevertheless
To illustrate	On the other hand
Today	Consequently
Therefore	Besides
Finally	Equally radical
Furthermore	Paradoxically

2. Overlap paragraphs. Use a word or several words as a common denominator to link two paragraphs.

"All these paintings" refers back to *paintings* mentioned in the previous paragraph.

The statement in one paragraph that "preliminary sketches were made from *photographs of models*" is echoed at the beginning of the next by "Sanden prefers to work with *professional models.*"

"Why?" she asked.

"Why?" he shot back. "You ought to know *why.*"

"I'm beginning to understand the importance of *your* job."

"Not *mine,* God's."

"keeps the *association's* financial wheels . . ."

"As *its* executive vice president . . ."

3. Use a symbol or gimmick to hold the larger segments of an article or story together. Recall how Anne Morrow Lindbergh used the phrases of the marriage ceremony as connecting links in her book, *Dearly Beloved.*

In an article about former Federal Judge Luther Youngdahl, then governor of Minnesota, I wanted to show how, because he is a Christian, his actions expressed his faith. I compared his hands to Christ's—I spoke of the governor's firm hands, of his loving hands, of his restraining hands.[2]

In another article a handicapped woman's struggle to attain success was likened to the climbing of a ladder. Each rung of the ladder represented a step of progress.

Calendar dates clarified the time sequence in one story of Dr. Paul Carlson's capture and martyrdom in Africa.

An adventurous life may resemble the turning of a kaleidoscope. Each turn a new surprise.

4. Connect article ideas through the use of questions. Questions helped link areas of involvement of the Billy Graham Evangelistic Association in an article I wrote about George Wilson, the association's executive vice president and business manager. I used questions, too, to unite segments of an article about Dr. Elving Anderson, a research scientist with the Dight Institute of Genetics at the University of Minnesota.[3] Here are some of them:

"I sense you are not pleased when genetic control is spoken of as manipulation. Why?"

"Before we get into a discussion of genetic control, will you tell me what made you decide to become a geneticist?"

"In layman's language, what is meant by human genetics?"

At this point Dr. Anderson spoke of other types of behavior conditioned by genes. The question that followed was simply, "For instance?"

"Can genetic disorders be corrected?"

"Is it possible to change the makeup of genes?"

Any of the above techniques may be used for specific transitions of time, locale, mood, character change, and viewpoint. In the following instances, note how transitions in each category are used effectively.

TIME

Two years later . . .

Later . . .

After preliminary sketches were made . . .

Today we ought to . . .

In the future I would advise . . .

The next spring planting took precedence . . .

LOCALE

Back at school, John looked for . . .

When he reached his father's office . . .

At the post office the next morning . . .

Once on the plane . . .

MOOD

Still boiling inside, Barkas snapped on the light.

When he awakened Jimmy forgot the gloom of yesterday.

She smiled sweetly, wondering how she could ever have been angry with him.

He greeted her cordially, but when she mentioned Phil he froze.

CHARACTER CHANGE

The Helen I knew had been a petite, gentle person. Before me stood a fat, slovenly woman who chewed gum with gusto.

I didn't recognize him. His hair had turned white. His shoulders stooped. Where and when had he lost the zest of youth?

Usually soft-spoken and mild-mannered, once at the podium he raged . . .

VIEWPOINT CHANGE

In nonfiction as elsewhere there are times when it is necessary to indicate a change of perspective—that is, of the viewpoint from which the topic or narrative is seen. In the article about George Wilson, I quoted Billy Graham's appraisal of the man.[4]

The next paragraph began: "Apparently Billy Graham isn't the only person who thinks highly of this man. Two colleges have honored him . . ."

In an article about two young nurses who responded to a plea for assistance in the Auca polio epidemic,[5] one of the girls thinks, "Whom can I get to go with me?" The next paragraph begins: "The first person who came to her mind was a Turlock High School classmate, Gayle Johnson. In San Francisco she too was between jobs."

A good transition never delays an idea, it pushes it forward. When transitions are expertly executed the reader will scarcely be aware that he has been taken from one place, one time, or one mood to another.

No doubt you have traveled over a good many bumpy bridges. Occasionally, however, you were scarcely aware you were on a bridge. So think of your reader as a passenger in your car. Build bridges where they are needed, but make them as smooth as you can.

Words, sentences, transitions—these are disciplines of style which, depending on how well they are used, determine whatever writing proficiency you achieve.

Your proficiency is your style. Like personality, it matures as you mature, for style is *you*.

CHALLENGE ASSIGNMENT

1. Examine a newspaper sports column as well as copies of *Sports Illustrated, Time* magazine, and *Boys' Life*. Make a list of strong verbs you find authors have used in writing for these publications.

2. Make a list of fresh similes, metaphors, and personifying figures of speech.

3. Make a list of picture-painting words you find in exploring several articles.

4. Without resorting to common religious jargon, explain what it means to be a Christian.

5. Check published articles and short stories for examples where emotion and action prepare the reader for dialogue.

6. Choose an interesting article. Underline all common connectives, as well as transitions which use the "paragraph-overlap" technique.

6. Writer Interaction

Those of us who write work alone, isolated from our colleagues. As a result we long for fellowship with persons with whom we can compare notes and enjoy a bit of creative "shop talk." I, for one, am glad there are several communication options that permit us to do this.

Writer's Conferences

One writer's magazine claims there are more than 200 conferences where writers can gather annually for instruction and inspiration. Held in different parts of the country, these conferences cover all types of secular and religious writing, with some specializing in a particular type—mystery, the short story, science fiction, the novel, juvenile writing, children's books, romances.

Writer's conferences give conferees the opportunity to meet with successful writers and book and periodical representatives. Lecture and workshop sessions teach skills, challenge, inspire, and help writers grow.

I have participated in conferences where each dining room table was assigned to a specific staff member or publication representative. Conferees were encouraged to take turns eating at these tables so they could meet and chat with professionals on a one-to-one basis. This book was born when Clayton Carlson, a Harper & Row representative, and I chatted together over the breakfast table at the Decision School of Writing in Minneapolis, Minnesota.

At such conferences leaders schedule workshops on practically

every phase of writing. Some designate certain sessions for beginners; others for more advanced conferees. For several years
the Decision School of Writing scheduled a "pro" session for
persons who had earned that status.

A few conferences allow pre-conference submissions of manuscripts conferees wish to have critiqued. These manuscripts are
sent to a select group of persons who evaluate them. Then con-
sultations are scheduled so author and evaluator can meet for a
brief period of time at the conference to discuss the critiqued
manuscript.

The May issues of the *Writer* and the *Writer's Digest* list dates
and locations of many of the writer's conferences held in this
country each year. *The Religious Marketplace* lists time schedules and locations of religious writing conferences. Check to see
which are held in your area.

Writer's Clubs

Several years ago I attended the Christian Writer's Institute
writer's conference in Chicago, Illinois. By chance I met Ronald
Keeler, a college English teacher who also lived in Minneapolis,
Minnesota, as I did. During our conversation Ron said, "There
must be other writers in our area. Wouldn't it be great if we
could meet for fellowship occasionally?"

"Why not?" I countered. "Let's go back and establish a writer's
organization."

We did. Once back in the Twin Cities we decided on a date
and a meeting place for our first get-together session. We sent
notices to local pastors, newspapers, and colleges.

Nine people attended that first meeting, at which time the
name, Twin City Christian Writer's Fellowship, was chosen.
Later, to accommodate persons living outside the Twin City area,
we changed the name to the Minnesota Christian Writer's Guild.
Today the guild has approximately 100 members. As many as
sixty of these people attend monthly meetings regularly.

If such an organization doesn't exist in your area, organize one.
Round up interested persons—beginners as well as pros. You

will profit greatly from the expertise of the latter group.

Once you have chosen a date and place of meeting, you will need to elect officers—a chairperson, a vice-chairperson, secretary, treasurer, publicity manager, etc.

Begin all meetings promptly with a short prayer and a roll call to which members may respond by giving their name and a *brief* report of sales, rejections, or special marketing news.

Programs may be planned to include:

1. *Guest speakers*. Periodical, book, and newspaper religion editors, professional authors, and television and radio personnel would all be good possibilities.
2. *A teaching session*. This could be on a subject interesting to all— marketing, the novel, interviewing, etc.
3. *A film*.
4. *Book reviews*. These should be specifically aimed at consideration of writing techniques.
5. *Book assignments*. One year the Minnesota Writer's Guild studied the *Art of Dramatic Writing* by Lajos Egri.[1] All members read the assigned chapter. Then they took turns leading monthly discussions that involved each chapter.
6. *Critique sessions*. If a membership is relatively small you may break up into groups and read and critique each other's manuscripts. In some instances, where groups are large, it may be necessary to pass a manuscript to the next person who, with pencil or pen, then proceeds to critique the manuscript received.

   If a writer's organization grows as they have in Minneapolis, Portland, San Jose, and San Diego, for instance, small groups may begin to meet in homes during the interim between regular sessions to accommodate persons in specific geographical locations.
7. *Panel discussions*.
8. *Demonstrations*. Possibly of the makeup of a children's book, the word processor, indexing procedures, records and files, and so on.

Small Group Critique Sessions

Critiquing is best done in groups of four or five participants. Groups may be organized to include persons on the same level of expertise. When all members are beginners it may be wise to hire a more knowledgeable person to sit in on the sessions and provide input. Occasionally a beginning writer may seek individualized help from a professional. In such instances the writer should be prepared to pay $10–$15 an hour for this assistance.

Members of critique groups should:

1. Be mutually dependable, hardworking individuals who take time to attend meetings regularly.
2. Earn the right to participate—read widely, be aware of what is happening in the world, write regularly, avoid being overly sensitive.
3. Strive for excellence; avoid allowing the group to become a self-admiration society.
4. Notify the leader when absence is necessary.

Further, as a critique group member you should:

1. Bring to the session a polished, well-researched, well-edited piece of writing—never a first draft.
2. Be prepared to answer questions regarding an outline of a book or article, ideas for a project, research resources, market possibilities.
3. Read so everyone can hear.
4. Come prepared to take criticism. Accept what is valid and beneficial; ignore questionable evaluations. Do not argue about a point with which you disagree.
5. Ask for further explanations if you don't understand an evaluation.
6. Listen attentively to each reader. Jot down comments you plan to make. Balance favorable with unfavorable. Present favorable comments first. ("Speak the truth in love.")
7. If you feel it is to the reader's advantage, suggest a different form, or a different approach. Explain why you feel as you do.
8. If you ask for an evaluation of a poem, it is wise to make duplicate copies for each person. Poetry is best critiqued when it is seen.

Critiquing by Mail

Perhaps you are thinking, "I don't know any writers in my area."

What about other areas? If you have attended a writer's conference you may have met persons in the same predicament as you. Don't be dismayed. Interaction with them is possible through the round-robin letter approach.

When some members of a Minneapolis, Minnesota, critique group to which I belonged moved, as I did, to other parts of the country, we felt great loss. "Couldn't we continue critiquing by mail?" I asked.

We could and we did. A round robin with five participants was born. It has been functioning well for a number of years.

A personal letter and a manuscript typed, double-spaced, on thin paper (to save postage) are sent on their round approximately once a month. Participants are asked to anticipate the "bird" and plan their schedules accordingly rather than dashing off a hurried critique the moment it arrives. However, we hold the "robin" no longer than four days.

Since all members are experienced writers we enclose material we feel is ready to market. We number each paragraph to simplify locating the area being criticized. We also include two extra pages (one a duplicate) on which we identify and type our comments. When we receive the robin we remove only one of the critique sheets so that persons who have not seen comments made by persons who follow them may be able to do so.

One-Day Writer's Workshops

One-day workshops may be planned and scheduled by an author or by a group of writers. Norman Rorher, founder of the Christian Writer's Guild, often schedules one-day workshops throughout the country for the benefit of his correspondence students.

A few years ago an Air Force chaplain I met at a West Coast writer's conference invited me to conduct a one-day writer's workshop at Beale Air Force Base near Marysville, California. In a series of lectures, using a variety of handouts, I tried to acquaint attendants with basic techniques, types of writing, and marketing procedures. Had these people been experienced writers, I may have been asked to speak in depth about a specific area of writing such as children's books, the novel, etc.

In both of the above instances one person assumed all teaching and lecturing responsibilities. In larger cities where attendance may be significantly greater, several persons, including editors and professional writers, may be asked to participate.

I am indebted to Ethel Herr, San Jose author, who has been involved in a Santa Clara Valley writer's workshop for several years, for providing information about their one-day seminar sessions.

"Advertising is of prime importance," Herr says. "We distribute brochures to libraries, bookstores, churches and to persons on the Mount Hermon Writer's Conference mailing list. We depend a great deal on word-of-mouth publicity, too."

At the first Santa Clara workshop 75 persons attended; now this number has grown to 125. A $10 fee is charged to pay for honorariums for special speakers and workshop leaders.

Speakers are chosen with a consideration of transportation costs, expertise and teaching ability. "We look for a variety in personalities, sex, and a balance between editors and writers," Herr says.

Workshops of this type require a facility with a large assembly room and adjacent rooms for workshop sessions. The Santa Clara sessions have been held in churches that have been able to accommodate them.

CHALLENGE ASSIGNMENT

1. Attend a local writer's group.
2. Seek out other writers with whom you can meet regularly to critique manuscripts.
3. Ask writers in your area to recommend a writer's conference you might attend. Make plans to attend.

2

Brief Forms

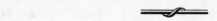

7.   Bits and Pieces

The quickest and easiest way for you to achieve publication is to try your hand at writing short items. Originally used to fill space at the bottom of a page or between articles and short stories, today these bits and pieces are often featured in special sections of the many periodicals whose pages they enliven.

Don't think, however, that because a filler is short it lacks significance. Many editors claim fillers of a page or less play a very important role in their publications. Persons who never get around to reading longer articles take time to scan short features. They read them while riding commuter trains and buses, or while waiting for the dentist or the doctor. They read them when they are tired and want to relax.

Usually a filler does not exceed five hundred words, though some editors place pieces up to a thousand in this category. Inspiration, commentary, and advice articles may be included in the latter length.

Because this type of writing provides apprenticeship training, many teachers urge their students to plunge into the filler field the moment they start writing. There are other reasons for this type of counsel.

1. You can write fillers in less time than longer pieces—anywhere, any time.
2. It's easy to learn how to write them.
3. You will never run out of markets. There's scarcely any periodical that doesn't use short items of one kind or another.
4. You already possess a great deal of knowledge you can use in writing fillers.

5. You know persons whose knowledge, experience, and skills you can tap for filler use.
6. You will find a vast number of filler ideas in the books, magazines, and newspapers you read.

Almost everything you do can be written as a filler. Cooking hints, teaching ideas, child-rearing advice, travel suggestions— all are likely subjects for you to pursue in the informal conversational style required in the writing of short items.

Each filler should be typed double-space on a separate sheet of paper. The reason is obvious: an editor can send them separately to staff members for their appraisal. And if he wishes to buy just one item of a group, he doesn't need to hold a page that has other material on it.

It's well not to send more than three or four fillers at a time to a particular editor. If you submit too many, he may think one who is so prolific isn't likely to maintain a high standard of excellence.

If an item is intended for a special feature page, send it to the editor of that page. If you don't know his name, simply type "(title of feature section) Editor" under the name of the publication. Under *Reader's Digest* for instance, you would type: "Life in These United States" Editor, or "Humor in Uniform" Editor.

When you plunge into the filler field, begin by studying many different types to learn how each is written. Don't let the fact that they are brief mislead you into thinking they can be dashed off in a few minutes' time. Good fillers are carefully planned and diligently polished before they are sent to market.

In your study, your first task will be to learn to identify the different types of fillers.

The Epigram

You may want to make your filler "debut" by writing just a sentence or two. An example of this type of filler is the epigram, a "bright witty thought, tersely and ingeniously expressed"— often a clever twisting of an old proverb or a play on words. It can be either prose or verse.

Before you lean on your own understanding, be sure it is strong
enough to support you.

Today is the tomorrow you either planned for or neglected yesterday.

If you intend to give someone a piece of your mind, make sure you
have a surplus to share.

In my Christian growth I often find that if I want to make progress
I need to stand still.

Quotations

Again just a sentence or two, short quotations may also be
used as fillers. Some editors glean those they use from other
publications. Others welcome free-lance contributions. History,
literature, speeches, advertisements, and interviews are good
sources for filler quotations. Used singly, they fill space at the
bottom of a page or between longer pieces. When used in a
group, they are usually given special placement space.

A group of quotations centered around a single theme is
called a survey filler. Publications use them most frequently
when they wish to call attention to a well-known person's birth
date, a special holiday, a historical observance, or some subject
of current interest.

If you check several periodicals around the time of Lincoln's
birthday, you will probably find survey fillers which quote him
on a variety of subjects. One that appeared in *Pentecostal Evangel* carried the title, "The President's Faith." The filler quoted
Lincoln himself and others, each of whom, in a brief paragraph,
commented on his religious faith.

You can prepare this type of quotation filler from living
sources by selecting a theme about which several persons could
make a brief statement: reverence for God; Christians in government; loyalty to country; love; incentives to success; devotion to the Bible; pet peeves; the book that interested me most
—the list is endless. Participants must, of course, be persons
vitally interested in the subject you choose.

After selecting participants, write them, describe the type of
statement you wish them to make, and tell them how you plan

to use it. Always include a stamped, self-addressed envelope for their reply. In submitting your survey filler to an editor, be sure each participant is given credit for the statement he made.

Hint and Advice Items

Brief, usually only a paragraph or two in length, hint and advice fillers begin with a topic sentence. This is followed by explanatory sentences which develop and detail the idea expressed. The last sentence clinches or confirms it.

Here you need to be a penny-pinching wordsmith. Spend words as you would money. Eliminate redundant, irrelevant, or unnecessary words. Avoid long words and technical terms. If you feel you must include a technical term, explain its meaning.

Note the progression in the following Sunday-school advice filler:

One way to give Sunday-school pupils personal attention is to remember them on their birthdays. Bake a cupcake for each child on the Sunday nearest his birthday. Decorate it and place a small candle on it. Display the cake either at the beginning or the end of the class period, and ask the rest of the children to sing a "Happy Birthday" song for the child being honored.

Most children like to take the cake home intact, without lighting the candle. However, should a child wish to light the candle, let him. Either way, because you have shown him this personal attention he will feel he is someone special.

Note that the first sentence pinpoints the idea, while the last sentence clinches it. The sentences in between logically explain procedure. There are no superfluous words. The piece is brief and to the point.

Now note this cooking hint:

You can poach eggs without having to worry about a messy-pan cleanup job. Place paper muffin-tin liners in the separate sections of your poaching pan. Break an egg into each paper liner. Season to taste and poach. When the eggs are done, remove them from the paper liners. They will be beautifully fluted. As important, you'll have no messy pan to clean.

Miscellaneous Facts

These brief informative items follow the same pattern as the hint and advice fillers: topic sentence, explanatory sentences, clinch ending. They may be written about a whole array of subjects, including travel, nature, animals, religious holidays, archeology, scientific discoveries, inventions, hymns, and art.

Taking his cue from Deuteronomy 8:9 and 1 Kings 7, Dr. Nelson Glueck, world-famed archeologist and Bible scholar, began to hunt for minerals in Israel.

In 1934 he excavated crumbled walls and furnaces blackened by copper slag a few miles south of the Dead Sea, indicating it had once been a copper-smelting site. Today the area is producing both iron and copper.[1]

Reading about the paths of the seas in Psalms 8:8 one day, Matthew Fontaine Maury, scientist who came to be known as "Pathfinder of the Seas," decided to investigate their existence. He found them and within a few years was able to chart the most significant ones, many of which are traveled by ocean-going vessels today.[2]

The Adaptation

A paraphrase is writing which rephrases another author's work yet retains the meaning of the text. An adaptation imitates form but alters details. If well done, adaptations can be marketed as fillers. The following example is an adaptation which imitates the style of 1 Corinthians 13:

If I teach with Harvard, Oxford, or Princeton skill and have not love, I am stalk and leaves, but never fruit.

If I parrot Scripture with verbatim ease and have not love I scatter crumbs; I do not share "bread."

Love mines knowledge with persistent zeal.

Love does not hoard what it has learned.

Love is not easily discouraged, never gives up.

Love is every-Sunday loyal.

Love inspires class rapport that invites counseling confidence.

Love is the shoe that steps into another's trial.

Love is the prism through which Christ's message of salvation captures rainbow hues.

Before I became a teacher I did not understand that this was true. Now I see that Sunday-school teaching is evangelism at its opportune best.

This does not mean that technique and knowledge are useless gifts. As a Sunday-school teacher I must possess technique, knowledge, and love, all three. But the greatest of these is *love*.[3]

The Anecdote

The anecdote is perhaps the most difficult short item to write. A miniature dramatic story, it has a beginning which introduces the characters involved, a middle which *shows* the action and conflict of the piece, and a satisfying ending, usually a punch line which clinches what has been said.

If you wish to write anecdotes well, study those published in mass-circulation magazines—the *Reader's Digest,* the *Catholic Digest,* and others. You may begin your learning adventure by putting your favorite jokes into written form. If well told, they follow this pattern too. Or you may choose interesting anecdotes from one of the magazines mentioned and type them just as they appear in print. After you have typed several you will begin to get the feel of the piece. When this happens you are ready to tackle original anecdotes. Besides being used independently as fillers, they are often used as leads (beginnings of longer articles).

Years ago an artist told me the following anecdote. It could be used effectively to show an individual's role in the body of Christ.

One day when Auguste Rodin put the finishing touches on one of his statues, the thrill of accomplishment pulsed through his veins. Feeling he had to share his joy with someone, he rushed out and brought back one of his students.

The student scrutinized every inch of the masterpiece. "Marvelous!" he said. Then his eyes focused on the statue's hands. "Those hands. . . . Such beauty, such reality."

Surprised and hurt, Rodin stormed at the fellow. He called in another student and asked his opinion.

"Miraculous! No other artist has ever produced hands like that."

A third critic echoed the same praise. "Those hands, they live."

Rodin stalked away, grabbed an axe, and before anyone could restrain him chopped the hands off the statue. His students stood by, appalled.

"Don't ever forget this," Rodin told them. "Those hands had a life of their own. They did not belong to the rest of the composition. No part is more important than the whole."[4]

The News Release

Any writer worth his publication salt will at some time or other be called upon to write a news release. Brief, not more than a page or two in length, it must concern a significantly newsworthy subject.

The format for the news release differs from most writing in that it presents the capsule whole in the first paragraph. This condensation is referred to as the five Ws— *Who, What, Where, When* and *Why*. It may also include *How*.

The news release resembles an isosceles triangle pointing down (see Fig. 1).

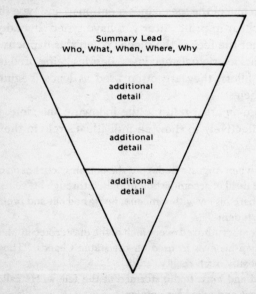

Summary Lead
Who, What, When, Where, Why

additional
detail

additional
detail

additional
detail

It is mandatory that all five Ws be covered in the first sentence or two, called the lead. Each succeeding paragraph presents details of declining importance. This permits an editor to adjust to space by cutting the bottom tip of the triangle wherever he wishes and yet retain the gist of the piece.

In writing news items you must adhere to the following commonly accepted regulations:

1. Be brief. One typed, double-spaced page will fill about six inches of one newspaper column.
2. Give exact date, December 10, not next Monday or next week. Be sure you synchronize date and day of the week accurately.
3. Use simple words. Skip the adjectives. If you say a banquet table was lovely, you are expressing your opinion. If you describe the table setting, that's a review of the facts which permits the reader to draw his own conclusions regarding loveliness.
4. Always spell out numbers one to ten (unless statistical); use figures from 11 on—usual procedure for news items. Do not begin a sentence with numerals. Spell them out.
5. Check every point of your release for accuracy: dates, time, place, spelling of names. Check newspaper requirements regarding the use of women's names (married, widowed, or divorced). Some editors may prefer the use of "Ms."
6. When you have finished your piece, go over it and cut out all possible adjectives and unnecessary articles (the, a, and an).
7. Finally ask yourself: If I weren't involved in this venture, would this news interest me? If you can't honestly answer in the affirmative, scrap the piece.
8. Research facts you aren't sure about.

In reporting church news, look for the human interest angle. If a church is installing a new pastor, learn all you can about him. If he is the father of a famous son, get the facts. Perhaps he left a lucrative position with IBM to become a minister. Find out why.

If you wish to publicize a guest speaker, call and get the title and a preview of his message.

When reporting a church dedication look for human interest stories. Is there a history connected with the site? How many hours of labor were donated by church members? What are the church's unique features? What are its projected plans?

If a member of your church, a high school or college student or a mother, accomplishes some achievement, write a report explaining it. Show tie-in between individual and church.

One Christmas the women in our church made bright, three-dimensional sequined-felt chrismons for our sanctuary tree. I called the religious editor for the local newspaper and described the project. I told her I'd be willing to write an article about the project if she would send a photographer over to take some pictures. She did and ran the article in the Sunday issue of the newspaper.

In a national survey of religious editors the following faults in material submitted in this category were listed again and again.

1. Lack of local tie-in.
2. Not genuine news.
3. Failure to meet publication deadlines.
4. Routine church announcement, nothing new.
5. Too long; too wordy.
6. Too promotional.
7. Lack of timeliness.
8. Insignificant detail.
9. Incorrect spelling of proper names.
10. Controversial or preachy.

The next time you write a news release check it against these faults. Be sure you are guilty of none of them. Too often church members lament the fact that they do not get enough publicity. Chances are they'd get all they want if they prepared releases properly, met deadlines, and included some element of human interest appeal.

CHALLENGE ASSIGNMENT

1. Locate six published epigrams. Now go through a book of maxims or the Book of Proverbs in the Bible. Choose one and

try to create an original epigram using the same idea.

2. Choose a subject. Query six people, asking them for an opinion on it. Now write a quotation survey filler.

3. Write a brief hint or advice filler.

4. Write a brief nature, travel, science, or history informative filler.

5. Write an original anecdote.

6. Select some event which is imminent or has already occurred. Write a news release informing the public of it.

8. The Devotional Meditation

Anyone can write impersonally about the many facets of the Christian life. The person who wishes to inspire, to comfort, to challenge, or to heal, however, becomes personally involved with people when he writes devotional meditations. In a sense he assumes the stance of a preacher. He takes from the storehouse of God's Word both what is new and what is old. Then he reshapes and reclothes that truth so that the reader gains new insight and inspiration.

In this he strives to emulate Christ, who through the use of relevant parables helped people understand what it means to be a vibrant, useful member of the family of God.

Not everyone can write this type of material. Here, more than anywhere, communication involves sharing what you yourself have experienced. John Bunyan clarified this sharing stance when he said, "What I smartly did feel, I did smartly preach." To test your aptitude, ask yourself if you are a person who really cares about other people, individually. Are you aware of their needs? Do you know where they hurt?

Determine, too, whether you are an observant person. Are you able to interpret events and encounters symbolically? Can you project what you see in such a way that your reader will say "How true!" or "I've never seen it that way before"?

A devotional filler may be presented as a narrative in which you tell the story of a personal experience or encounter that helped you understand some spiritual truth. Narrative writing is discussed in chapter 15; here we are dealing chiefly with the brief devotional meditation, which can be used either as a filler in some periodical or as a one-page meditation in one of the many daily devotional books being published today.

I began writing brief meditations in a column I called "This I Know," which I syndicated myself. Several of the meditations consisted merely of the retelling of a news item or observation which I hoped would convey the emotional impact I felt when I shaped it for publication. One of these meditations was titled "Are You?"

A police sergeant in Toledo, Ohio, asked his superiors to remove a case of dynamite which had been stored in the basement property room directly beneath his offices. Knowing that dry, corroding dynamite explodes with the slightest jar, he was extremely perturbed.

Reporting the situation, he said, "I believe this condition should be checked before some desk sergeants or reporters take a ride into oblivion." Then he added words far more frightening than the imminent danger of physical death: "I'm not ready to go."

For Easter publication I wrote the following piece, titled "Do You?"

Do you remember the time when an attempt was made to take the life of President Harry Truman?

Quick to respond to the responsibility of his position, one of the guards intercepted the bullets and met death at the assassin's hand.

Of special significance are the words the president released for press publication when he was questioned about his reaction to the incident.

"I never knew what it meant to have someone die in my stead."

Later I wrote meditations which appeared on the back cover page of *War Cry*, the official Salvation Army publication. From time to time the editor sent me a packet of photographs. From them I picked those that stimulated ideas for relevant meditations to be printed when the photographs were. A meditation accompanying the picture of a lighted torch being passed from one hand to another was titled "Torch Relay."

"The torch has from earliest times been the symbol of knowledge. . . ." I heard these words for the first time when, as a senior in high school, I was made a member of the National Honor Society at its annual initiation ceremony.

I was delighted to have met membership requirements, proud to accept the torch, but I must admit I didn't recognize its spiritual symbolism at the time.

Now, however, this part of the ceremony has special meaning to me. It has made me reconsider my spiritual heritage. Simple, hardworking, honest people, my parents knew what it meant to carry a torch for God. And because they made it such a vital part of their lives, I reached out to accept it, too.

This is something everyone must do. No one can accept faith's torch for you, nor can you pass it on to others unless you reach out to receive it yourself.[1]

In some instances you will not relate an anecdote or refer to a meaningful experience. You will merely explain some new insight you have gained about a particular Bible passage. Such was the case when I wrote "United We Serve."

It was just a chance remark heard in a Sunday sermon. Yet it started the wheels of my mind turning toward the concern of man for man. "I'd like to believe," the clergyman said, "the four men in Mark 2:3–5 who carried their palsied neighbor to Jesus were not of the same household; not even of the same religious persuasion."

Who were they then? I asked myself. Imagination supplied the answer. The Roman centurion to whom Jesus said, "I have not found such great faith, no, not in Israel." A Jewish tax gatherer, despised by his own people for collaborating with the enemy. A publican, a mason perhaps, a man for whom Jesus had shown special concern. Lastly, a Samaritan merchant in Capernaum on business.

Socially, materially incompatible, possibly not even liking each other very much, they were drawn together by a common concern, a palsied friend, and by a common faith that Jesus would make him well.

When they approached the Master they were thwarted in their plans. Like erupting lava the crowd spilled into the courtyard and surrounding streets. There was no way to get through. The tile roof? The mason suggested the possibility. Rope? The Roman army commissary, of course.

Finally the tense dramatic moment arrived. The men lowered their palsied friend and Jesus healed his frail, useless body.

This time Jesus did not say, "Thy faith hath made thee whole." It is recorded, "When he saw *their faith*, he said unto the sick of the palsy, 'Son, thy sins be forgiven thee.' "[2]

Did you notice that I included a challenge only in the torch-relay meditation? In two of the examples, the titles supplied the spiritual impact; in the last, it became an inherent part of the whole.

This is not always possible. Some material doesn't lend itself to such treatment. Too, some editors expect you to spell out your directive. In such instances, restrain yourself; avoid the sledgehammer approach.

You will be required to summarize or challenge when you write devotional meditations directed toward daily-devotional pamphlet or book publication. Here an editor usually assigns the Bible passage he expects you to comment about. Word length and format may be stipulated, too. The format with which I am most familiar is used by several publications. It demands that your writing have freshness and vitality without being preachy.

1. *Title*
2. *Assigned Bible passage*
3. *Key verse* (you may be asked to choose the one that appeals most to you from the passage assigned).
4. The meditation
   a. A catching lead: a startling statement, a relevant anecdote, a news item, an observation, a poignant memory.
   b. A paragraph which relates the lead to the scripture.
   c. A paragraph which applies the scripture to life (*b* and *c* may be reversed).
5. *Focus* (a brief capsule-thought which clinches or summarizes, or challenges the reader).
6. *Prayer* (a short informal sentence-prayer in the first person).

All parts of the meditation must be relevant to each other and project one message only.

Here are two daily-devotional meditations written on assignment for *The Quiet Hour,* a David C. Cook publication.

"Antagonism Toward Jesus"
Read: Mark 2:1–12
Remember: "Why doth this man thus speak blasphemies? Who can

forgive sins but God only?" (Mark 2:7)

A trio of young people were apprehended some time ago for subjecting an evangelical university professor to several weeks of vicious harrassment. Because the man was what they called a "religious bigot" they besieged him and his family with fake deliveries, abusive telephone calls, obscene letters, and false death and accident messages.

When charges were filed, the young people admitted they had discontinued their antics because: "It didn't seem to make the slightest difference to the man. He's just as religious as he's always been."

Harrassment didn't faze Jesus Christ either. Instead it challenged performance. Why? Because he had a task to perform regardless of opposition. He came to prove that he, the Son of God, had power over sickness, sin, and death.

If we commit ourselves to tasks we believe Christ has assigned, we too will pursue them to completion, unmindful of those who ridicule or strive to thwart our efforts.

Focus: Christian commitment is not touched by ridicule or scorn.

Prayer: Help me to be faithful to you no matter what people say.[3]

"The Friend of Sinners"

Read: Mark 2:13–17

Remember: "They that are whole have no need of the physician, but they that are sick: I came not to call the righteous, but sinners to repentance." (Mark 2:17)

One of my friends is terribly excited about her work in the poverty program. When she speaks of the alien, the migrant, the welfare recipient, the homeless man on the street—each unemployable because he cannot read—she does so with concern.

Nor is this concern dulled when folks ask, as they frequently do, "But aren't some of these people awfully obnoxious? How can you stand them?"

"Because I have learned to love them," she tells. "It isn't what they are but what they can become that counts. I look at their potential. I think of them as they will be once they have gained self-respect. It's a totally new experience for me."

When Jesus dined with sinners there were people who reproved him for this type of involvement. He too may have heard, "How can you stand them?"

We know his answer. It was to such persons he came to minister. And it's for such people Christ expects us to be concerned.

Focus: Christian love knows no boundaries.

Prayer: Help me to love the unlovely and to give myself in service to them.[4]

When you write family daily-devotional meditations always include something each week that appeals chiefly to children. Shun pompous, literary language and allusions that only an English major would recognize and understand. Write as if you were talking to a family you know. Here is an example taken from my book, *Happy Moments with God.* Though it follows a different format, it was written for families with young children. Most of the meditations in the book begin with anecdote or narrative leads garnered from personal experience with my own or someone else's children.

Jimmy Hit Me

Sandy came into the house crying as if her heart would break.

Mother sat down and took Sandy in her lap. She hugged her close and wiped the tears that spilled down her cheeks.

"Now, now," Mother comforted, smoothing Sandy's hair away from her eyes. "It can't be as bad as all that. Tell me what happened."

Sandy sobbed some more. Mother waited.

"Can you tell me now?" Mother asked.

"Jimmy hit me!" Sandy blurted. Jimmy was the little neighbor boy who often played with her. "We were playing in the sandbox and he hit me."

"What were you quarreling about?" Mother asked.

"We decided the sandbox was a big farm. But Jimmy wasn't fair. He said he should have a bigger part of it just because he's a couple years older. And he hit me!" The tears began to fall again.

"And what did you do? Did you hit him back?"

"No," Sandy said as she sat up in Mother's lap, clenching her teeth in anger. "I hit him first."

Something to think about: Do you feel sorry for Sandy? Why? Or why not?

This story proves there are always two sides to a quarrel. If Sandy hadn't hit Jimmy, he might never have hit her. Sometimes our selfishness makes enemies. Perhaps Jimmy had a special reason for wanting the bigger part of the sandbox. Sandy should have talked about it instead of getting angry. Suppose Jimmy had been angry anyway. What would you have done if you had been Sandy?

Bible verse: "Thou shalt love thy neighbour as thyself." (Leviticus 19:18, Matthew 22:39)

"He that is slow to anger is better than the mighty; and he that ruleth [can control] his spirit than he that taketh a city." (Proverbs 16:32)

Prayer: Dear Lord, You know how easy it is for us to get angry when we don't get our way. You have taught us that this is wrong. Forgive us for the times we have forgotten Your teaching. Keep us in Your love this day. Help us by our actions to prove that we love You. In Jesus' Name. Amen.[5]

Other authors have written books of devotional meditations for teenagers, nurses, teachers, clergymen, the single woman, the adult church member.

In some instances a number of these meditations appear in periodicals first, having been submitted on a "book-rights-reserved" basis about which you will learn in chapters 20 and 32.

If the writing of devotional meditations appeals to you, write an editor of one of the many daily devotional books and ask for a trial assignment. Enclose two or three sample meditations you have written to the pattern presented in this chapter. Or submit one or more meditations to periodicals you have learned use them.

CHALLENGE ASSIGNMENT

1. Choose a Bible passage that is meaningful to you.

2. With the daily-devotional pattern in front of you write a meditation—one you believe could be used in homes with children from six to fifteen years of age.

3. Go through a daily newspaper and clip items you believe would make good leads for devotional meditations. Indicate the thought you would want to stress.

4. Set down a personal observation or memory which would make a good lead for a meditation.

5. Write a one-paragraph meditation which could be used as a filler in a periodical. Name the periodical.

6. Make a list of publications which use meditations.

9. *Poetry, Light Verse, and Greeting Cards*

One of the unaccountable assumptions about writing is that, though a person may lack both the ability to interpret life meaningfully and a knowledge of poetic forms, he can (he believes) sit down and write poetry which some editor will be delighted to publish. Of such people it has been said, "They think they can run before they learn to crawl."

The sad thing is that God is often given credit for inspiring these "masterpieces." Such credit is misplaced. These people don't write poetry, they write doggerel rife with time-worn word, rhyme, and allusion clichés.

When I say this I do not mean to imply that a person becomes a poet simply by learning poetic forms. This would show lack of understanding of what a poet is.

The Stuff of Poetry

A poet stands out from other people in the way he looks at life. He has a unique sense of wonder. He describes, interprets, and analyzes what he feels. Too, he hears, sees, touches, and tastes more perceptively than most people. And because he possesses this kind of sensitivity, he expresses himself more meaningfully and clearly through well-chosen words that say precisely what he means them to say.

If you aspire to write poetry, shun the mistakes made by novices who begin by searching for pretty phrases, tapping out rhythms with a pencil, or hunting for words that rhyme. Rhyme should be your last consideration. For though it has rhythm, much good poetry doesn't rhyme. Inherent in it, however, is a significant idea born in a poignant, provocative emotional experience.

Poet Edith Lovejoy Pierce says it takes some kind of an emotional upheaval to inspire her to write a poem, whether it be associated with love, sorrow, anger, joy, or despair. "Lines leap to my mind, but only out of a matrix of feeling, past or present, active or quiescent."

A grieving friend discovered this truth one day when, some months after the death of her husband, she traveled across an Arizona desert. In full, startling bloom, it reminded her of an earlier trip when it lay dormant, devoid of any sign of life.

The experience struck her so forcefully that the desert immediately became a symbol of her own life. Drab and dormant, temporarily robbed of hope, could it—would it, she wondered —bloom once more?

A poem! she told herself. *I must write a poem!*

From this woman's experience we come to realize that poetry takes all of life into consideration, for poetry is primarily concerned with truth, with the ordinary as well as the strange, with the poor as well as the rich, with the sad as well as the joyful, and with death as well as life.

Author Joseph Bayly realized this when he wrote his book *Psalms of My Life.* Here is the last part of "A Psalm on the death of an 18-year-old son."

> I cannot see
> such waste
> that You should take
> what poor men need.
> You have a heaven
> full of treasure
> could You not wait
> to exercise Your claim
> on this?
> O spare me Lord forgive
> that I may see
> beyond this world
> beyond myself

Your sovereign plan
or seeing not
may trust You
Spoiler of my treasure.
Have mercy Lord
here is my quitclaim.
                —Joseph Bayly[1]

Poetry requires that a writer develop an idea gleaned from experience as concisely, precisely, as vividly as possible. Though not concise, Joseph Bayly's poem does say precisely what he meant it to say, in a vividly memorable way. Such writing may require use of the fresh simile, the strong metaphor, the carefully chosen picture-painting word.

The Home-Going

Let it be light . . .
As the ripe release of an autumn leaf
Tired of clinging . . .
As a bird's swift flight
From the quivering bough
. . . Singing!
                —Helga Skogsbergh[2]

Give Me a Drum

Give me a drum to march by
That never misses beat,
That leads me through the fog of doubt
And fires weary feet.

Offer me faith that laughs at fear
No matter who may scorn
And I will fight the hate of man
Till love itself is born.

Show me a cause that asks for all
The courage I possess
And I will raise my banner high
And stop for nothing less.
                —Charles A. Waugaman[3]

Poetic Language

It's true, of course, that poetry makes more use of musical language than prose does. Edgar Allan Poe described poetry as "music . . . combined with a pleasurable idea."

You acquire a musical quality or rhythm by a careful choice and arrangement of sounds, accents, and cadence. Just as a musician varies the repetition of melodies, you will vary the sound of words, both individually and in phrases, long or short, being especially sensitive to what they accomplish in getting across the *feel* of what you have in mind.

Rhyme, on the other hand, involves the repetition of the final sounds of a word with the same accent pattern. It is called masculine rhyme if only one syllable rhymes, as in *box* and *fox*. It is feminine rhyme when two or more syllables rhyme—*hurdle* and *curdle; rightfully, spitefully*. Rhyme is referred to as internal rhyme when one or both rhyming words appear within the line (fairly rare); as end rhyme when both rhyming words appear at the end of lines. The latter is the most frequently used sound repetition in the English language. To achieve a musical rhythm, a poet may also repeat whole words, phrases, lines, or groups of lines, as in the refrain of a song. Poems that rhyme are often favorites with children.

> **Puddles**
> Every wee raindrop
> Falls alone,
> All the way from the sky
> On his own.
> They all run
> To talk about the trip,
> Gathering in puddles
> Drip by drip.
> —Ruth Cox Anderson[4]

Note the effective rhyming in this meaningful adult poem.

The Wall

Here as we kneel,
Shoulder to shoulder at the altar rail,
Each stone slips into place
To form the Temple wall.
The Evil One cannot mount or assail
The rocklike face;
No matter with what zeal
He tries to strike
Or climb, he can but fail.
No storm can breach this dike.
Here at the altar no one is alone;
Each draws his strength from the great Cornerstone.

—Edith Lovejoy Pierce[5]

Then one of my own:

My Legacy

I err if I
Safeguard antiquity,
Keep it intact
To leave posterity;
Then fail to will
As parent or trustee
The heritage
That Faith and Grace decree.[6]

Rhythm and Rhyme in Action

In his book, *Sound and Sense*, Laurence Perrine likens rhythm to any wavelike recurrence of motion and sound. Meter, he says, is the kind of rhythm we can tap our feet to. In writing that is metrical there is a regular beat of rhythm and accents.

Meter means measure. For measuring poetry we use what we call the foot, the line, and the stanza or verse.

Since it is impossible to cover meter thoroughly here, I

merely call your attention to the basic types of poetic feet. Note that the curved line over the syllable designates the unaccented syllable; the straight stress marks the accented syllable.

EXAMPLE	NAME OF FOOT	NAME OF METER
ădōre	iamb	iambic
vāllĕy	trochee	trochaic
ĭntĕrvēne	anapest	anapestic
sȳmpăthȳ	dactyl	dactylic
sūnlĭght	spondee	spondaic
bōx	monosyllabic	

The line is measured by determining the number of feet it contains:

monometer	– one foot
dimeter	– two feet
trimeter	– three feet
tetrameter	– four feet
pentameter	– five feet
hexameter	– six feet
heptameter	– seven feet
octameter	– eight feet

Scansion is the term used for scanning or measuring a particular poem. This involves identifying the predominant foot, determining the number of feet and whether they follow a regular pattern, and noting the stanza pattern.

Though you will be more concerned about substance and meter than about the rhyme of a poem, you need to familiarize yourself with a few basic rhyme patterns. (Here is where you learn to crawl.) By employing letters of the alphabet to identify lines of a poem that have the same rhyme, you can learn to use these patterns in your own writing.

1. The two-line stanza or *couplet*: *a a*
2. The three-line stanza: *a a a*; *a b a*
3. The four-line stanza or *quatrain*: *a b a b*; *a a b b*; *a b b a*; *a b c b*

4. The five-line stanza: *a b a b a*; *a b a a b*; *a b a b b*

The sonnet, used a great deal by English poets, is a fourteen-line lyric poem with a fixed rhyme and rhythm pattern. It is divided into two sections. In the "Italian" or Petrarchan form the first eight lines present the idea or theme and the last six comment upon or resolve it. The meter is iambic pentameter —the great classic rhythm of English poetry:⌣‒ ⌣‒ ⌣‒ ⌣‒ ⌣‒.

The basic rhyme is *a b b a a b b a* for the eight lines and *c d e c d e* or *c d c d c d* for the six (technically called the *octave* and the *sestet*). There are other possible variations, such as *a b b a c d d c* for the octave, but the sestet must not end in two rhymed lines.

The "English" or Shakespearean form has a longer development of twelve lines (three quatrains) and a brief ending in a single couplet, with compressed poetic effect. Thus you might have *a b a b c d c d e f e f*, or perhaps *a b b a c d d c e f f e* or other slight variation before the final two lines with their separate rhyme.

The two kinds of sonnet together have constituted a basic poetic form in the language for nearly five centuries, and show no sign of disappearing. The following illustrates the Shakespearean type:

The Prodigal's Father

He has reclaimed the shelter of my roof,
And finds secure, albeit guilty, rest.
But will my eldest son withstand the test
Of love? Angered, he holds himself aloof
And has no ready welcome in his soul
For one who sought and scattered to the wind
My freely-given substance. Will he find
Some understanding which will make him whole?
I yearn to heal him now, but hold my breath.
A generation hence, his son may seize
A rocky path and stumble to his knees,
Envying swine and facing hungry death.
Will he, as I, in this way and no other,
Learn to forget he is the elder brother?

—Joan Truitt[7]

The haiku is a three-line poem originated by the Japanese. Almost always containing some reference to nature, its first line has five syllables; its second, seven; its last, five.

> Haiku
> Strawberries are ripe
> Eat as many as you can
> June in a teaspoon.
> Lois Leurgans[8]

In any group of writers questions about the terms *verse, free verse, metered verse,* and *blank verse* come up frequently. What do they mean anyway?

Verse is a sequence of words arranged metrically, guided by some rule or design, as a verse of a hymn. However, verse often refers to metrical writing that is light as well.

Free verse is poetry which ignores rhyme as well as specific line units. It contains no set number of metrical feet per line.

Yet free verse may be said to have a general rhythm, often spoken of as *cadence,* which is achieved through a subtle handling of balanced rhythms and a sense of the arc or span through which meaning moves to its completion.

Though many line breaks occur at the end of grammatical phrases, some of the finest and most powerful poetry plays the language against the metrical pattern, while free-verse poets especially may even end lines by dividing words.

Perhaps beginners start writing rhymed and metrical verse because this is the type of poetry they know best. The meter becomes a tune, and all they have to do is to think up words that fit. They seem to need the support of a definite stanza form and recurring rhyme. You may be one of these people.

If you are, let me challenge you to try your hand at free verse. Begin by putting on paper some meaningful words in any arrangement you wish. The important thing is that you say something significant using imagery that is relevant, consistent, and fresh. You may use incomplete sentences, internal rhymes, short lines, whatever. Such freedom is bound to make you think *message* rather than form.

Yet do realize you are free to use rhymed verse forms. Good poets learn to write all types of poems even though free verse is currently in style.

In *metered verse* the length of the lines is measured by a definite number of metrical feet (discussed earlier).

Blank verse is iambic pentameter metrical verse which doesn't rhyme. In this form much of the great poetry of English literature up to the twentieth century was written.

Joseph Bayly's poem (pp. 69-70) is free verse. Here is another example.

Film Take

Since You chose to make
such a dark and lifeless
flimsy drab flammable
piece of celluloid
You'll have to thread me, Lord
to project light.

You'll have to
            clean the film gate
            throw the switch
            adjust the frame
            focus the lens
            make sure I'm on track.

Perhaps then You can transform
the obvious negative
to dazzling positive
and display the splendor of Yourself
through a transparent human heart
on the screen of life.

—Morris Anderson[9]

Our chief concern in writing poetry should be that we write *poetry*, not doggerel. *Writer's Digest* columnist Judson Jerome, distinguishes between the two: "The difference between a real rose and a wax one, between a living human being and a plastic surrogate, and between a vibrant enduring poem and a mere versified sentiment, is complexity of tone."[10] The failure to achieve this tone occurs before the poem is ever set on paper. Authors fail to grasp life and experience it sufficiently. Poetry, he notes, is like "a cavern of endless echoes. Its mystery and profundity and resonance arise from a sense it conveys inexhaustibility. We stand back in awe because our capacity to explain, describe, or contain is overwhelmed."

Light Verse

Light verse differs from other poetry in that it is less exhaustive, less meaningful. Called doggerel by some poets, or even just *verse* as opposed to *poetry*, its purpose is to entertain, to chide, or to needle.

Light verse resembles an epigram. A flash-in-the-mind illustration of life, it is usually written humorously. It speaks of the commonplace, the homely, the universal experiences of man.

Richard Armour, popular light verse writer for many years, says that such verse is playful poetry written about practically everything. As such it does serve a purpose, though this is not the same as that of the serious poem.

Don't assume however that, because light verse is brief and seemingly very simple, it is easy to write. To achieve publication in the highly competitive market for this specialty requires that you follow specific rules and employ rhythm, rhyme, and meter.

Top-notch light verse rhymes must be exact. You will employ assonance, consonance, and polysyllabic and internal rhyme. You will also play with words, twist and make puns of them. It's wise to jot down unusual, catchy rhyming words whenever they pop into your head. Though iambic tetrameter is the most popular line used in this type of writing, deviations can be challenging and fun.

You can learn what editors are looking for by studying magazines which publish light verse and by analyzing the examples to be found in Richard Armour's book, *Light Armour*.

In this type of verse as in serious poetry, you must begin with

an idea—something universally significant. I have found that an
original epigram can be changed into this sort of poem. A verse
which won a Burma Shave contest prize was written after I had
set down an original epigram on the same subject.

Drinking drivers,
None are worse;
They put the quart
Before the hearse.

You may be wondering if there is a market for light verse in
the religious field. I have found there is. Here are some pieces
which earned publication on a simultaneous-submission basis.

'Tis Better
Do not regret when folks accept
Your good ungratefully;
That's better than to own some wrong
For which you went scot-free.

Easy Does It
Good leadership
Is never badgering
To prove this truth,
Just try to push a string.

Do You Dare?
If you are inclined
To offer a friend
A piece of your mind,
Think twice.
Do you dare?
Are you sure
That you have
A piece
You can spare?

Not So!
Why, I wonder, do we think
    Approval we can win,
By spreading the statistics
    Of other people's sins?

Mistaken Identity
"Please sit in front," the preacher pleads,
In tones he hopes sound mellow;
Yet each and every member thinks
He means the other fellow.

Greeting Cards

If you are like most poets, you have probably at one time or another looked at a greeting card, read its message, and said, "That looks easy. I ought to send some of my verse to a greeting card publisher."

It does look easy. But don't let that supposition mislead you. Writing greeting card messages, be they long or short, involves creative ideas, empathy, research, concise writing, and knowledgeable marketing.

Greeting card verse isn't dashed off in a few moments. It is "reflected upon in tranquility" just as any good poetry is.

If you are a competent writer and want to try writing for the greeting card market, you should first study greeting card verse. Be aware that the market is not static. It continually changes. What was accepted ten years ago may not sell today. Types of cards, however, do not change.

VARIETY

Contemporary cards. Upbeat cards that reflect the times.

Conventional cards. Formal or sentimental; customarily verse or simple one-line prose.

Cute cards. Can be either verse or prose; informal, gentle humor tied closely to illustrations.

Inspirational cards. Usually poetic and religious; purpose is to inspire; many are Biblical in nature.

Juvenile cards. Geared to children and their interests; often utilize animals in verse or illustrations.

Mechanical cards. These involve action of some kind; may have some type of pop-up or punch-out feature. Some are for children to color.

Seasonal cards. Christmas, Easter, Graduation, Halloween,

Mother's Day, Father's Day, Hanukkah, etc.

Topical cards. These speak to a specific subject: sympathy, wedding, anniversaries, congratulations, gratitude, love, friendship, or any other special interest.

IDEA EVALUATION AND EXPANSION

Ideas bloom all around you. Pluck them immediately; examine their color, form and emotional response. Program your mind to latch onto catch phrases in converstions, on radio and television, in literature, in song lyrics, in quips you hear.

Store these ideas in a notebook at once or they will fade before you have time to expand them at your leisure. Ideas need to be contemplated in quietness. You need to be alone without disruptions. Open your notebook. Concentrate. A title such as "No Longer Lonely" may leap at you. Think: Who would no longer be lonely? To whom would the expansion of that thought be addressed? Is the idea general enough to be marketed widely?

You might decide to alter the phrase. You may have been lonely and you want to send a card to some empathetic person who responded to your needs. Inherent in that thought is another title, "To Someone Who Cared."

Many people are lonely; many people care. Could this be a gratitude card from a sender who has been lonely to someone who cared? Can you write it clearly with warmth and sensitivity? You are perceptive enough to answer these questions honestly with insight. And you are the person, the *I*, who will be addressing the recipient as *you*.

Note this *you* emphasis in phrases garnered from cards I have received:

> Hope *your* Christmas . . .
> . . . bring happiness to *you*.
> as *you* celebrate . . .
> . . . to help *you* get well.
> Do *you* know what makes . . . ?

When you write, aim for warmth, readability, individuality, and excellence.

Sharon Harris, who is a concert soloist, decided to write and have an artist illustrate cards that she would market herself. When the first twelve-card printing found a ready market with friends and associates, Harris decided to expand her list. At this writing she has sixty religious greeting cards on the market.

Noting her success, a Christian bookstore offered to print, package, and market the cards on a royalty basis. My friend agreed to the arrangement. As a result she decided to expand her line to include children's cards.

Innovative and creative, the cards are printed on cream-colored paper with sepia line drawings. Her adult cards have personal appeal. I chose to send one to my son on his birthday. The illustration: a sturdy, beautifully executed sequoia pine. The verse:

> My son . . .
> So often
> I've wanted to tell you
> How proud I am
> That you are my son.
> But certain sentiments
> Are difficult to express.
> It's easy, I know,
> To tell you what you aren't,
> But today I want to tell you
> What you are—
> And that is everything
> I could ever
> Ask God for
> In a son.
>
> **Sharon Birdwell Harris**[11]

It takes courage and ingenuity to strike out as Harris did. Most of us prefer to begin by submitting greeting card verse to publishing firms who make up, illustrate, and market our work.

If greeting card verse appeals to you, collect ideas, ponder their expansion, write and polish each one as you would a gem. Then, and only then, submit your creations to the most promising publisher without delay.

Customarily, greeting card messages are submitted on 3″ × 5″ or 5″ × 7″ cards. Number each card and its duplicate, on which you will indicate the names of greeting card publishers to whom you send it. (This will prevent you from duplicating submissions.)

You can usually submit five to seven card ideas at one time.

CHALLENGE ASSIGNMENT

1. Study several publications or poetry anthologies. Locate *(a)* a rhymed poem, *(b)* a blank verse poem, *(c)* a free-verse poem. *(d)* a sonnet, and *(e)* a haiku poem.

2. Choose one of these types and write your own poem.

3. Try writing some light verse.

4. Do further research on greeting card preparation. (Your library can locate instructional books for you.)

5. Make a list of types of cards you would like to write.

6. Make a list of the most promising markets.

7. Now write, revise, polish, and market several greeting card submissions.

10.   Columns

Columns are features which appear regularly in newspapers and magazines under permanent titles. Usually they occupy the same spot in issue after issue. They carry the by-line of the author and reflect his opinions.

A columnist may present facts, advice, or news, or he may answer questions or comment on a variety of subjects. He must have competence in his field, empathy for his readers, and a generous supply of psychological understanding of the age group for which he is writing. The Christian writer possesses an additional qualification: he is dedicated to the tenets of his faith.

The Question-and-Answer Column

A familiar and popular column follows the question-and-answer format. Readers supply the questions, which a person who is an authority in a specific field answers.

A doctor answers questions about medical problems as they relate to the Christian life. A Sunday-school specialist answers questions about Sunday-school involvement. A pastor or youth minister answers questions young people may ask about problems that concern them: courtship, marriage, loneliness, career choice, family relationships. A psychologist answers questions which deal with tensions, mental breakdowns, temperament.

The merit of such a column is measured by its reader appeal.

The Commentary Column

This type of column also handles topics of universal interest. Some vary in subject matter from week to week. One author has divulged his opinions about death, dogmatism, deviant lengths of hair, editorial policies, Biblical interpretations, morality. A certain woman columnist writes only about one specific subject, a woman and her automobile.

If you consider writing a commentary column you should realize that you will need to strive for originality and freshness of expression and content. Keep your readers guessing as to what's coming next. Far better that they should say, "I wonder what he's talking about this time—" than "Oh, not that subject again!" Four pertinent requirements: write to space limitation; meet deadlines; avoid preachiness; research facts you don't know. Make a mistake, and you can be sure your readers will let you know about it by return mail. In many instances research will involve checking facts with informed people who are especially knowledgeable in their particular fields.

Through reading and in querying several columnists I have garnered the following column-writing directives:

1. Read extensively. You never know when an item in a newspaper or magazine will start the wheels of your mind whirling.
2. Keep an idea file.
3. Broaden your associations. Be alert to other people's views.
4. Be able to laugh at yourself. And if you can, strive to make your readers laugh at themselves.
5. Don't copy another's style; develop your own.
6. Be willing to admit a mistake.
7. Honestly and openly speak your convictions.

Because a columnist is given a great deal of latitude in subject matter and idea approach, Christian writers, whether they are pastors, housewives, business or professional persons, or students, should avail themselves of column-publication opportunities.

One high-school senior persuaded a newspaper editor to give him column space in the weekly high-school insert to counteract what was otherwise totally secular.

A housewife in Illinois writes a weekly column about interesting Christians she meets.

Many clergymen write weekly columns about religion for their daily newspapers. One of these men likens the boundary between the secular and the religious to a no man's land which is being constantly taken over by the secular. He feels Christian writers should invade this territory to build rapport, to persuade, and to clarify misconceptions about the Christian faith.

If you would like to attempt writing a column, send several editors samples of what you have in mind. Don't allow yourself to be easily discouraged. Keep trying until you find an editor who agrees to give your submissions a trial run. If you prove yourself, he may give your column permanent space. Eventually you can branch out and secure space in other publications, too.

Letters to the Editor

Want to influence public opinion? Speak your mind freely? Accomplish speedy publication? Then write a letter to the editor of a daily newspaper, a mass-circulation magazine, or an official church organ—all of which allot special column space for this type of communication. Such columns appear under a vast array of interesting titles: "Sincerely Yours," "Pros and Cons," "Blasts and Blessings," "Speak Your Mind," "Feedback," "Assault and Flattery."

The letters-to-the-editor column provides a democratic opportunity for persons of divergent views to express themselves about subjects of current interest. By writing responsible, authoritative, constructive letters you can become what one editor called contributors to this column: a community builder.

Most editors welcome responsible letters to the editor and try to print two sides of an issue, be it a local school controversy, traffic problems, taxes, building and industry locations; or religious editorial policies, doctrinal interpretations, and personal bias.

In writing a letter to the editor be brief, authoritative (know your facts), not too personal. Avoid a "hot-under-the-collar" approach. Present your viewpoint logically, with clarity.

The average letter should contain three parts: (1) identification of the subject to be discussed; (2) an explanation or interpretation of your viewpoint; (3) suggested action or persuasion. Though the letter may comment on the divergent opinions of another writer, you should not attack your opponent's character nor the manner in which he makes his presentation. You should understand that an editor will not print anything that might subject him to a libel suit—anything that would injure someone's reputation or threaten his employment opportunities.

You increase your letter's chance of being published if you keep it brief, not more than 250 or 300 words in length, and sign it. Editors do not, as a rule, print anonymous communications.

You may be wondering whether letters to the editor are effective. Often they are. One small California community wrote several such letters urging the installation of traffic lights at a very dangerous corner. It took a number of them, including one from a woman whose car was severely damaged at that crossing, to spur the city into action.

You must, of course, feel sincerely about a particular issue on which you express an opinion. Two symphony orchestra patrons in a midwestern city disliked being required to pay their share of the cost of liquor they did not drink at promotional dinners. After trying unsuccessfully within the organization to remedy this situation, the wife wrote a gracious yet very pointed letter to the editor of the daily newspaper saying that she and her lawyer husband would cease attending such functions until the policy was changed. The letter accomplished its purpose; the policy was changed.

Note that the woman tried conventional channels before she wrote her letter. Suppose you have some complaint against city officials. Don't write a letter to the editor if a call to City Hall would accomplish the same purpose. This policy applies to letters written to religious publications, too. Refrain from airing a personal complaint which could be settled in a personal letter to the editor. Refrain, too, from insisting that an editor do something about a matter which can only be settled by an official church body. You may urge a particular line of action, if you approach the subject kindly and fairly. There are people who delight in airing the failures of a corporate group who would never dream of exposing the failings of their own family. Let Christlikeness be your direction.

Book Reviews

If you love books and enjoy appraising them, writing book reviews may be the perfect assignment for you.

To latch onto such an assignment cultivate a local or regional newspaper editor in your area. Identify yourself, state your qualifications, and offer to submit a sample review for his approval. If you prove you can deliver honest, well-written book reviews, he'll latch onto you.

As a rule, your only pay will be the books you review. Not a bad arrangement if you like to read. You may keep the ones you like for your own library. Give surplus copies as Christmas and birthday gifts to your relatives and friends.

Once you have proved your worth, you can reach out and approach other editors by submitting copies of your published reviews. Do consider religious magazines and church-school papers in this outreach. They need good book reviews, too.

Your first step in writing a review is to read the book, *every word of it.* If you don't, your review will give you away. I recall reading a one-paragraph review of a book I felt was very poorly written. I knew immediately the reviewer had failed to read it. He had merely mouthed the praise of the book jacket. Had he read the book in its entirety, he would have tempered his praise.

As you read, place paper tabs of some kind between pages you wish to refer to later.

Now put the book aside. Take as much time as a deadline will permit to mull over the book's contents. Jot down phrases that describe your reaction to content, purpose, and journalistic appeal.

Ask yourself:

1. What are the writer's qualifications in this particular field?
2. What is the author striving to do in the book?
3. Does he achieve his purpose?
4. What facts can I present to rouse interest in the book? (Do not include so much that you stifle interest to begin with. You want to let the reader find some things out for himself.)
5. Has the author done enough research? Is the book well documented?
6. How well is the material organized?
7. Does the book contain controversial material I should bring to the reader's attention?
8. To what extent can I recommend the book?

If the work is biographical, add the following questions to those listed above:

1. Does the book give a comprehensive picture of the subject?
2. What phases of the subject's life receive the greatest attention? Is this justified?
3. Does the author prove the subject's significance?
4. To what extent are weaknesses and idiosyncracies noted?
5. Has he presented new facts about the subject?
6. Does he exhibit any one-sided bias toward him?
7. How does this book compare with other biographies by the same author?

If the book is fiction, ask yourself (in addition to the preceding questions):

1. What is the theme of the book?
2. What specific phases of human experience are dealt with?
3. Do the characters come alive? Do they change or do they remain the same?
4. What is the book trying to do—present adventure, mystery, character growth, a basic attitude toward life?
5. Does it achieve its goal?
6. Are settings so sharply defined that I feel myself living in them as I read?

When you write your review, be concise, precise, and honest. Avoid exaggerated praise—"this book is a must," "no one should miss this book"—except, of course, in the very rare instances where such language is deserved. Keep within the designated word limit. Avoid distortion of facts; quotations out of context; misrepresentation or omission of facts because of personal bias. If you feel it advisable, you may tell something about the author (layman or specialist) and why he wrote the book.

Your review will be written with a plan: a beginning, a middle, and an ending. Immediately arrest the attention of your reader. Then in an ordered, unified manner introduce the book to your reader. Your ending may clinch or summarize what you have said, or it may challenge the reader to obtain the book. You will tread cautiously here—you will want to be fair to the writer who has spent a year or more writing it; at the same time you must think of the reader who is being asked to pay several dollars for it.

CHALLENGE ASSIGNMENT

1. What type of column do you most frequently read?

2. Pretend you wish to interest an editor in a commentary column. Choose a permanent title for your column. Write two sample columns which would be relevant to that title. Give them subtitles.

3. Write a book review following the suggestions given in this chapter.

4. Clip and file a variety of published columns that appeal to you.

5. Choose a publication which deserves commendation of some kind. Write a letter to the editor voicing this commendation.

3

Feature·Length Nonfiction
General Suggestions

11. Groundwork

After repeated filler sales you are apt to receive a letter from one or more editors saying, "We appreciate the material you have sent us. We'd like to see you try something longer now."

This something-longer direction means you expand your writing to include feature-length articles of various kinds. As a rule a feature article is said to be one that receives special-placement space and emphasis in a given issue of a publication. We shall deal in this section with longer articles, any one of which could receive this special-placement treatment.

The feature-length article differs from most fillers in that it requires more research, investigation, and deliberation. Varying in length from twelve hundred to two or three thousand words, with fifteen hundred the most acceptable in the religious press, it borrows techniques of fiction, a fact you will understand more fully when you have studied the section devoted to fiction.

The thought of developing a longer article may frighten you. It need not. Since thousands of magazines publish millions of words on a regular basis, editors are always looking for new talent. When they find a creative, trustworthy writer, they encourage him as much as they can.

Because these magazines cover practically every topic you could name, you can begin writing feature-length articles about subjects you know. If you have overcome a handicap you will be able, through your writing, to help others overcome theirs. If you have developed and tested a Bible study intended specifically for young married couples, you can share your plan with individuals who teach this type of class. Or perhaps you have accumulated a great deal of knowledge about archeology. Share what you have learned.

You will, of course, familiarize yourself with the different types of articles and topics currently accepted by editors. Article patterns vary according to content. One which tells readers how to avoid a mental breakdown differs from one which describes the changes that have taken place in Israel in recent years. The first is a psychological advice article, the second may be classified as reportorial. In part 4 you will learn to recognize a variety of article patterns.

At present, however, you need know only that an article has a beginning, a bridge, a body, and an ending. The beginning is the eye-and-mind-catching bait that hooks a reader's attention. Once you have caught it, you take him across a transitional bridge into the *tell* and *show* section, called the body, which explores the subject of your article. Then when you have made your point, you wrap up the whole thing in a satisfying ending.

You may wonder what constitutes a good feature-length article. One might say that a writer who concerns himself only about financial remuneration would consider an article good if it pays well. Though a Christian writer is as interested as anyone in fair payment, he considers a good article one which provokes thought, inspires, and challenges the reader to a worthwhile response.

A good article is recognized, too, by its timeliness and its universal appeal. It is written with one theme in mind, and one premise or point of view about it—a premise you should be able to state in a single sentence. A good article also zeros in on a specific angle of a general subject.

Note how published authors handle general subjects through a specific-angle approach. An article about cigarette smoking titled, "They Buried the Cigarette Habit,"[1] describes a California city's one-month crusade against cigarette smoking. An article about art begins by focusing on artist Annie Vallotton's line drawings in *Good News for Modern Man.*[2] A very different article about art explains what to look for in an art show. A piece about senior citizens suggests how churches can utilize the talents and skills of the retired.

Anatomy articles in the *Reader's Digest* assume "specific" significance when titled, "I am Joe's Heart"; "I am Joe's Ear"; "I am Jane's Ovary."

After you know the specific angle you want to develop, you are ready to begin to research your subject. Using the *Reader's Guide to Periodical Literature* in your public library, check to see if this idea has been handled before. If it has, consider whether you can approach it from a different and a fresh angle, or if, by adding new information, you can come up with a better article.

Because you can never know too much about a subject, you will begin your research by reading relevant books, magazine articles, and newspaper reports. Here a librarian can help you. You will also interview persons who have special knowledge about the subject.

Record every incident, anecdote, conversation, name, date, statistic—everything and anything you feel may enhance your article. For the most part you will not copy notes verbatim but will put down your findings in your own words (unless you wish to use a specific quotation). In that case you must copy the material precisely as it is printed.

After you have researched until facts begin repeating themselves, you are ready to select those you feel are most pertinent to your presentation. *Number* these notes and type them out in full detail. Don't be concerned about sequence here. Study the notes, fix them in your mind. They represent your proof-text inventory.

Let's begin by assuming you have already selected the article pattern you wish to use. Following this pattern, outline your article proceeding logically from beginning to end.

Now go back to your numbered research notes. Insert under each division the number designating the reference or references you will want to include in that spot. Check off the numbers of the reference notes as you transfer them to your article outline. As a double precaution, check off each number in the outline when you incorporate that particular proof text in your article as you type it.

Let me illustrate. I once wrote an article about a photographer, a Benedictine nun, Noemi Weygant, who taught photography in a Chicago ghetto one summer.[3] Though *Good Housekeeping* magazine used only a portion of the article, preferring more pictures than text, I did follow this procedure in preparing the manuscript.

In researching the article I studied the beautiful coffee-table poetry-photograph books she and a Lutheran pastor had compiled. I talked to the minister, the Rev. Herbert Brokering. In doing so I learned what circumstances in his life had fostered his interest in nature and in the church. I learned how he had met Noemi Weygant and what had led to this particular collaboration.

I also interviewed Sister Weygant, who told me the story of her Montana childhood. I learned about her work as photographer-teacher at the priory where she lived. I spoke to photographers who knew her work. I learned about national honors she had won.

Then I flew to Chicago and talked to the woman responsible for the ghetto assignment. I spoke to the Mother Superior at the St. Ambrose parochial school. From her I learned what part the school played in the program.

Then I visited Sister Weygant's photography classes and talked to the boys she taught, asking questions about their involvement in the class. I collected facts, anecdotes, statistics, ghetto jargon, ghetto descriptions—everything I thought I might need when I wrote the article.

When I returned home I typed my findings on sheets of paper. Not bothering about any kind of sequence, I numbered each proof text. After deciding on my angle of approach, I outlined the article, inserting the number of each research note in the spot where I believed it belonged and where it would appear in the finished product.

As you incorporate research notes in your article outline you may discover you have more material than you need in that particular piece. Some of it may be irrelevant to the main thing you want to say about your subject. Don't discard this material, however. Instead, try to come up with another angle of the same subject—one which will utilize material left over from the first article. Or you may find that you have enough information to write a series of articles, each from a different approach to the same general subject.

A final word: as you put your article together, be yourself. Let your personality show. No one else will ever approach your subject exactly as you, because of your background and experience, approach it.

CHALLENGE ASSIGNMENT

1. List factors that make a good article.
2. Make a list of five topics which are currently in the news.
3. Choose and identify specific angles of each.
4. Select one specific angle of one of these subjects. Check the *Reader's Guide to Periodical Literature*. Locate all the articles published during the past year on that specific angle.
5. Obtain one of the articles in the library. Read it and try to discover the avenues of research used by the author.

12. *Article Segments*

In most editorial offices the departmental editors or members of their staffs do the preliminary reading of a manuscript. It is their attention you must capture if you expect your manuscript to be read.

Titles

Next to an article's illustrations, the article title is the first thing these readers notice. In the shuffling of a moment it must persuade them that the entire piece merits consideration.

To be effective a title should be concise, precise, and accurate. You make it concise by assembling a few apt words in the most deft manner—which means that the title is short and contains no unnecessary *a, an, the,* or *that,* etc.

Your title may be classified as precise when it says exactly what you mean it to say. Suppose I were trying to find a title for an advice article telling women whose mates travel a great deal how to handle home responsibilities while their husbands are on the road. I could mistakenly entitle the piece, "How to Carry On While Your Husband Is On the Road" (as one author almost did). Far better to say precisely what I mean, "Cope, Don't Mope," "A Daily Chat and a Welcome Mat," or "Plan your Strategy, Together," depending on the specific angle from which I approach the problem.

Accuracy means that the title describes the subject matter truthfully. If an article titled, "The Fastest-Growing Sunday School in the State," tells the story of a Sunday school whose growth doesn't approximate that of two or three faster-growing schools in the state, it may be said to be dishonest. The writer, we assume, failed to do his homework.

Beware of such superlatives as *biggest, most significant, greatest.* Use them only when they represent personal opinion. I may title an article, "My Most Disastrous Experience," since this represents my opinion. I may title an article involving another person, "The World's Most Beautiful Scenery," if I make it clear in the writing that this is that person's opinion.

Title selection can be simplified if you learn some of the types most frequently used. Titles fall into specific categories with which you should be familiar.

BALANCE AND CONTRAST

Tit for Tat	Loud and Clear
Christ or Chaos	For Better or for Worse

DECLARATIVE SENTENCE

A Heart Is an Inn	There's Potential in Those Years
Sex Isn't Everything	Prayer Changes You

DIRECT ADDRESS

Cry Not That He is Dead	Dare to Discipline
Salute Your Uncle Sam	Memorize

EXCLAMATION

It's Tremendous!	Help!

LABEL

The Torch Relay	The Canvas Message
The Shepherd Song	Bach's Fugue

WORD PLAY

Practice What You'd Reach	Assault and Flattery

PROVOCATIVE OR MYSTERIOUS

No Toys for This Man	Malagasy Interlude
Wrapped in a Maxim	The Man From Mars

QUESTION

Is Your Latchstring Out?	Can You Face Death?
Who Needs God?	Are You Killing Your Pastor?

RHYME OR ALLITERATION

A Call is Not All	Ban the Can
March of Manners	Car Caution

STARTLING ELEMENT

Last Warning to the World	No Place to Hide

WHAT, WHEN, WHY, HOW

Why Babies Cry	When Talking Fails
What Makes Churches Grow	How to Buy a House

One editor may prefer the pun, another the matter-of-fact or declarative-sentence title. And some editors will expect you to submit a subtitle with your article. A subtitle—an extension of the title—is brief, just a phrase or two (preceded by a colon and beginning with a capital letter), in which you try to state the essential coverage of the article. For instance, a *Decision* magazine article was titled "The Other Man on the Bench." Its subtitle: "EVER WONDERED WHAT A JUDGE THINKS ABOUT?" "We're Going to Crash!" titled an article in *Good Housekeeping* magazine. Its subtitle: "Last year a train slammed into a busful of children and five of them died. Sorrow, outrage—and fear it could happen again—have turned strangers into neighbors, neighbors into friends." It's your job to find out which periodicals use these explanatory subtitles.

Occasionally subheads are required to identify various sections of your manuscript. Again, note how they are used.

Beginnings

The beginning of an article, the lead, is a captivating, eye-and-mind-arresting show-window display that says, "This is a sample of my merchandise. There's more inside."

As a window display, your beginning must be subject-relevant and so enticing an editor will want to investigate the product found in the body of the article.

Article beginnings vary according to type. The following examples should help you understand some of these variations.

THE ANECDOTE LEAD

You have already learned that the anecdote is a miniature story. It has a beginning which sets the stage for the story, a middle which presents the story drama, and an ending which clinches what has been said. I have found that the most meaningful and useful anecdotes are not those I read but those which, through experiences of one kind or another, belong solely to me.

We were packing, hoping we would be ready when the moving van came to load our household goods.

My husband, dressed in his most dilapidated togs, was busy cleaning the garage. A couple of small neighbor children stopped to watch him work. After a bit, one of the youngsters, a puzzled note in his voice, asked, "Say, mister, are you really a preacher?"

"Yes, I am," my husband answered. "Why do you ask?"

"Oh, I just wondered." He paused, hesitated a moment, then added, "You sure don't look like one."[1]

Good-natured, kind, self-effacing, Uncle Oscar gave unstintingly of his time, energy, and substance to help support the small northern Minnesota church to which he belonged.

Unfortunately diabetes complicated the last years of his life. As the disease progressed doctors found it necessary to amputate both of his legs. Yet he never complained; his joy in the Lord never wavered. When he died, one of his sons who had weighed the significance of his father's entire life said, "Even a man without legs can leave eternal footprints in the sands of time."[2]

THE CONTRAST OR COMPARISON LEAD

In this type of lead you use contrast or comparison to hook your reader.

It's a mammoth step from an affluent, middle-class, Protestant-sheltered home in Hinsdale, Illinois, to New York's Sixth Street, Ave-

nue D, East-Side ghetto area. Nevertheless, I took that step. And
though I had been properly warned, my first contact with city smells,
broken glass, crumbling concrete, and streets teeming with children
filled me with apprehension.[3]

Many people think contemporary artists are mop-headed, scruffy-
looking individuals bent on painting indiscriminate distortions of all
that is real. A person who does not fit this picture is young Howard
Sanden, tall, chic Minneapolis artist whose work is attracting world-
wide appreciation because it does not distort that which is meaningful
and real.[4]

THE DESCRIPTION LEAD

To be good, a description lead should be brief and vivid. It
should paint a clear picture of the individual, scene, or object
you will be writing about. It will include action when that is
possible.

It happened the second year we were in California. By that time we
were accustomed to Christmas without soft, downy snow blanketing
lawns, shrubs, and trees.

The sun shone summer warm; the lawns were green as New England in May. The poinsettia trees stretched their flaming fronds high
along the sides of the Spanish bungalows in the section of Los Angeles
where we lived. White calla lilies stood like proud sentinels against
stone foundations.[5]

You've met him frequently in cartoons, on magazine covers, posters,
and highway billboards. Tall, angular, clad in flamboyant red, white,
and blue clothing, he is as familiar as the American flag, as traditional
as the Fourth of July.[6]

THE DIRECT-ADDRESS LEAD

The direct-address lead speaks directly to the reader by using
terms such as *everyone, many people, most of us, you.*

"Teenagers!"
You've often heard this word applied to the segment of society to
which you belong. Yet how the word is spoken, what tone of voice is
used, depends not so much on the person speaking as on the circumstances involved.[7]

Many people remember the *Look* magazine article about the Jesus People. Few, however, know that I, Jack Cheetham, and my wife Betty researched and photographed the story. Identity is important only as it helps people understand what happened to us while we worked on the project.[8]

THE INCIDENT LEAD

Though many writers do not make any distinction between the incident and the anecdote lead, I think of them as two different types. The anecdote lead is a miniature story with a beginning, a middle, and a clinch ending. The incident lead, on the other hand, does not end with a punch line. It merely relates a significant, highly interesting occurrence relevant to the subject matter discussed in the article.

The high-school music instructor raised his hand. "Hold it," he said. He walked over to one of the musicians.

"Take that run alone, Sherman."

The boy took the run—and flubbed it.

"Again," the instructor directed.

Sherman tensed. What's he trying to do? Show me up or something? he thought. He adjusted his instrument and with grim determination took another stab at the score.

The director shook his head. "Not quite." "Try practicing that part at home. You're too good a musician to let a few hard notes trip you up."[9]

THE NARRATIVE LEAD

The narrative lead begins a story presentation, often a personal experience adventure. It differs from the anecdote lead in that it doesn't have a beginning, a middle and a clinch ending. It merely presents the beginning of a story which continues to the end of the article.

The giant plane rolled down Chicago's cloud-blanketed O'Hare runway. Then it lifted to soar into a sun-bright sky. When the signal was given, passengers loosened their seat belts and relaxed. A few began to read, others to chat.

One passenger, a pleasant, motherly woman, did neither. Her heart beat rapidly. She felt she ought to pinch herself to make sure it was she who had begun the first lap of a journey that would take her into Zaire bush country. In her wildest imagining, Esther Johnson, a pastor's widow, had never dreamed that one day she would return to the people she had served as a young missionary bride.[10]

THE NEWS-PEG LEAD

The news-peg lead presents a news event of significant interest and relevance to capture reader interest in the article.

A few years ago the phrase "give the shirt off your back" was dramatized, literally, when members of the Los Angeles Advertising Club responded to an appeal for Korean refugees. To a man, the five hundred men present removed their shirts and contributed them to the cause.[11]

"Doctor Gordon Bengtson and family left Saturday for Batavia, Illinois, where they will spend the holidays with Mrs. Bengtson's parents. . . ." This paragraph from our small-town newspaper shouldn't have surprised me. Such items are tidbits that make local journalism palatable. Yet it did. "How does he do it?" I asked my husband. "He took time off during hunting season, too."[12]

THE QUESTION LEAD

Here the lead asks a pertinent question which relates to the subject to be presented and arouses the curiosity of the reader.

A friend lamented the fact that so many church members fail to entertain newcomers, visiting ministers and missionaries.
"How does your church handle this problem?" she asked.[13]

How would you like to witness to several thousand people at one time about things you believe are pertinent to the Christian faith?[14]

THE QUOTATION LEAD

The quotation lead contains a recognizable quotation from a living person, from an historical figure, from a book, newspaper, or magazine.

"It's when you give yourself," the poet Kahlil Gibran wrote, *"that you truly give."* Across the nation, generous individuals from many

walks of life are sharing their time and talents with the deprived. One such helping hand is offered by Noemi Weygant, a Benedictine nun of Duluth, Minnesota, and a prize-winning photographer. Armed with enthusiasm and affection. . . .[15]

"Ban the Can!"
This is the ecological battle cry of James F. Carlson, Director of Library Services at the American River College, Sacramento, California, who is out in front warring against can and bottle pollution in the United States.[16]

THE STARTLING STATEMENT LEAD

This arouses interest by startling the reader. It presents facts, statistics, anecdotes that shock and jar without exaggerating.

What an accomplishment! Millions of records—7,000,000 to be exact —gratis to 170 countries of the world! One shipment of 100,000, weighing 15 tons, to Indonesia alone. For such an achievement credit Gospel Recordings, the missionary endeavor founded by Miss Joy Ridderhof.[17]

More or less sensationally, newspapers and magazines seem bent on frightening us about scientific control of man's genetic future, referred to by some as genetic manipulation.
According to Dr. Elving Anderson, University of Minnesota professor, scientist and Christian at the Dight Institute of Human Genetics, no one needs to fear genetic control unduly. He says . . .[18]

THE STATEMENT-OF-PURPOSE LEAD

A type of lead which needs no explanation—it simply tells the reader immediately what he may expect to find in the article.

Here is an excellent hospital-gift idea that involves the participation of a group of individuals. Called a one-a-day gift, it is especially appreciated by the person who expects to be hospitalized for a week or more.[19]

THE SUMMARY LEAD

This resembles the summary lead of a news item in that it gives a brief synopsis of the entire article. It provides the reader with a quick panoramic view of the subject.

Three lives. That's the story of graying, sandy-haired Enoch S. Christoffersen, mayor of Turlock, California—up-and-coming city of 16,000 in the heart of the fertile San Joaquin Valley.

Mr. Christoffersen is a businessman, a civic official, and a Christian —on whom, he says, "God has priority claims."[20]

THE SURVEY LEAD

Here we are presented with two or more examples of a given problem or situation the article explores. Use this lead to prove your subject has universal interest and concern.

In a remote village of the Alaskan interior, a small band of Eskimos gather around a transistor radio. Static crackles through the crisp arctic air as someone adjusts the tuning knob. Then loud and clear the strong voice of Theodore Epp of the Back-to-the-Bible broadcast from Lincoln, Nebraska, is heard.

Later in the day fishermen along the Alaskan coast cut their outboard motors. Inland trappers pull transistors from their parkas. It's time for the "Eskimo Hour" to break the silence of the far north.[21]

A school principal dictates his last letter, an application for his retirement pension. A business executive hands his office keys to an eager colleague who trails him on the promotional totem pole. A gray-haired librarian stamps her last "date-due" in an avid reader's armload of books. A minister folds his clerical robe and heads for home.

To what?[22]

THE COMBINATION LEAD

When you employ two or more kinds of leads in the beginning of an article you are using a combination lead. Here is an example which is both a news-peg and a direct address.

If you are like most people you do not like to attend funerals. You share very poignantly the pain mourners experience in the loss of loved ones. This is only natural.

Had you been in Turlock, California, some time ago, you might have attended a funeral devoid of sorrow. This unique event, called a "Coughin," was held to dramatize the final results of smoking. After a ceremony of uncomplimentary eulogies, with proper pomp and mock soberness, the "loved one," the *cigarette habit*, was laid to rest.[23]

Endings

If an editor likes your title and your beginning, chances are he will bypass the body of the article temporarily to see how you end it. Note the following examples of the most common article endings.

THE SUMMARY ENDING

This recaps what has been said in the article.

"You see, as a scientist I delve into man's physical and chemical makeup. Yet as a Christian I believe man is also a spiritual being, able to respond to God and therefore responsible to Him for what he does with his life. This is why, in the field of genetics, my work is undergirded by faith, not by fear."[24]

THE CHALLENGE ENDING

This type of ending is directed to the reader. It challenges him to act on what he has learned.

Challenging? Indeed. Let's give retirees jobs of dignity and worth.[25]

THE PROJECTION ENDING

The projection ending looks into the future. It speaks of an individual's or an organization's contemplated plans.

His ambition?
To be one of America's most effective interpreters of the Christian faith. He says, "After all, an artist who is a Christian does more than interpret a scene. His work is the projection of a message."[26]

THE CLINCH ENDING

This ending ties the article together in a neat, satisfying package. Often it does this by referring to something said in the beginning.

"I know, Mom, and I've been thinking. That fancy tree was all right for the store. But let's have one just like we've always had. It really takes years to trim a tree."[27]

By the time an editor has checked the title and read the beginning and the ending of the article, he knows pretty well whether he wants to consider it for publication. To make certain, he now reads the body of the piece. This is the final test. For in the body, the proof section of your article, you will or will not have explored your premise and documented and authenticated (with anecdotes, facts, quotes, examples, and statistics) everything you said initially about your subject. If the editor is satisfied, the word is *go*.

CHALLENGE ASSIGNMENT

1. Using six or seven periodicals, locate apt article titles which illustrate each type presented in this chapter.

2. Clip and paste, on separate sheets of paper, samples of article beginnings that have been discussed. Under each, indicate the type.

3. Follow the same procedure—clip and identify samples of the four types of article endings just cited.

13. Article Illustrations

To illustrate or not to illustrate, this is the question you must resolve before you mail your manuscript. Almost all publications use illustrations. Some use pen-and-ink drawings; the majority (90 percent, some people say) illustrate their articles with photographs. Study of a magazine will alert you to its policy as well as to the type of photograph used, black-and-white or colored. It's best to settle the matter of illustrations in your query letter. Tell the editor what types of illustrations you can supply.

Picture Requirements

Periodicals that do use photographs look for pictures which

1. *Reproduce sharply.* An editor isn't as much concerned about the size of the negative from which a photograph is enlarged as he is about its sharp focus. Most editors prefer an 8″ × 10″ enlargement, though some will accept a 5″ × 7″.

Be sure the picture you have enlarged is in sharp focus and that it is printed on glossy paper. Discard pictures which reflect light from eyeglasses, windowpanes, and bodies of water.

2. *Relate to the substance of the article.* In submitting an article about an artist you may have a choice of *(a)* a mug shot of the artist; *(b)* a photograph of some of his work; *(c)* a photograph of him at work painting a picture. Obviously the latter photograph would more precisely reflect the substance of your article, especially if it referred to specific painting techniques. Since several pictures are better than one, you could include photographs of the man's work, too.

3. *Incorporate relevant props.* The photograph submitted with an article I wrote about the woman in charge of shipping for Gospel Recordings (an organization which supplies missionaries with gospel records) showed her at her desk talking to a customer. A large map, pinpointing world ports to which shipments are made, hung in full view on a wall behind the desk.

Photographs which illustrate how-to articles may show your subject in action in a step-by-step demonstration of the procedure you describe.

A word of caution—don't allow anything in the background to distort a picture. Some object may appear in the finished print as an extension of your subject's nose or as a strange-looking hat.

Photograph Sources

1. YOUR OWN PICTURES

You are money ahead if you are able to take your own photographs. You need not invest in costly equipment. A good reflex or single-lens camera can be purchased reasonably. Many models have built-in light meters and range finders which simplify picture taking.

If you need assistance in choosing a camera ask one of your photographer friends or a local newspaper photographer to help you. Watch for used-camera sales advertised in your local newspapers. The professional photographer is constantly upgrading his equipment. The camera he sells will very likely serve you well. Before you buy, however, have it checked by someone who knows camera quality.

To achieve picture-taking confidence consider enrolling in a college or adult-education photography class. Or join a local camera club where members evaluate each other's work and share picture-taking knowledge. Read books about photography. Upon request the Eastman Kodak Company, Rochester, N. Y., 14650, will send you a free index of their publications.

The book *Visual Impact in Print* by Gerald Hurley and Angus McDougall (experts in the field), American Publishers Press,

812 W. Van Buren St., Chicago, Ill., 60607, is considered a classic text as subtitled: "How to Make Pictures Communicate: A Guide for the Photographer, the Editor, the Designer." You may be able to obtain this book from your local library.

Good photographers advise: never skimp on film. Shoot many more pictures than you need. Then you will be sure to get one or more shots which are superior to the rest. Visualize and plan pictures before you take them. This will mean posing your subject engaged in some activity. Don't forget relevant props.

To make sure that a picture was taken with the subject's knowledge and permission many editors ask that a model release be submitted with the photograph. You should secure one for your own protection, too, since you rarely sell more than a one-use right to photographs. You may have occasion to sell the print separately for other purposes.

A suggested model release form:

I,_____, of _____, consent to the use of the picture taken by _____ in which I appear. I waive all claims for any remuneration for such use.

_____
(Signature of subject)

Date _____

_____
(Signature of witness)

Most free-lance writers do not try to do their own film processing. Top-quality processing is an exacting art which, if you wish to free-lance extensively, you won't have time to pursue. Let professional custom-lab processors handle the dark-room detail.

I am sure you realize you won't get this type of service through your local drugstore or through a film-drop firm which specializes in speedy service. By hand-developing films, custom labs are able to correct minor exposure mistakes you may have made in taking a picture. And upon request they will prepare a contact sheet of negative-size positive prints of each roll of film. By studying these contact prints with a strong reading glass you will be able to select the ones you wish to have enlarged.

The Astra Photo Service, 6 East Lake Street, Chicago, Ill., 60601, does top-quality work and is centrally located geographically for most writers. If you prefer working with a custom lab closer to you, write the American Society of Magazine Photographers, 60 East 42 Street, New York, N.Y., 10017, and ask them for the name and address of a photo specialist in your area.

2. YOUR SOURCE OF INFORMATION

In many instances the person or organization you write about will offer to supply photographs you need. This was true of the story I wrote about Annie Vallotton, the artist who illustrated *Good News for Modern Man*. The American Bible Society, for whom Miss Vallotton did the drawings, provided the photographs.

From two students who spent a year in Europe I obtained the photographs for an article written about their experiences. The Westinghouse Electric Corporation supplied photographs for an article describing the use of the computer in compiling the concordance for the American Revised Version of the Bible.

3. PROFESSIONAL PHOTOGRAPHERS

There will be times when you are unable to obtain the photographs you need, either by taking your own or from your source of information. In such instances you may have to turn to a professional photographer who, for a price, will take the pictures you require. While collecting photographs of the Benedictine nun who taught photography in a Chicago ghetto, I learned that a New York photographer had visited her class and taken a picture I had failed to get. He gladly released it for my use.

Do not despair if the only available picture is a colored print. A good studio can make black-and-white copies from a sharply focused colored photograph.

4. NEWSPAPERS

If you recall having seen newspaper pictures of your subject, you may contact the newspaper's photograph librarian for prints you wish to use. I could never have taken as good pictures of my subject in one instance—a handicapped woman—as the *Minneapolis Star* photographers had already secured. Upon request, and for a fee, this newspaper made several prints for me. To facilitate location of newspaper photographs you should supply the date the pictures have appeared in print. Some newspapers charge less for the pictures they release if they know they will be used to illustrate articles in religious publications. As a rule they ask to be given a credit line.

5. TRADE AND NATIONAL SERVICE ORGANIZATIONS

An article telling readers how they could help the blind was illustrated with pictures received free of charge from the American Foundation for the Blind, 15 West 16th Street, New York, N.Y., 10010. The American National Red Cross, 17th Street between D and E Streets, N.W., Washington, D.C., 20006 distributes free photographs of disaster scenes, safety practices, volunteer services, and nursing.

The Shell Oil Company, 50 West 50th Street, New York, N.Y., 10020, stocks a vast number of black-and-white, no-cost prints about the oil industry, vacations, camping, and fishing.

The American Telephone and Telegraph Company, 195 Broadway, New York, N.Y., 10007, can supply pictures about telephone history as well as all phases of telephone operation, telestar, and satellites.

The Westinghouse Electric Corporation, 300 Stanwix Street, Pittsburg, Pa. stocks more than a million service pictures.

Doubtless a good many other foundations and corporations can provide photographic materials to the person who will take the trouble to discover these sources.

6. GOVERNMENT AGENCIES

The U.S. Department of Agriculture, 14th Street and Independence Ave. S.W., Washington, D.C., 20250 will supply pictures about agriculture, conservation, and home economics. The Children's Department of the U.S. Department of Health, Education, and Welfare, 330 Independence Ave. S.W., Washington, D.C. 20201 is a source for pictures of children at play or engaged in craft and hobby activities.

The Library of Congress, Prints and Photograph Division, 10th Street S.E., Washington, D.C., 20540 stocks material dating from the fifteenth century on.

Photographs from the National Archives, Still Picture Branch, 9th and Constitution Avenues N.W., Washington, D.C., 20408 touch all phases of U.S. Government activities.

The U.S. Fish and Wildlife Service, 18th and C Streets N.W., Washington, D.C. 20240 provides black-and-white photographs of wildlife and conservation.

Local and state government organizations also supply photographs relevant to their particular area of concern.

7. RELIGIOUS ORGANIZATIONS

The Religious News Service
43 West 57th St., New York, N.Y., 10019
U.S. National Catholic Conference
1312 Massachusets Ave., N.W., Washington, D.C., 20005

8. PHOTOGRAPH SUPPLY COMPANIES

Special companies maintain complete stocks of for-a-fee photographs on almost any subject you can name.

Ewing Galloway
420 Lexington Ave., New York, N.Y., 10017
Cobb Shinn Services
721 Union Street, Indianapolis, Ind. 46225

Once more, resources for an enterprising person are far from being limited to those listed here. In New York City alone the Manhattan yellow pages (classified telephone directory) carry more than two columns of names of persons or firms with photographs for sale.

9. READER'S GUIDE TO PERIODICAL LITERATURE

This may seem an unlikely source for photographic material. It isn't. If you can't find a picture relating to the subject you are writing about, look for that subject in the *Reader's Guide*. Take note of articles on the subject. When you locate them in the library's magazines, you will find a paragraph which lists "Il" (illustration) sources. By noting these credit lines you will know to whom to write to secure similar pictures.

A special section in *Writer's Market* is devoted to picture sources, too.

Occasionally an article requires submission of a chart or drawing of some kind. Though few writers prepare their own, you may if you can. Illustrations done in india ink are almost always required when submitting puzzles and how-to articles. Even if you do not draw well, you can come up with a crude sketch which will serve as a guide for the artist who prepares the illustration for publication.

Cutlines and Captions

Unless a picture or illustration is used only to decorate, prepare an explanatory label for it. Most publications print this under or to one side of the picture. A few also use a heading, printed in larger type, above the picture or above the explanation. The explanation is called the *cutline* or *legend,* while the heading is the *overline* or *caption.* Cutlines may be a few words or up to a paragraph in length.

A cutline may be typed on a strip of paper which approximates the width of the picture, minus an inch or two. If a caption is used it is typed above the cutline. The top of the strip is pasted (I use rubber cement) to the back of the photograph across the bottom so that the cutline extends below the picture. In mailing, the typed area is folded up over the picture.

An increasing number of editors, however, ask that photographs be numbered somewhere along the edge of the print side (not on the back). Then the cutlines and captions are typed on a separate sheet of paper and numbered to correspond.

You should learn how to write catchy, interesting cutlines. Avoid the sameness so common in cutline texts.

1. Maintain a present tense reference.
2. Avoid trite phrases: "This picture shows—"
3. Avoid *the, an, a* beginnings. Study picture cutlines in the *National Geographic, Ford Times, Friends Magazine,* and *Sports Illustrated.*

Note these examples of beginnings of cutlines taken from Chevrolet's *Friends Magazine:*

Ocean breakers surging . . .
Logging has been a major industry . . .
Browsing in her library . . .
Ready to pull the pin . . .

In checking an issue of *Time* magazine I found that captions were used frequently together with cutlines. For instance, each of three pictures of Lyndon B. Johnson identified him and the role he was playing at the time. Below, a running cutline summarized the photo thought: "Shaped and shadowed by the hill country, he was a whole cast of characters—folksy, frugal and patriotic."

Under a caption identifying a well-known basketball player the cutline read: "Going all out all the time at both ends of the floor."

4. Use picture words. Strive for sensory impressions.
5. Keep cutlines brief—adopt the economy of a telegram.

Do not write on the back of a picture or use a paper clip to secure it to cutlines and captions. Ink marks or an indentation will show through the picture when it is printed.

In mailing, sandwich photographs between sheets of sturdy corrugated cardboard which may be cut from grocery cartons. It's wise to have the rib-grain run in one direction on one side and across it on the other.

Editors prefer that color transparencies be submitted in the transparent plastic sleeves in which they are returned from a photo lab. Captions and identifications should be typed on pressure adhesive labels which can be attached to the plastic sleeves. Protect transparencies with cardboard, too.

Unless the editor specifies otherwise, do not submit the original color transparency. Send a copy of it. Remember, you sell one-right use to a photograph. You will, of course, mail article illustrations in your manuscript package.

Repeated photo submissions will convince you that editors *do* think pictorially. Your job is to please them by submitting the most meaningful, sharp, subject-relevant photographs you can secure.

CHALLENGE ASSIGNMENT

1. Describe a good photograph.
2. From what sources are you most apt to obtain your photographs?
3. Select a photo from your home collection. Write a caption and a cutline for it.
4. At the public library pick up several illustrated magazines. Make a list of illustration sources you find in the paragraph of photograph credit lines.

4

Feature·Length Nonfiction
Article Patterns

14. The Reportorial-Explanatory Article

You can pick up any number of magazines and find several articles which follow the first and most basic feature-article pattern: the reportorial-explanatory. In writing this article you choose and research a subject you are vitally interested in and one you believe readers will enjoy. Then you report and explain your findings.

Unlike the brief newspaper report, the reportorial-explanatory article reflects more extensive research—material you garner from printed sources and from talking to informed individuals. This article also permits you to analyze the facts you have presented or to express a personal opinion about them.

Each reportorial-explanatory article has a beginning which hooks the reader and a bridge which ties the beginning to the body of the piece and nudges the reader to continue reading. The body contains the *tell*-and-*show* data of the article. Here you authenticate everything you have said about your subject. The ending may clinch what has been said, or it may summarize, challenge, or make some projection based on the knowledge presented.

One of Walter Campbell's students came up with some very catchy designations for these article segments: *Hey!*, *You!*, *See!*, and *So?*[1]

Hey! says, "Stop—this is interesting!"

You! says, "Look—this is important to you!"

See! says, "Listen—here are the facts and their documentation."

So? says, "Act! Evaluate what you have read, do something about it. Think about what has been said."

I suggest you pick up a current magazine and study the many advertisements which, for the most part, follow this outline precisely.

Note the following example, an office copier advertisement, which said in effect:

> *Stop!* Here is a copier that excels many on the market.
>
> *Look!* No waiting in line! (The significance of this fact was illustrated by a speed-blurred photograph showing how secretarial traffic moved quickly leaving the machine.)
>
> *Listen!*
>
> 1. The machine has a special feature that permits continual copy feeding.
> 2. It's automatic.
> 3. It's versatile. It copies practically everything.
> 4. It produces copies which are crisp and sharp.
>
> *Act!* Get in touch with the manufacturer for more information. Don't be a copier's servant; let this copier serve you.

A UNICEF advertisement used reproductions of its holiday cards to attract attention to another example of the reportorial-explanatory outline pattern.

> *Stop*, readers, and *Look!* Most holiday cards talk about peace, good will, and joy; UNICEF cards do something about it.
>
> *Listen:*
>
> 1. They provide nourishment, medicine, and school supplies for needy children around the world.
> 2. The cards are beautifully executed by well-known artists.
> 3. They are no more expensive than other cards. So,
>
> *Act*, readers! You are going to buy Christmas cards anyway; why not buy UNICEF cards and give hope to some child?

The reportorial-explanatory article, though longer and more extensively documented, is written like these advertisements. By appropriating this outline you can write articles about:

missionary endeavors	controversy
history	inspirational subjects
science	opinion and commentary
new ideas and discoveries	medicine

government   the church
travel   the home

You should be aware, however, that many of these subjects lend themselves to other article patterns, too, depending on the particular angle from which you approach your material. Take missionary work as an example. If you use the reportorial-explanatory pattern you may write about: a new missionary dormitory in Japan; new trends in missionary work; the financing of missionary work. If you write about one missionary's personal experiences on the mission field, you may choose a different pattern—the narrative most likely.

I can best illustrate this point by referring you to two very different missionary articles. One, titled, "The Voice of the Arctic,"[2] follows the reportorial-explanatory pattern. Its subtitle: "Across the frozen tundra of the Far North come broadcasts of dog-team races, the Eskimo Hour, and a regular schedule of gospel programs."

The beginning (Stop!)
A survey lead (referred to in chapter 12) sets the stage. It describes Alaskans occupied in many activities, listening to Radio Station KICY in Nome, Alaska.

The bridge (Look!)
This transitional section points up the effectiveness of the station, identifies the founder, the Evangelical Covenant Church of America, and suggests that the station has broken through the long silence of the Arctic.

The body (Listen!)
1. See! The before-and-after picture explaining contrasting conditions. Example of a teacher in a remote village who didn't hear of President Eisenhower's heart attack in 1955 until several weeks after it happened.
2. See! The programs used to break the silence of the Arctic.
   a. World-wide programs with specific examples.
   b. Local news. Live coverage of dog team races; coverage of high school sports events. Report of a submarine's visit as it stopped in Nome by way of the North Pole.

  c. Public health programs. Examples of broadcasts which inform
     parents of the exact time a government plane will arrive in a
     remote village to bring help to a sick child. News broadcasts of
     the condition of persons in city hospitals.
  d. The "Swap Shop"—a program which identifies items to be
     traded and the price and owner of each. Items: wolverine and
     wolf pelts, dried fish for dog food, a walrus tusk and jawbone,
     a pair of gold scales, a set of reindeer harnesses.

The ending (So?)
This contains a projection: "As more folks migrate to this newest of
the fifty states (Alaska's population has already doubled since 1950), the
'Voice of the Arctic' should become even more influential."

Another missionary article, however, might be of the personal-experience type. I recall one, for instance, which described
a short-term missionary's adventures in the Malagasy Republic.
It followed the narrative pattern, about which you will learn
later. Had the reportorial-explanatory pattern been used, it
might have expounded the merits of short-term missionary
work. Then, as with the KICY article, it would have included
anecdotes, narrative incidents, quotes—whatever—to report,
explain, and prove its particular theme: the value of short-term
missionary work.

The account of a spiritual happening at North Park College,
Chicago, Illinois, also serves to illustrate the reportorial-
explanatory pattern. Title: "Then Jesus Came."

The beginning
The survey lead establishes, through a paraphrased version of the
song by the same title, the need for such a happening.

The bridge
"These paraphrased references represent a sample of lives trans-
formed when the Holy Spirit moved across Chicago's North Park College campus last January."

The body
1. How it all got started
   a. Need to make the college "Religious Emphasis Week" more
      meaningful.
   b. Name changed to "Festival of Faith."
   c. Circumstances leading to the selection of an evangelistic team

    headed by Don Williams, associate pastor of the Hollywood Presbyterian Church.

2. Team personnel
   a. Names and descriptions of each of the nine persons involved. Their significance.
   b. Means by which the team members established rapport with the students. They asked for no special accommodations; they moved into college dormitory rooms; they slept in sleeping bags; were constantly available.
3. The festival procedure
   a. Breakfast Bible study
   b. Chapel services
   c. Afternoon seminars on prayer, personal commitment, the role of the Christian woman, and so on.
   d. Evening evangelistic sharing services
4. Effectiveness of the "Festival of Faith"
   a. Testimony of students whose lives were changed
   b. Testimony of faculty members
   c. Comments by President Lloyd S. Ahlem

The ending (a projection)

What happens now? Students are determined to prove the experience wasn't just a transitory kick. Plans for next year's religious emphasis involvement.

The reportorial-explanatory article can be used effectively in writing controversial material. Some editors like to present two sides of an issue. They may choose two authors whose viewpoints differ. One reports, explains, and attempts to prove his conviction; the other takes an opposite stance.

Frequently such articles are printed together, on facing pages. One discussion which received this placement treatment dealt with euthanasia. Another presented pro and con views concerning the practice of encouraging children to believe in Santa Claus.

Simple, direct, logical, the reportorial-explanatory article pattern ought to become as familiar to would-be writers as their *ABC*s.

CHALLENGE ASSIGNMENT

1. Study several ads in a current magazine. Outline one of them as was done with the office copier ad.

2. Select a published reportorial-explanatory article which interests you. Outline it following this particular outline pattern.

3. Choose a subject you feel would make a good reportorial-explanatory article. Plan an article about this subject.

4. Research and outline the article.

5. Write the article.

6. Name two or three controversial topics on which opposite viewpoints could be presented together to show the basis of divergent opinion.

15.   *The Narrative Article*

"I recall the time . . ." "What an experience, let me tell you about it . . ." When you hear these words, listen! They may introduce you to a story about an exciting adventure, a meaningful struggle, or a life-changing experience which you can write up as a narrative article.

Of all types of articles the narrative, a dramatic tale with an emotional impact, most closely resembles fiction. It involves the reader vicariously, just as a short story, a novel, or a play does. Unlike fiction, however, it is true. The tale you tell must actually have happened to you or to someone you know or can persuade to tell his story.

The narrative may be an adventure story in which the experience is highly unusual. You could write about a young couple who were shipwrecked in the English Channel; a family under attack by a wild bear; a miraculous escape from a burning building. Although suspense or entertainment may be primary goals, the religious writer tries to find an additional ingredient: the spiritual impact of such an experience.

Another type of narrative is one that relates a personal experience which is typical rather than unusual. It may detail a person's struggle with a particular problem: health, personal relationships, marital difficulties, church involvement, parent-child tensions.

Such articles might be titled

> I Was "Committed" to Death (church involvement)
> I Am a Sensitive Kid (blindness)
> We Couldn't Cope (parent-child relationship)

The confession is a much more intimate revelation of personal experience. In it the writer bares his soul. Confession articles might be titled

> I Was a Teenage Witch
> I'm Glad I Wasn't Aborted
> My Mastectomy
> My Husband Wouldn't Talk

"My Son, My Son" by Bernard Palmer[1] (later expanded into a book) represents this type of confession article. In it the author reveals his inmost feelings in recounting the struggles and heartbreak of trying to cope with a wayward son.

Such a piece is extremely difficult to write. If genuinely done, it drains the author emotionally. I wept as I wrote the article, "If Senility Strikes,"[2] telling how our family coped with problems that faced us when a parent suffered from cerebral arteriosclerosis.

Occasionally the personal-experience narrative relates intimate details involving some other person's life. (Think of the many published articles written by persons closely associated with presidents of the United States.) Narratives of this sort might be titled

> I Was President _____'s Secretary
> I Worked for a Defense Lawyer
> My Father Deserted Our Family
> I Learned to Live with Alcoholism

Of all narratives, those involving life-maturing experience and spiritual discernment are the most meaningful and popular. Note their frequent use in all types of periodicals. No doubt the fact that they appeal to a great many people accounts for the growing popularity of *Guideposts* magazine, the publication which specializes in "spiritual take-away."

Suggested titles might include

> Born Again? I Was
> Courage to Face Tomorrow
> I Gave My Son the Keys to Death

Land of Beginning Again
I Found God Through Sorrow

The first person, the "I" approach, may be used in writing narratives both about oneself and also about other people. Since you aren't apt to have a vast number of meaningful personal experiences to relate, you may turn to others for material. You may recount the adventure of a friend, or investigate and write a story that involves some person you have read about in your newspaper. Let's say you see a news item about a man who was stranded on a mountain in Alaska following a plane crash. Interview the man. Ask him to describe the experience in detail. Try to discover the emotional and spiritual impact of the ordeal. Then write the article.

Though such an experience may be written in the third person, it sometimes has greater impact when written from a first-person point of view. Here is where you, the writer, have an advantage. Since most people are not writers, they will need someone else to tell their story. When an author writes another's story in first person the by-line will appear: "Jim Downs as told to Mark Stanley." The experience is Jim's. He tells it to Mark, who becomes Jim and writes the story as if it had happened to himself, from the "I" standpoint.

There are times, especially in as-told-to confessional pieces, when for the sake of family or for business reasons the person who has had a particular experience prefers not to have his name appear in the by-line. In such instances he may use a pseudonym (a pen name).

The ending of a personal-experience narrative should give direction and encouragement to readers who may have to cope with a similar struggle.

You will hold suspense if you begin your narrative at an exciting point in the adventure, or at a climactic point in a confession. Then, using a flashback of some kind, you can feed in antecedent material—events which happened before the opening episode.

This is the most common approach. You set your reader down

in the midst of action, struggle, or involvement. Your story will follow a broken sequence pattern: 4, 1, 2, 3, 5, 6; or 3, 1, 2, 4, 5; or the like. The story about the widow who spent a one-year missionary interim in Zaire began, as we saw in chapter 12, in an airplane as it lifted off Chicago's O'Hare runway. Then, in a flashback, the article tells why the woman decided to go to Zaire. After this information is presented, the article takes the reader step by step through the new experiences she has in the country she served as a young missionary.

The other approach is strictly chronological: 1, 2, 3, 4, 5, 6. There are times when no other sequence will do. You start at the very beginning and tell the story in the sequence in which it happened.

A narrative about a young mother's miraculous rescue of her five-year-old daughter from a burning building started at the very beginning. It told

1. Where the members of the family were before they discovered the fire.
2. Why the child had been sent back into the house.
3. The discovery of the fire.
4. How the mother's attempts to reach the child were thwarted by a burning stairway, the only means of escape.
5. The breaking of a second-story window.
6. The miraculous escape with the child to a roof below and to one side of the window.

The narrative ending described the impact of the experience on the family's spiritual life.

When you study the section on fiction you will understand how closely the adventure and struggle narratives follow the purpose-accomplished short-story pattern. You set your character (which may be you) down in the midst of an adventure or struggle, then flashback to the beginning and feed in antecedent material. You continue your narrative by showing your character striving to overcome one complication after another until he reaches a climactic situation. Then he decides what course of action he should take to resolve his difficulty.

As you write personal-experience articles, try to recapture the bewilderment, the frustration, the agony, the remorse, or whatever emotion the viewpoint character felt during the experience. You see, you have to *care* to *share*. If you do, your reader will share that caring.

CHALLENGE ASSIGNMENT:

1. Check at least five magazines, religious or secular. Jot down titles of the narrative articles you find in each.

2. Underline those that involve adventure.

3. Which ones follow the 1, 2, 3, 4, 5, 6 sequence, and which the 4, 1, 2, 3, 5, 6 or some other order?

4. Think back over your own life. List experiences involving adventure which were meaningful to you.

5. What personal struggles have you won?

6. Whom do you know who has experienced an adventure or personal struggle you would like to write about?

7. Check the daily newspaper for items which tell about other people's experiences. Clip those you believe have narrative potential.

8. Outline and write a narrative article about your own or some other person's experience.

16. The Personality Sketch

People enjoy reading about other people. There's an element of empathy in such reading. There's empathy involved in writing about people, too. You must care for and identify with the person you write about. To present him most effectively you need to step into his shoes and *be* him.

An English biographer, Lytton Strachey, referred to biographical writing as the "most delicate and humane of all branches of the art of writing." He might have said it is also one of the most difficult undertakings. By this I do not mean burdensome, but rather exacting and challenging. It is rewarding, too. My life has been broadened and enriched by the people I have written about.

Here as in no other writing, "the medium is the message." The personality sketch is the person. Everything you bring into such an article should project the specific image you wish to leave with your reader. You do this by describing your character's appearance, his dress, his mannerisms, his interests, his motives, his achievements, and his goals—anything and everything that will make him come alive for your reader.

You may choose to write about any number of people:

> Persons of achievement
> Persons engaged in an interesting kind of work
> Persons who have overcome handicaps
> Unusual persons
> Persons with interesting hobbies or special skills
> Persons who have known adventure

In some instances the narrative pattern will serve your purpose best. This is especially true in writing about people who have had adventures or have overcome handicaps. The problem-solution pattern may be used in writing about someone who has overcome a handicap, if the purpose of the article is to suggest solutions your character has discovered in his struggle—means of coping with difficulties which will help others in a similar predicament.

Today's personality sketch usually explores an individual's achievements, whether they relate to a particular career, job, or service involvement. Or it may zero in on a person's philosophy of life. The following procedure is recommended when exploring a given subject's achievements.

The beginning

Introduce your character in one of the following ways: describe him physically; in an anecdote convey a particular image of the man or woman or describe one of his or her achievements; suggest the premise of the article; summarize his (or her) work.

The bridge

This transitional section will tie the beginning to the body of the article. Here you show the significance of the person's achievements and quicken the reader's interest.

The body

In the body of the article you prove the premise of the piece. You speak further of achievements, of a person's contributions to his field, enlarging on their significance. Under each section include human interest anecdotes, statistics, incidents, quotes, opinions of others—all the proof-texts you need to authenticate and illumine the statements you make about your subject. The body of the personality article may follow this sequence:

1. Achievements; contributions to his field.
2. Significance of these achievements.
3. Background—family, environmental influences, education, training. Note: the background information shows your character's growth; it suggests why he is what he is.
4. Come back to present involvement.

The ending

You may refer back to something in the beginning to clinch the article, or you may summarize or challenge. Many personality sketches end by making some projection regarding the subject's future.

If you intend to stress a person's philosophy you may follow this procedure:

The beginning
In some way, with a quote, anecdote, or illustration point up the person's philosophy of life.

The bridge
Show the significance of this philosophy and tie the beginning to the body of the article.

The body
1. Explore your subject's philosophy more fully.
2. With anecdotes, incidents, quotes, show that he lives what he believes.
3. Background: note influences which have shaped his outlook.
4. Talk about the present. You might show how this philosophy is influencing others.

The ending
The ending may clinch, summarize, challenge, or project.

I used a simplified version of this particular pattern when writing about a dentist who believes his work must not become his god. The article titled, "Not By Bread Alone,"[1] suggested the man's philosophy of life. The beginning clarified it. In the body I proved that he lived what he believed: he took time for recreation; he assumed city, school, and church responsibilities; he did not neglect his family. The article ending spoke of future plans, which included time for travel.

Before you write a personality sketch you must find a person to write about. Not a difficult task, for people are everywhere. Be sure you choose a person with whom you can empathize, however.

Look around you. Whom do you know who has won special recognition for some achievement? Whom do you know who has changed career-horses in the midstream of life?

Whom do you know who has overcome some handicap? The article for which I secured the Minneapolis Star photographs described a woman who was born with arms that terminated at the elbow, with one leg that terminated at the knee, and the other so crippled it had to be amputated when she was a teenager.

After earning a Ph.D., she became superintendent of a school for educable handicapped children; achieved the honor of being named "The Handicapped Person of the Year" by President Eisenhower; and traveled extensively abroad assisting other nations to set up programs for their handicapped youth.[2]

Read newspapers, magazines, and professional journals. These publications are idea gold mines. Contact, interview, and write about persons you meet through these channels. Once I read that a musical, very talented couple, parents of college-age children, had resigned challenging positions in the states to join the staff of a foreign-based radio station. Why, I wondered. This could have been a good article had I pursued it. I didn't, and missed the ball some other writer may have caught.

Listen to local news releases; watch television interview programs. By chance I heard a radio program on which the man who photographed and researched the *Look* magazine article about the Jesus People was interviewed. Interest prompted me to contact him and write an article about him.

Keep your ears and eyes open at conventions and conferences. Several periodicals have published articles for which writers have garnered their material at the Laymen's Leadership Institute, held in different parts of the country each year. When you attend writers' conferences, take special note of conferees who would make good subjects for personality sketches. This kind of alertness led to the writing of an article about a Detroit Ford Motor Company executive who served his Sunday school as superintendent of its nursery department.

If you plan to visit an area unfamiliar to you, ask your editors if there is any person in the area they would like you to contact for a personality sketch. One such assignment resulted in an article about the regional director of a national detective agency.

Choosing your subject is just the beginning of a personality writing project, however. Now you must learn all you can about him. Make an appointment; ask for an interview. Indicate the approximate time you will need for it.

If you know little or nothing about this person, his work, achievements, and interests, get busy and acquire the information. You'll want to ask intelligent questions during the interview. I possessed only a thimbleful of knowledge about genetics when I was asked to write an article about a research scientist in the field. With the help of the *Reader's Guide,* I located articles which supplied the background I needed. I also read books on the subject and talked to the man's associates. The more you know about your subject, the more effective your interview will be. Besides, you won't waste your own time or his if you have done required pre-interview homework.

You may check the particular *Who's Who* in which your subject might be featured. Read articles and books, if any, he has written. Read speeches he has given. Talk to members of his family, business associates—yes, even people who dislike him. From this cross section of people you will learn about your subject's education, pet peeves, weaknesses, leisure-time activities, anecdotes, achievements, and honors received.

Be a bloodhound when it comes to tracking down human interest anecdotes that involve your subject. Better than anything they will help you understand his philosophy of life, his hopes, and his dreams. According to Dr. Howard Thurman, "As long as a man has a dream in his heart he cannot lose the significance of living." It's this significance you are hunting for.

Plan your interview ahead of time. More correctly, be your reader when you plan your interview. As the reader, what would you like to know about your subject? Jot down these areas of interest. Then plan questions that cover them. Ask *who, why, when, how,* and *where* questions. Avoid asking questions which can be answered simply by yes or no.

Rehearse the introduction and conclusion of your interview. Your leading question should be aimed at putting your subject at ease. "What do you believe is the most important qualification for your type of work?" "What qualities do you look for in an employee?"

Try to catch your subject at leisure. It helps, too, to arrange some time with him while he is engaged in some activity: driving, fishing, playing golf, at lunch, in a family situation.

Be on time for your interview. And do realize that, once you have put your subject at ease, *you must not relax*. Sit up, look your subject in the eye. Act interested. Listen! You didn't arrange the interview to hear yourself talk. Besides, alert listening means you will catch significant cues which may lead you to ask pertinent questions you could not have foreseen.

If you fail to understand a point, say so. You wouldn't be interviewing your subject if you knew all he knows. Ask him to spell names of people, cities, organizations he mentions. If you don't understand terms he uses, ask him to explain them. If the man isn't specific enough, ask: "For instance?" "Can you illustrate?" "Will you give me an example?" "Can you prove that?"

The methods used to record an interview vary according to the personal preference of the author as well as the person being interviewed. Writers gifted with good memories may jot down only a phrase or two as they go along. Others may take very complete notes. I prefer to use a tape recorder, if my subject doesn't object, for then I capture exactly what is said. In considering the use of a tape recorder you should realize, however, that you must allow time to transcribe the tapes.

If, in doing an in-depth interview, time runs out, don't hesitate to ask for another appointment. Remember, too, that the interview is the time to take pictures or arrange to obtain them. Be sure they are pictures that tell a story and in some way relate to your subject's work and achievements.

As soon as possible after an interview, jot down observations you made while talking to your subject. What did you notice about his clothing, his mannerisms, his temperament, office furnishings, speech habits?

There will be times when you won't be able, because of distance, to arrange a personal interview with your subject. It's then that the postal service and the telephone come in handy. Either type of interview will cost you a great deal less than a trip across the country.

You prearrange a telephone interview by synchronizing time schedules and determining the exact time of your telephone call. You also prepare your subject for the interview by mailing, beforehand, a list of questions you wish to discuss. Tell your subject if you plan to record the interview (a legal requirement). If you interview by letter, mail questions to your subject, leaving sufficient space between them for him to fill in the answers.

Let your subject check your finished manuscript for possible errors or misunderstandings. It's easier to deal with them before than after publication.

When your subject is an authority in a special field, you may include this statement of certification at the end of your manuscript. "This article has been read and verified by _____ _____."

Don't hesitate to tackle a personality sketch even if you feel inadequate. You have to start sometime—why not now?

CHALLENGE ASSIGNMENT

1. Make a list of the types of persons you might interview. Under each category list names of individuals you believe would make good subjects for a personality article.

2. Choose one of these names and plan a personality article. Begin by researching your subject. Plan and make arrangements to interview the person you have chosen.

3. Determine the age group which would be most interested in your subject.

4. Outline your personality article, then write it.

5. Indicate the type of pictures you would use to illustrate the article.

17. The Problem-Solution Article

A young mother discovers she is a born storyteller.

"Please," her children beg, "tell us about the boy fisherman again."

Mother tells the story again. Her children stop her. "Mo—ther," they chide. "That isn't the way you told it last time."

I should write down my stories so I could remember exactly what I said, she tells herself. Hmmm, that's an idea. Perhaps I could get them published somewhere. She hesitates a brief moment, then shakes her head. No, I couldn't do that, I wouldn't know how.

This mother represents a cross section of people—college students, educators, psychologists, clergymen, housewives—who want to write but feel they don't know how. This lack of knowledge means they limit their sphere of influence.

Yet none of them needs to stifle this writing impulse. The college student can take any number of journalism classes to help him learn how to write. The psychologist, the educator, the clergyman, and the young mother can start by reading this or other books about writing technique. They can attend evening college and adult-education classes which teach creative writing.

If they are persistent persons who can work alone, they may study by correspondence. Or they might choose to attend a writers' conference in the area where they live. There they would meet other novices as well as professional writers and editors.

In time these individuals could join a local writers' organization where manuscripts are read and appraised by members of the group.

Can one learn to write by following this advice? Indeed. A widow who has been widely published began her writing career in a college English class where the teacher stressed basic techniques of nonfiction writing.

A high-school student joined a private writing class taught by a published writer. Sharp, hard-working, quick to grasp techniques, he soon outdistanced the adults of the class. By the time it disbanded he had successfully marketed several articles.

Many published writers owe their start to university correspondence courses. Wanting to earn college credit and unwilling to pay the exhorbitant prices some independent organizations charge, they sought help through this avenue.

Many would-be writers have gained self-confidence in smaller critique groups planned by local writers' organizations. They accepted and profited from this type of criticism.

So if you are one who yearns to become a writer, set your feet on one of these learning paths. You won't be sorry you did.

There, much simplified and abbreviated, is a problem-solution article. It is written to this pattern:

> Problem
> Significance
> Solution
> Proof of solution
> Challenge or projection

Problem
The young mother, the gifted storyteller mentioned above, identifies the problem: a lack of writing knowledge.

Significance
This transition shows the range and meaning of the problem: others are in the same predicament.

Solution
College journalism classes
Private reading
Correspondence courses
Writers' conferences
Local writers' organizations

Proof of solution

Examples of persons who have learned to write through these specific avenues.

Challenge

"Try one of these learning paths!"

I am indebted to Curtis Mitchell, for many years a *Reader's Digest* writer, for calling my attention to this particular article pattern. Without recognizing it, I had been using it in one form or another. He clarified the procedure, however, and caused me to note its frequent use in mass-circulation magazines.

Most of these articles begin with a survey lead, no doubt to show the universality of the problem. A *Reader's Digest* article titled, "Let's Fight the Bad-Driver Menace,"[1] may be designated a problem-solution article.

Problem

The article presents the problem (ineffective driver licensing) by describing two fatal accidents, one in Columbus, Ohio, and the other in Minneapolis, Minnesota. In the Ohio accident the driver responsible for the mishap held a driver's license, though he had been charged with fourteen traffic violations in four years. The second driver had no license and had been involved in five previous accidents.

Significance

Case histories and startling statistics were used to show the growing menace of indiscriminate, careless licensing.

Solution

Fail-safe cars? A thing of the future

Best method: upgrading licensing procedures

Better screening tests (written, film, and vision)

New enforcement techniques (restricted licensing, stiffer punishment, impounding of cars)

Proof of solution

Instances where these techniques have worked in several states.

Challenge

The article advises proper funding, putting the 1966 Highway Safety Act to work, changing attitudes regarding driver licensing.

Another *Reader's Digest* problem-solving article was titled "California Cleans Up Its Welfare Mess."[2]

Problem

The article presented the problem by quoting Governor Ronald Reagan and supplying startling facts about welfare abuse.

Significance

Overwhelming statistics and case histories

Able-bodied hippies supporting communes with welfare aid

Thousands of employed persons drawing welfare aid. Several checks issued to one name. Teachers with $11,000 incomes on summer welfare.

Solution

Governor and local authorities fought for and achieved California Welfare Reform Act (1972).

Specific examples of problems tackled and solved

Absentee fathers forced to pay family support

Proof of solution

One billion dollars saved

40 counties able to lower property taxes

Allotment raised for the needy

Projection and clinch ending

Other states are or will be adopting the same solution techniques. "Welfare can be controlled."

In my problem-solution article, "There's Potential in Those Years,"[3] I presented the problem through a survey lead (referred to in chapter 12). Then I asked, "And what does the church do in this dilemma?" I called attention to the importance of the problem by showing that ordinary activities do not provide a lasting sense of fulfillment. Then the solution: engage the aged in work which utilizes their talents, knowledge, and skills. That this policy is effective was proved through references to specific individuals who have served the church effectively during retirement years. The ending, a lengthy challenge, spelled out areas where these people could serve competently with a feeling of dignity and worth.

We can understand why this type of article is so popular when we realize that wherever we have people we have problems.

Universally significant, they include:

pollution	unemployment
energy crisis	education
health	crime
welfare	church involvement
inflation	immorality
family tensions	spiritual concerns

Should any of these problem categories appeal to you, select a specific angle. Then identify the problem with two or more persons in various careers, economic levels, or geographic locations and write a survey lead which will alert your readers to the problem. Show its significance. Offer a solution. Prove its merit. End with a challenge or a projection of some kind.

In some problem-solution articles you may not be able to separate each solution suggestion from its proof. In that case present them together.

This article pattern may also be used for the advice article, which is much more personal in content. Again you pinpoint the problem immediately. Stress its significance and indicate its relevance to the reader. In the body of the article give advice showing how the problem may be resolved—in many instances this would be how you, the writer, resolved it. Prove that the solution works. End with a challenge to follow the advice you have given.

Each of the following titles suggests a problem about which advice may be given:

Dress Up and Keep the Price Down
Shape Up
When Death Strikes
After a Poor Start
Practice What You'd Reach
When You Can't Forgive

Page through any issue of any popular magazine and you will find at least one advice article with a similar title. Editors welcome such articles because they know readers are always looking for ways to improve themselves. They want advice about finding the right mate, making marriage work, handling time, stretching the budget, living a worthwhile life, coping with health problems.

In an advice article a dramatic lead may present a given problem. A bicycle safety article began with a single dramatic incident in which a newsboy who ignored bicycle safety rules was struck by an automobile and killed, an episode I personally witnessed.

An advice article about the proper use of time began with an episode which involved two young teens.

Bang! Jack slammed his locker door and dashed down the school corridor, meanwhile trying to adjust the papers which kept falling out of his notebook. That's when he almost knocked his friend, Matthew Andrews, down.

"Watch it," Matthew flung at him. "Where's the fire?"

"No fire. It's just that I have to see the band director before I peddle my papers. And I promised Hank I'd help him fix his bike before dinner. Wish there was some way to make time stand still. Then maybe I'd have enough."

"Know what you mean," Matthew answered, for like Jack he was always short of time too.

Do you identify with this problem? Most kids do. . . .⁴

Jack and Matthew are hypothetical characters, yet their peers identify with them. Handling time is a mutual problem.

When writing advice articles, strive for a light touch, particularly with teenagers.

1. Avoid pointing a finger. After you have identified the problem, instead of saying, "I'm sure you've done this many times," say, "Could this be you?"
2. Avoid a direct command. Use diplomatic words: *perhaps, maybe, sometimes.* Say *should* and *if* instead of *surely, positively, must.*
3. Address the reader as "you" when describing favorable traits. Use hypothetical characters (others) to point out failures.
4. Rather than "You're wrong, this is the right way," say, "That's a touchy problem. Ever thought of trying this?" Or, "Want to know how I handled that problem?"

Whatever the age of your reader, be sure your advice is psychologically sound. In spite of extensive research, I had a psychiatrist check my senility article before I mailed it. This is not always necessary, I know. Often just good common sense determines what you say. However, if you are in doubt, check your material with someone whose knowledge you trust.

CHALLENGE ASSIGNMENT

1. Choose a universal problem relevant to a particular age group.

2. Now choose a specific angle of this problem and begin your research. List all items of documentation and number them. Insert the numbers in the outline where they belong.

3. Write a survey lead which will pinpoint the problem. Write a challenge ending.

4. Write your article and title it.

5. Now write an advice article following the problem-solution pattern. Choose your readers: grandparents, mothers, teenagers, children. Decide which problem your readers need advice about. Pinpoint the problem with a single episode or anecdote lead.

18. The How-to Article

If you are a stickler for detail and an able teacher, you may find you are well equipped to tackle the how-to, (or how-to-do) article. Exactly what its name implies, this type of writing encompasses a vast area of know-how: crafts, art, carpentry, and mechanical techniques; party, program, administration, and teaching procedures. Editors prefer articles that describe something you have actually done (which they are apt to refer to as "how-'twas-done" articles).

Ideas for how-to articles are found everywhere. Examine your own experience. What have you done or made that you believe is unique, which you can share to benefit others? Everyone has some talent he has used creatively at some time or other. Yet you need not possess a particular skill or knowledge to explain a process or procedure. A friend may have come up with an original camping idea. Another may have made an original birdhouse; still another may be particularly adept at creating interesting bulletin-board displays. Ask these people if you may describe their projects in a how-to article. They'll feel honored that you believe their ideas merit publication.

Be alert to newspaper items which inform you of how-to article sources. Interview the persons involved. To gain the knowledge you will need, watch a demonstration of the project.

As with other types of writing, you should check to see what periodicals publish do-it-yourself articles and what types they prefer. You wouldn't submit a Sunday-school teaching how-to to a music magazine. Nor would you submit sewing and food how-tos to publications which maintain their own home economics staffs.

In checking periodicals, note too the great number of religious publications which accept how-to articles on a number of subjects, including

flower arrangements	church publicity
photography	letter writing
Sunday-school promotion	bulletin boards
parties and programs	church libraries
crafts	Sunday-school teaching

Once you hit upon an idea, research enough to enable you to write a good query letter. At the public library check material already written on the subject. Go through individual articles and jot down pertinent features mentioned in each. Ask yourself: Do I have a simpler approach? Additional information?

Your writing should include what is pertinent in all the articles, plus knowledge and methods you have discovered which would make your contribution an improvement over the others. No idea is ever obsolete if you can come up with a new twist, new information, or a better procedure.

When you have completed your research, write a brief query (except for the very short how-tos, such as we have seen under "Bits and Pieces"). Include a skeletal outline of your proposed article. Indicate photograph and drawing availability.

The how-to article requires a personal, logical approach. You put yourself in the position of the least informed reader and answer every question he is likely to ask. Put on a demonstration for him and say, "These are the items you will need. Here's how to proceed."

In writing the article explaining this demonstration, select a title—usually a label, a declarative sentence, or a *how* title—which identifies the subject matter.

The title must also appeal to the specific reader you have in mind. I titled a resin project, "Glamor Lights." A friend suggested a boy's market. This necessitated a title change. "How about 'Chemical Lights'?" she asked.

"Excellent," I answered. "What could be more appropriate for a boy's magazine?"

Your how-to should follow this pattern:

The beginning
Use a simple direct-address lead telling precisely what is to be explained, made, or planned.
The bridge
Show the significance of the project.
The body
This is the *how* of the article.
a. Materials needed
   Include size and color. Tell where each item can be purchased. Indicate approximate cost.
b. Procedure
   Present logically the step-by-step process or procedure of the project.
   Include special warnings or helpful hints on points about which your reader might not be aware. Take nothing for granted; be specific.
The ending
This is the challenge to do.

When you have written your article, ask someone who knows nothing about the process to read your manuscript. If he says he doesn't understand certain directions, you can be sure your reader won't understand them either. Rewrite and clarify parts that are obscure.

The article length is determined by the amount of information you wish to convey. Some ideas may be compressed into a paragraph or two. Others will require several pages of explanation.

In preparing for a Christmas candlelight service one year, a member of the planning committee said she disliked using ordinary wax candles because they were a fire hazard. "I always hold my breath during the choir processional," she said. "I'm afraid a candle will ignite somebody's hair."

"We can get around that," a young man countered. "We can make our own candles with small flashlight batteries." And that's exactly what we did. He showed us how.

This is too good to keep, I thought; it ought to be explained in a how-to article. With the young man's consent I wrote the piece. Titled "Candle Lights Without Fire,"[1] it began with a question which I hoped would arouse interest in the subject.

The beginning

When planning a candlelight service, have you ever wished you could locate candles which would preserve all the charm and beauty of wax candles without being a fire hazard? Though such candles are marketed commercially, you may find their cost prohibitive if you need a great many of them.

The bridge (this tied the beginning to the body of the article)

We solved the candlelight problem in our church by making our own. If you purchase and assemble the following materials, you can make yours too.

The body

a. Materials needed:

Approximately 18" of no. 18 or no. 20 gauge wire (any wire will do if it bends easily yet retains its shape)

One size AA battery

One no. 112 prefocused flashlight bulb. Transparent cellulose tape—3/8" wide

One sheet of white bond paper; letter size, fairly heavy

White paste

White touch-up lacquer

Paintbrush

b. The procedure

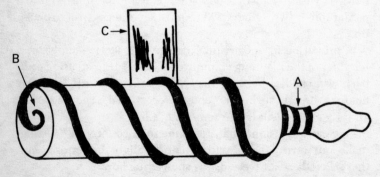

Figure 10

Wrap one end of the wire around the metal base of the light bulb *(A)* to form a socket thread for its contact with the top end of the battery. Then wrap the remaining wire around the battery and turn the end back sharply at its base *(B)* to hold firmly in place. (Fig. 10).

A short piece of transparent tape *(C)* wrapped around the sides and the end of the battery holds the wire in place.

Screw the light bult into the makeshift wire socket to make sure the contact is complete and that the light operates successfully.

Now wrap the battery diagonally in the white bond paper, beginning at the lower left-hand corner of the sheet. Give the candle a tapered effect by tightening the rolled paper at the top as you wrap it and widening it a little at the bottom (Fig. 11).

Figure 11

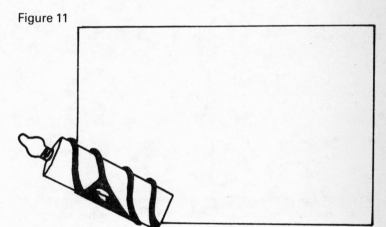

As the last of the paper is rolled around the battery, fasten all edges securely with white paste. Fold under the top and bottom edges. Fold the top unevenly *(A)* to give the illusion of a burning taper. Double the base edge back evenly to whatever length you wish. The sturdiness of the candle is determined by the amount of paper turned back inside of the bottom edge.

Since the light from prefocused bulbs usually has too much brilliance, daub the tip of the bulb *(B)* with a drop of white touch-up lacquer to give it a diffused look (Fig. 12). This can be done with a small brush or by dipping the tip of the bulb into the paint.

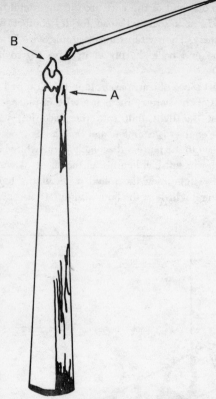

Figure 12

To light the candle screw the bulb into the wire socket until it touches the battery. To extinguish the light, unscrew just enough to break contact.

The ending

Make as many candles as you need. The payoff: hazard-free candle-light comparable to the most alluring candle flame.

By this time I am sure you have come up with several ideas you are convinced will make good how-to articles. Now all you have to do is write them.

CHALLENGE ASSIGNMENT

1. Make a list of periodicals which accept how-to articles.
2. Choose a how-to project you would like to write about. (It may be your own or someone else's.)
3. Outline your article.
4. Check your outline against the following questions:
   a. Is my directive lead clear?
   b. Have I listed all materials? Have I noted size, color, and cost (if this is important)?
   c. Are directions presented in logical order?
5. Write your article.
6. Ask someone who knows nothing about the process to read what you have written. When you are convinced he understands each step, secure whatever illustrations you need and mail the article to an editor you know accepts this type of material.

19. Article Variations

Just as there are exceptions to rules, there are variations of article patterns. This chapter will acquaint you with four of them: the interview article, the symposium article, the survey article, and the photo story.

Almost always these articles are set in a frame made up of the beginning and the ending of the piece. The beginning sets the stage. It introduces the subject and identifies the article premise. It also introduces and describes characters involved.

The ending relates back to the beginning and ties the article together. Sandwiched between these two segments is the specific article variation.

The Interview

The interview article, a first cousin of the personality sketch, supplies information about someone's specific achievements or philosophy, or his opinions regarding a given subject. It may provide information regarding a specific organization, too.

This type of article utilizes a simple question-and-answer format. The author asks questions he believes his reader would ask, and the person being interviewed answers them. Note the procedure:

QUESTION:
ANSWER:
QUESTION:
ANSWER:

In planning an interview you will need to know the direction you will take. Your questions should follow the sequence of one of the article patterns you have learned. The exact questions you plan to ask should be prepared beforehand. You may decide to take off in an entirely different direction while it is going on. Or you may find you need to vary or amend prepared questions. But foresight in preparing them ahead of time will help you proceed logically.

Remember, you set the stage and prepare the reader for the question-and-answer presentation in the beginning of the article. Then, after you have presented the question-and-answer section, you complete your frame—tie the article together with a satisfying ending.

I used this format in an article I wrote about George Wilson, vice president and executive director of the Billy Graham Evangelistic Association.[1] I set the stage by describing Mr. Wilson, identifying his work, and showing its significance to the association. The question-and-answer section focused on the breadth and effectiveness of the association's outreach under George Wilson's direction.

The ending picked up where I left off in the beginning. It described Mr. Wilson's family life and presented a projection of the work as he sees it.

The Symposium

Much like the interview, the symposium presents questions in the body of the article which are answered by a panel of people—persons who should be well informed about the particular subject under discussion.

QUESTION: (Interviewer)
ANSWER: (First participant)
ANSWER: (Second participant)
ANSWER: (Third participant)
ANSWER: (Fourth participant)
QUESTION: (Interviewer)

This procedure may be varied by changing the answering sequence, at times permitting only one or two of the participants to answer a given question.

The Survey Article

The survey article resembles the survey lead (see p. 111). Here, however, the cross-section report occurs in the body of the piece. One specific topic unifies the article, which may contain revelations, commentary, or confessions of as many as eight or more different people. Each person speaks to the issue as he interprets it.

Again the beginning, which sets the stage, and the ending, which ties the article together, constitute the frame for the survey revelation. If sufficient information is provided in the beginning, an ending may be omitted in this type of article.

A mass-circulation publication once published a survey article in which a select group of people commented on "My Most Meaningful Christmas." In another article, participants revealed, "What I Remember Most About my Mother."

You could research and write survey articles about:

My Most Poignant Childhood Memory
My Most Meaningful Travel Experience
My Most Meaningful Christmas (neither idea nor title can be copyrighted)
What I Remember Best About My Mother
A Mistake That Changed My Life
A Person Who Greatly Influenced My Life
What Impressed Me Most About the Holy Land

You will begin by choosing the persons you want to include in the survey article. Write them asking if they will participate. Explain exactly what you expect of them. Determine ahead of time the word limit for each commentary and give each person a deadline for the submission of his material.

The Photo Story

If you find your photo skill approximates or even excels your writing ability, you might consider combining talents to produce a photo story. A photo story is a narrative in which the photos tell the story. It may portray a sequence of any activity or involvement. Or it may show a specific character in a variety of activities.

A photo story in *Teen Time* titled "Sailing on Ice"[2] contained nine black-and-white pictures, showing two high-school students involved in various phases of ice sailing. The narrative text which described the boys' experiences occupied approximately one fifth the space allotted to the pictures.

Often picture stories are made up of posed pictures where the persons involved act out the sequence of the narrative text. Following any one of the article patterns, the photo story requires careful planning.

If the text is brief, it may be presented in cutlines accompanying the photographs it describes. If it is long it may appear in a block, with the entire script separated from the story photos.

Follow the same rules in writing cutlines as you would follow when you submit photographs to illustrate your articles.

Train yourself to look for photo stories. One day a small neighbor boy came to visit me. A typical child, he snooped around the house as I worked. Suddenly he discovered a new spoon-shaped telephone on my bedside table. His brown eyes grew round as he saw the dial numbers on the base of the telephone. Here's a picture story, I thought. I dashed for my camera. Immediately I began to plan the story sequence, which I felt should be illustrated by the boy (1) looking at the telephone intently; (2) holding it, examining the dial base; (3) hunting for his home telephone number; (4) dialing the number; and (5), smiling as he made contact and began to talk to his mother.

By the time the pictures were developed and enlarged I had

come up with a series of rhymed couplet cutlines which carried the story line.[3]

>   Fun with a New Telephone
> Fig. 13 My neighbor has a brand new phone.
>   It's not like others I have known.
> Fig. 14 She claims the bottom is the dial,
>   Said I could put it to a trial.
> Fig. 15 Here's Mother's number printed small;
>   I think that she would like a call.
> Fig. 16 B, R, one, seven, eight, six, three—
>   She'll be surprised to hear from me.
> Fig. 17 Why, hello, Mom! Can you guess who
>   Has telephoned to talk to you?

A series of photographs may depict the sequence of a child learning to swim; a child meeting his baby brother for the first time; events that fill a pastor's day; a family's camping trip; the list is endless.

Take camera, a little bit of imagination, interesting models, and a captivating story line, put them together and—who knows?—you may come up with a prize-winning photo story.

Article Series

You may find you can approach a given subject from many significant, related angles. In such a case you can write and market a series of articles. Article series may be written about

hymn writers	mental health
religious holidays	archeology
famous missionaries	Bible customs
Holy Land travel	Bible children

Since you may wish at some later date to compile your series of articles into a book, it's well to write "Book rights reserved" under each article's word count.

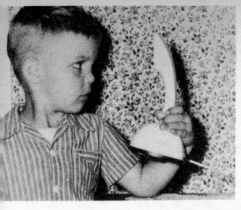

Figure 13

Figure 14

Figure 15

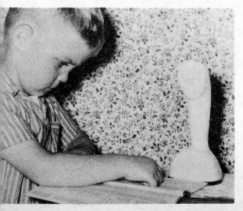

Figure 16

Figure 17

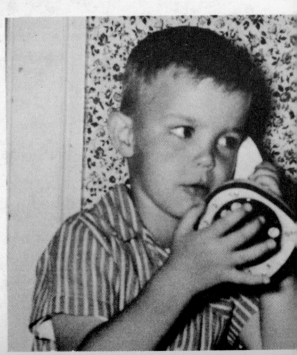

CHALLENGE ASSIGNMENT

1. Study several magazines. Try to locate at least three inter-view articles.
2. Note frame of each.
3. Locate a symposium article. Indicate subject matter discussed.
4. List questions you feel could have been improved. Also list questions you feel should have been included and weren't.
5. Locate two survey articles. Indicate subject matter.
6. Make a list of subjects (other than those listed) which you believe would make good survey articles.
7. Plan a photo story. Tell which pictures you would include and how you would handle script.
8. Name an article series you would like to write.

20. *Be Your Own Judge*

As a beginning writer you will be tempted to send your manuscript to some editor the moment it is completed. Don't. Put
the article aside and begin working on something else. Then
when you believe you can approach the first article objectively,
go back to it. Judge it according to the following suggestions.

1. Read the article aloud, rapidly, as if you were reading someone
   else's work. Ask:

Is it interesting?
Is it significant?
Is it believable?
Are there any blind spots?
Is it properly slanted for the periodical for which you wrote it?
Did you raise questions you didn't answer?
Does the article have reader rapport?
   Make marginal notes to specify changes.

2. Read the article a second time. Ask:

Is the article logical?
Does the ending tie to the beginning? Does it come full circle?
Can you tighten sentences?
Can you improve word choice?
Are transitions clear?
Does it conform to periodical's requirement as to word-length.
   Change parts that need changing.

3. Read the article again. This time probe deeper. Ask:

Is the lead sufficiently interesting?
Is it honest and relevant?

Does the article open on a strong note?
Does it sustain interest?
Does it have a suitable climax?

4. Read the article again, this time from a literal viewpoint. Verify sources, dates, quotations, facts, spelling (particularly of names), punctuation.

5. Now ask someone you trust to read the article. Watch for initial reaction. If any of the material doesn't grab your reader, find out why.

It may help you in your revision to know what faults editors claim most often earn a rejection slip for a manuscript.

1. Poor organization. Information isn't presented logically.
2. Lacks significance.
3. Contains irrelevant material.
4. Doesn't read smoothly. Sentences are phrased awkwardly and-/or too long.
5. Transitions are either weak or missing altogether.
6. Contains few relevant anecdotes.
7. Lacks convincing documentation.
8. Is verbose (a dozen words where two would do).
9. Language is pompous.
10. Contains factual errors.
11. Lead is weak, ending unsatisfactory.
12. Dialogue unrealistic.

Before you mail your article, check also to see whether it is too didactic or too pietistically unreal. If your article is controversial, be sure you approached your subject with a search *light*, not a branding iron.

Satisfied? Good, now send it on its way. Begin work immediately on something new or revise one of the pieces you wrote while the first one cooled.

Then, when the article is published, compare the printed copy with your carbon original. Note editorial changes that were made. If you feel they improve the article, study them carefully. The lessons you learn can be applied to future writing.

5

Curriculum

21. Writing to Teach

I recall with dismay the day I answered an editor's request that I consider writing curriculum for his publishing firm. After I expressed my appreciation for his confidence in me I declined, adding, "For the present, I prefer doing more creative writing."

Shame on me! Curriculum demands as much (perhaps more) creativity as other types of writing.

In retrospect I believe I shunned this opportunity because I feared its restrictive structure. I've learned since then, however, that structure can be a challenge rather than a handicap. All types of writing require structure.

I now believe curriculum stands at the top of the publication ladder in helping persons experience Jesus Christ and in the personal satisfaction it brings the writer. Consider the fact that, to survive, Biblical information must be passed from one generation of Christians to another, as well as to those alien to the Christian faith.

In an article in *Interlit*, Robert Meyers wrote, "Curriculum is the easiest, quickest—in short, the most painless way to communicate this [Biblical] information."[1]

Qualifications

To be a curriculum writer you need not attend a seminary, Bible college, or secular college, or secure a communication degree. Of course the possibility that persons with such training may have an edge on writers not as well equipped is not ruled out.

Carol Noren, who has her master's degree in Instructional Technology and will soon complete her doctorate in Educational

Systems Development, with a supplementary emphasis in films and television, has done a great deal of creative curriculum. Her specialty is teaching techniques, handwork, supplementary activities, and layout. "I'm actually a religion instructional designer," she says. "In my writing I have often supplied activities for lessons other persons wrote. I became known as an 'idea' person."

On the other hand, Janice Hermanson, though she attended college and took several Bible and Christian education courses, does not have a degree. Yet she has earned an enviable niche in the curriculum writing field. "I keep abreast of current innovations by attending as many Christian education workshops as possible," she says.

It was at a writer's conference that Hermanson approached her denomination's curriculum editor expressing an interest in this type of writing. Since his immediate need centered on young adult material, he agreed to send her some assignments. In one three-year period she did forty additional assignments for this editor.

A year later this persistent writer showed her work to two nondenominational publishers. "I'm certain they thought I was a bit 'pushy,'" she told me. Pushy or not, her work caught their attention and earned her their respect—and further assignments. One publisher arranged for her to attend a curriculum training session, which helped her understand their particular needs. From then on it has been uphill all the way. Very soon Hermanson had more requests than she could handle.

As you study curriculum writing you will learn how long-range programs are developed. In a March 1981 issue of *Writer's Digest*, Wesley Tracy says, "Sunday school is not a random study of the Bible and Christian beliefs. Curriculum developers employ experts in education, Biblical studies, psychology, and theology to work with them in developing a curriculum program."[2] Aldersgate's Graded Curriculum, he tells, is jointly produced by cooperative efforts of nine denominations. On the other hand, large denominations such as Lutheran, United Methodist, and Southern Baptist develop their own curricula for all age groups.

Independent publishers such as David C. Cook, Gospel Light, and Scripture Press develop curriculum plans for markets that cross denominational lines.

Tracy believes writers need to know the long-range plans of these curriculum producers. This gives the writer a definite idea of subjects, themes, and goals, and facilitates the creation of pertinent lesson plans. It's wise then to query organizations for whom you wish to write, asking for curriculum charts and brochures.

Be aware, too, that editors of "take-home papers" (usually for Sunday school) look for articles, short stories, puzzles, and quizzes that correlate with material used in class.

Some publishers expect curriculum writers to supply both the student's manual and the teacher's guide. Today there appears to be a growing trend toward using books written on various subjects, by people considered authorities in the field, as adult students' manuals. In such instances the curriculum writer prepares only the teacher's guide with creative suggestions for teaching the contents of the book. Ordinarily less research is needed in such writing, because the book's author is considered an authority who has already done his or her research. You will, however, need to research areas that need further study.

To research effectively, a curriculum writer needs a variety of resource books—several versions of the Bible, a Bible dictionary, a concordance, a Bible atlas, and Bible commentaries among other things. The writer will, in time, acquire valuable clipping, anecdote, and activity files.

Before you accept an assignment for a particular age group, make sure you understand the group well. Read psychology books that speak of the characteristics of that particular age. If they are children, visit classes they attend, in Sunday school or public school. Talk to them and to their parents. Watch them at play. Explore their needs and problems.

Specifications

Though specifications differ, most publishers use a format that requires you to give title, Scripture, key verse, and goal. Goals are identified as major, unit, and individual lesson goals. Lesson goals should be brief, specific, and clear so that their fulfillment may be realistically evaluated in retrospect.

You will plan your lesson in four sections:

1. *Approach (Introduction).* Strive to capture the students' interest immediately. Take them from a "so what?" stance to one of interest and attention. They must be led to feel the lesson has something important for them personally.
2. *The Bible Lesson.* Here you teach. Attempt to make Scripture interesting and relevant to your students. Apply a variety of teaching devices and supplementary material. Meaning is of prime importance.
3. *Application.* Allow students the opportunity to respond. Ask questions that apply to their lives—"why" and "how" questions that require thoughtful answers, not merely yes and no responses.
4. *Decision and Projection.* Work toward some kind of commitment or decision on the part of students. It need not be voiced. Aid the students in projecting the lesson into the future, into their lives during the coming week.

In moving from one lesson assignment to another, the curriculum writer should pick up some thought from the previous lesson that links it to the one that follows it. Also watch transitions between lesson segments. They should flow into each other just as instruction and activities should move smoothly one to the other.

Activity and Discussion Techniques

Short stories. These can be relevant stories from take-home Sunday school papers, from magazines, Bible stories, or stories created by class members or the teacher.

Buzz sessions. The class may break up into small groups in which members discuss the lesson according to directions you have given them.

Quizzes. These may be garnered from outside sources or you may include some you have devised for the teacher's adaptation or use.

Audiovisual aids. Films, slides, filmstrips, music, maps, exhibits and graphs can be used to convey information and spark discussion.

Talks. The teacher may assign, to one or more of the class members, a subject pertaining to a particular phase of the lesson. They will be asked to report back the next Sunday. Occasionally outside speakers who have special expertise in a certain area can provide valuable information concerning the lesson.

Interviews. Again, persons with special knowledge who live in the community may be interviewed by the teacher or some capable class member.

In each of the above areas, participants should be informed of the purpose of the session and time limit. Ask the teacher to allow a specific time when class members may ask questions.

Panel discussions. This approach is especially valuable when controversial subjects are involved. The panel director should keep the discussion lively and pertinent. This person also controls the time, tactfully moving from one panel member to the other.

Role playing. This activity provides an emotional interaction not possible in other discussion techniques. Members of the class assume specific personality roles and act out a sequence relevant to the lesson. They may argue, contradict, orate, and so on.

In a session on aging at a conference on gerontology I attended, the workshop leader, a college professor, set up a role-playing situation where a conflict ensued between an aging parent and her daughter who wanted her mother to live with her. The mother, on the other hand, insisted she remain in her own home. The actors assumed their roles in a realistic conflict that prepared the group to discuss the pros and cons of the situation.

Skits. These may be created by class members or selected from books featuring discussion skits. One such book by Daniel Seagren uses fabricated skit situations which may be read or acted out by young people. The aim is to spark a meaningful discussion.

Questionnaires. The teacher may prepare a questionnaire relating to the session—or you the curriculum writer may do so.

Questionnaires may be used in class or handed out ahead of time so the students have an opportunity to study them in the interim between classes.

In a series of lessons I taught about aging, I used the following questionnaire as a lesson assignment titled, "Age and Youth: Harmony or Discord?"

1. At what age may a person be considered old?
2. What can an older person learn from young people?
3. What can young people learn from older persons?
4. What do you believe causes the most friction between the old and the young?
5. Recall and list Bible characters who enjoyed special affinity with someone younger than they.
6. How can older people's time be directed most effectively:
   a. In society
   b. In the home
   c. In the church
7. How can young people help the elderly?
8. How can older persons help youth?
9. Come to class with suggestions that will encourage interaction between the old and the young.

Book reviews. Suggest the teacher locate one or more books relevant to the lesson and ask, prior to the lesson, certain students to read and report back to the class facts they believe relate to the lesson.

Periodicals and newspapers. Class members may be asked to read a specific magazine or newspaper article and report to the class. Or at the beginning of a particular unit the teacher may ask class members to bring to class articles and news items which add light to a particular lesson.

Field trips. I was once a member of an adult class that visited a Jewish synagogue where we met with the Rabbi before and after the worship service. He explained the significance of the order of service as well as provided information concerning the culture of the Jewish people in the Old Testament.

A children's class could visit a nursing home residence following a lesson on love for others.

Handwork. A great deal of handwork is needed for the youngest Sunday school children. As a curriculum writer you need not be an artist to explain a particular piece of handwork. Make rough drafts and the artist and editor will take over from there.

Writing Specifications

Unless your editor sends you copy sheets which indicate characters per line and lines per page, type your manuscript on 8½″ × 11″ paper, leaving wide margins on all sides.

Be sure to keep a carbon copy for your files.

Identify the project in the upper left-hand corner of the first page (for example): Junior Teacher, October–December 1983.

Give exact source, title, author, publisher, and page for quoted material. Also give source for statistics. Secure source permissions if this is expected of you. Quote Bible (whatever version used) accurately, together with location of the quote.

Make and test all handwork before you prepare instructions and rough sketches.

Mail first class—flat and protected by cardboard.

To write curriculum you will need to pace yourself so you don't have a flood season followed by drought. Hermanson says she blocks out writing time on the calendar, working back from her deadline, constantly checking other deadlines and engagements.

Knowing the subject she will be writing about conditions her to be alert to related materials, articles, anecdotes, statistics, and news clippings.

If you enjoy writing how-to material, if you can honor deadlines and understand and interpret Scripture, if you can teach and don't object to writing within the framework of another person's direction, you may enjoy curriculum writing. Remember: It is the quickest, most challenging way to communicate Biblical information.

CHALLENGE ASSIGNMENT

1. Choose the age group for whom you would like to write curriculum.

2. Learn about them; visit some of their classroom sessions.

3. Ask your Christian Education director for a published lesson plan and teacher's guide for this age group.

4. Choose a specific portion of Scripture. Write a lesson plan and teacher's guide following the format you have studied.

5. Send this "sample" to a publishing firm for which you want to write curriculum. Following suggestions made in this chapter, ask for an assignment.

6

Church Outreach

22. Brochures and Newsletters

Brochures

Brochures are created to attract strangers, instruct visitors, and reaffirm a church's purpose and strengths to church members. As advertising tools they should be creative, well-written, clear, and significantly enticing.

In many instances the pastor or a staff member of the church will assume responsibility for a brochure. Other churches or religious organizations utilize the skills of a professional writer.

Should you, as an author, be asked to write a brochure for your church, prepare for your task by asking for definite instructions regarding size. Ask if a logo or a photograph of the church will be used as a masthead or headline enticement.

Before you begin, collect and study brochures from other churches in your city and from other areas. (Include return postage when asking for information outside your area.) The brochures you study need not be church-related. You will learn a great deal from those produced by business firms and nonprofit organizations.

Become emotionally involved as you study these samples. Which makes you *feel* most responsive? To which do you fail to respond? Brochures ought to shout, *Stop! Look! Listen!* Will you be able to convey that message with a logo, a photo, or an illustration of the church combined with a lead sentence or phrase that grabs?

Evaluate and zero in on your church's strengths. Does it have ample parking space? An elevator or ramp for handicapped persons? An unusually capable choir? What about facilities? Nursery care? Children's church? A counseling staff? Drama groups? Talk about people—the pastor, the organist, the choir director, Sunday school teachers, and others. If the church has a unique location or an interesting history, mention that fact.

Write down anything and everything you believe might be a selling point, no matter how insignificant it seems. You will sift the wheat from the chaff later. Be sure all names are accurate. Dates may be included in a church history but are not needed in current news. Instead of a specific date, which soon may be outdated, use terms such as "recently," "last year," or "a short time ago."

Printing costs can be reduced if your brochure is typed on a good typewriter that produces clear, bold type. Mastheads can be laid out using letters of various sizes purchased from a stationery or art supply store. Photographs and illustrations may be included and the brochure photographed and reproduced by a printer that handles this procedure.

Many church offices have electronic equipment that cuts a master stencil used to duplicate in numbers needed.

Whatever the method, the brochure should not be printed until it has been thoroughly checked for errors in grammar, spelling, and punctuation.

Newsletters

Though newsletters also serve to advertise, they are intended specifically to instruct, inform, and inspire church families. They should be written with all ages in mind.

The author-editor of a newsletter, like the author-editor of a brochure, will collect and study a great many newsletters before attempting one. Again, this study need not be limited to church publications. Much can be learned by examining those prepared by business firms and organizations of various kinds.

Anyone undertaking the writing of a newsletter should learn how to design material pictorially. Photos and illustrations often need to be cropped for effectiveness or to conform artistically to the space allotted them. Gutter margins (space between columns) should be less than those at the top and bottom of the page.

Penciled thumbnail sketches of the page layout are helpful. They will indicate where pictures and text should be placed. Groups of pictures should be horizontal as well as vertical. It's wise not to use too many pictures. Two larger ones may occupy the same space as five or six small ones, yet provide just as much impact. Be aware, too, that people should face into the page.

The examination of published newsletters indicates that headlines are staggered—they do not appear monotonously side by side across the page. An adequate amount of white space keeps the newsletter from appearing cluttered.

An *Interlit* article on layout by Ed Elsner advises, "Don't let layout become blocky or tiresome. Throw in surprises. . . ."[1] Use bleeds; jump the gutter; vary column width. . . ."[1]

Time must be carefully scheduled for each task with intermediary deadlines to ensure the newsletter's being completed on schedule.

If and when you have written a number of newsletters, you may want to venture into the business world for additional assignments. All you need to do is approach business firms and organizations of various types offering your services to them. Though some newsletters are written and edited "in-house," others are prepared by outside writers who are familiar with production procedures.

You may be hired to produce a first newsletter or to take over the writing of an existing one.

Again, familiarize yourself with what has been published. Establish a number of news sources. Determine your fee. Some writers charge an hourly rate—usually $10 to $20 an hour. Others charge a project fee, which can vary from $300 to $700 depending on the size and the anticipated time involvement.

You can determine your charge by listing anticipated involvement in:

Research

Discussions with client

Telephone expense

Interviews

Writing time

Time spent securing approvals

Rewriting

Time spent taking pictures (if this is one of your responsibilities)

Delivery to and pickup from the printer

Galley proofreading

Rough layout designing

Proofreading of printer's blueprint

Ordinarily business people understand such costs. This may not be true of a church. Yet, a worker is worthy of his or her hire.

With business newsletters, as with church newsletters, you will need a news "source," which will include employees as well as officials in the company.

Where business firms may wish a newsletter specifically for personnel, others—nonprofit organizations for instance—because they reach out to contributors will want material that interests outsiders.

A newsletter that is prepared each week alerts church members to coming events, birthdates, persons currently hospitalized, etc. It may relate interesting news of the church. It need be no more than a page or two in length—depending on the size of the church.

The monthly newsletter is longer and will include more data. It is not a preaching medium, however. Too many newsletters feature sermonettes by the pastor and his associates, who forget sermonizing belongs in the church service.

What then should monthly newsletters feature?

Allow space for poetry (not doggerel), book reviews (for both young and old readers), epigrams, cartoons, photo-stories, and creative parables or anecdotes that convey a message without sermonizing.

Each issue of a Houston, Texas, monthly newsletter prepared by my son carried a modern parable he had written that involved a fictional character named Adam (Everyman). One story related that at work Adam made an irresponsible mistake, which cost the company thousands of dollars.

Adam was called into the chief executive's office. The man spoke frankly about the error and what it cost the company. Then he said, "Adam, we consider you a valuable employee. But we cannot afford such errors. However, I have decided not to fire you. I will give you another chance. Just don't let this happen again."

Adam thanked the man profusely and left.

At home he discovered his young son had done something (I don't recall what) that had dire consequences. Adam, however, showed no mercy. He punished the boy and sent him to his room.

The episode caused a strained relationship between father and son, until the following Sunday when they attended the morning worship service at their church. Adam squirmed when the pastor named his text and began relating the story of the unforgiving debtor (Matt. 18:21–36).

Duly penitent, Adam placed his arm around his son's shoulder and drew him close in a gesture of conviction, forgiveness, and love.

Many newsletter author-editors won't be able to create their own parables. Yet they can locate published stories and anecdotes to use, if permission is sought.

One newsletter that is sent to our home by mail devotes an entire page to interesting happenings concerning children, young people, adults, a recent move, a trip, an honor received, a special promotion, the adoption of a child, involvement in sports, in the school band, or a symphony orchestra. The creator of this newsletter knows that people enjoy seeing their names in print and that they are interested in what happens to others.

Such information takes time and effort to assemble. That's why each author-editor needs a staff of "reporters" (young and old) who have a nose for news and a commitment to deadlines.

The most effective newsletters include a calendar of scheduled church events. They should also allot separate pages for the Sunday school, church board and church business meetings, women's work, volunteer involvement, and youth interests. Some include a children's page with short stories, puzzles, quizzes, poetry, and news.

Reporters (in time the whole church should be involved) should hand information to the author-editor in written form. Oral messages are easily misinterpreted or forgotten. It's the author-editor's responsibility to correct grammar, clarify, and re-write what is submitted for publication. If reporters know they need not submit a professional piece of writing, they will be more apt to cooperate. The author-editor should be given leeway when it comes to discarding material that does not seem pertinent.

CHALLENGE ASSIGNMENT

1. Collect several brochures and newsletters.
2. Study them as you have been instructed in this chapter.

7

Short Stories

23. Story Ingredients

Through the ages man has cried, "Tell me a story!" Moses admonished the Israelites to tell every generation the story of their escape from Egypt.

Jesus told stories. The Bible says, "All these things spake Jesus unto the multitude in parables [stories]; and without a parable spake he not unto them." (Matt. 13:34)

Shakespeare wrote stories which have lived for centuries. And despite rumors to the contrary, fiction lives today. Parents tell or read bedtime stories to their children. Speakers and teachers use stories to illustrate their messages. A great many short stories and novels are published every year.

Yes, fiction lives and will continue to live as long as civilization endures. Good fiction will always find a market.

In learning how to write good fiction, you soon perceive that stories are contrived, that they are *fiction* as the word implies. Real-life incidents, no matter how meaningful, are not stories. A story may contain real-life incidents. When it does, they are altered in such a way as to become an integral part of the fabricated whole.

Let me illustrate. One day as I sat looking out of my living-room window, a yellow station wagon drove up and stopped in front of our house. The driver, who remained in the car, maneuvered the rear window so that it opened, closed, opened and closed again.

Meanwhile I glanced over the tops of the houses across the street. Behind a window in a distant multilevel apartment building a woman watched the man maneuver the window, too. When he drove off, she turned away from her window.

In relating this experience, I have cited specific details of a real-life incident. I have not told you a short story. Yet when the incident occurred, I—a fabricator of tales—immediately sent my imagination in pursuit of one. Had the man devised a window code by which to signal the woman? Could be. The incident might be used in a mystery story, a teen mystery story. Pondering further, I asked, about whom? When? Where? Why?

When you begin putting together stories you will give your imagination five story ingredients to work with: *people, problem, place, perspective, premise.*

People

Of these elements, people deserve first and extensive consideration. For relatively speaking there are only so many plots and so many settings about which you can write; but there are millions of people, no two exactly alike. Besides, more than any ingredient, people make your story live, make it plausible. Readers—being people—relate to and are interested in other people.

To begin with you'll need a lead character, a protagonist who struggles to achieve some goal, to make some decision, or to come to an understanding with himself regarding some basic concept about life.

If you are wondering whether it is wise or fair to grab an acquaintance and put him to work in your story, forget it. A real person is a complex individual. He may have some trait you need in a story, but other characteristics will get in your way. Think of yourself as a creator, fashioning an entirely new being to live and act in an environment and amid circumstances you have devised specifically for him. However, this person, if you will it so, may be made up of composite characteristics of people you know.

Your lead character should fit your story problem as a custom-tailored suit fits the man for whom it is made. In fact, the chief character faces a specific problem because he is the person you have made him.

To insure story conflict it may be well to equip your lead character with two opposing characteristics. A man who is an excellent provider may be exceedingly generous; so much so that he is an easy mark, unable to refrain from helping other people. A tough cop may be a pushover with children. A good mother may be a negligent housekeeper; a very intelligent person may have an inferiority complex.

In many stories, whatever the conflict, the outcome will be determined by the victory of one trait over the other.

When the conflict involves man against man, the protagonist must be given a believable antagonist who is as strong as he is. Yet he should possess traits which in some way are opposed to those of the protagonist. Lajos Egri calls this contrast of characteristics an "orchestration" of character traits.

A penny-pinching husband may be given a wife who is a credit-card abuser; a quiet executive an extremely vocal subordinate; a perfectionist wife a sloppy husband; a very restless, active man a slow, patient wife or business associate.

The number of characters you use in a story depends on its length, its complications, and the time it consumes. Keep the number at a minimum, however. Too many people confuse the plot just as too many cooks spoil the broth. Introduce minor characters only when they serve the story in some way.

Occasionally a minor character may act as a "foil" or a "stooge." A foil is a person whose tone is different from that of the lead character, with whom he often appears in close contact. He is brought into the story to set off by contrast the qualities of the main figure—sometimes to his advantage, sometimes to his frustration. Horatio, Hamlet's quiet friend, acts as a foil in Shakespeare's play, for in talking to him Hamlet is able to make his own disturbed feelings clear and to reveal much of the background of the play. Laertes, the impetuous brother of Ophelia, on the other hand, is a foil to Hamlet in the antagonistic sense.

A stooge may be introduced to heckle or bait the chief character, as in comedy routines. In some instances he supplies needed information.

A minor character may act as a judge, a person whose opinions are usually right. It is from him that the central personality seeks advice. He may be a grandparent, a teacher, a chum, or an old-timer. A judge strives to set the chief character straight. He may guide, but he may not make a decision for the lead character. In one magazine story an uncle dispensed advice by quoting meaningful maxims to help the lead character, his niece, decide her course of action. In a teen story by Ethelyn Parkinson, the doctor who gives two high-school students their physical examinations acts as a judge, sharing information with guarded candor, yet never spelling out the boys' course of action.

You conceive each character in your mind. During the gestation period you live with and dream about him long enough for him to become a real person to you. If he doesn't come alive for you, you may be sure he won't come alive for your readers either.

Most beginning fiction writers think chiefly of a character's physical makeup when they begin to create him. They forget that he has psychological and sociological qualities which must be accounted for, too. That's why you should consider each of the following character-determining factors when you create story people:

PHYSIOLOGICAL FACTORS

actions	health
body build	tendency toward illness
color of hair and eyes	outstanding features
color of skin	mannerisms
handicaps	posture

SOCIOLOGICAL FACTORS

race	family relationships
nationality	hobbies
occupation	recreation
suitability to work	place in community
close friendships	political affiliation
enemies	religion

PSYCHOLOGICAL FACTORS

mental equipment	creativity
temperament	recollections of childhood
ambitions	security/insecurity
frustrations	self-image
imagination	attitude toward law and order
judgment	fears, superstitions

When you have explored each of these factors you may like to follow your story people around for a day. Take the protagonist first. Get up when he does. Eat his breakfast. Go to work with him. Listen to him talk. Observe his mannerisms as well as his reactions to associates, family, and friends. Finally, ask the following questions about him:

1. What does your character most sincerely believe in? On what faith does he stake his life?

2. What is his most noticeable mannerism? I have a friend whose eyebrows go up and down whenever she gets upset about something. Another draws figure eights with the toe of her shoe when she is deep in thought.

3. What music does he prefer? A man on skid row may enjoy classical music; a quiet, introspective person band music.

4. What is his attitude toward the person who is closest to him? If the lead character is a mother, is she overly protective of her child? A scholarly husband—does he demean his wife? A young newlywed—does he defer to his mother because he is a mama's boy?

5. What comments does he habitually make? "Doesn't that slay you?" "How about that?" "Cool it, man!" "I'll have to give that some thought."

6. What is his favorite entertainment? Televised football? Reading? Concerts?

7. What is his greatest fear? Failure? Death?

8. What is his pet peeve? Lack of ambition in his child? People who smog up a room with cigarette smoke? People who are always late?

9. What is his attitude toward members of the opposite sex?

10. What are his favorite foods? Lasagna? Lobster? Pizza? Peanut butter sandwiches? Apple pie?
11. What is his greatest psychological need? To belong? To overcome an inferiority complex?
12. How does this need affect his actions? Does he try to buy his way into the hearts of people? Does he clown?

Once your story people have come alive for you, make them come alive for your readers. You succeed in this attempt through a revelation of their

PHYSICAL APPEARANCE (OFTEN JUST A LINE OR TWO WILL DO)

"Gram says her hair is dark because she gives it 'loving care,' whatever that means. She's quick as a kitten. Not very tall—about as tall as I am and I'm only average size for a thirteen-year-old boy."

A small boy with eyes too old for his face.

Flamboyantly bearded and monocled, he carried his walking stick with a flourish.

ACTIONS

Contemplatively he moved the silver back and forth as he would chessmen.

She slumped in her chair, pouting.

Craig hurried to her side. He took her hand and started down the hallway. Abruptly he stopped. He knew he would flub his chances, yet he had to do it. He knelt and turned Sheryl so she faced the committee. He hesitated briefly, then he said, "This is my sister. She's a mongoloid, you know."

SPEECH

"What's got into Sammy?" Gram asked. "Always making a molehill out of a mountain—"

Bitterness crept into his voice. "Why don't you just say, 'Boys, here's my brother. Oh, he isn't president of the United States or anything, but he's a top-rate construction worker.' Anything wrong with that?"

THOUGHTS

Inside the house she listened tensely as Bob Dixon nudged his car away from the curb.

Good! He hadn't gunned the motor. If her folks heard him leave, Lori knew she'd be in hot water again. . . .

. . . she pulled the covers over her and sighed. She realized she wasn't completely off the hook. Not yet. Come morning she'd have to answer some very pointed questions. . . . When they went any place, she didn't ask them where they were going, or how long they'd be gone. Not that she needed to. They always told her exactly where they would be, and how long.

OPINION OF OTHERS

Sara Whiteside! It seemed all Dola's frustration revolved around this matronly perfectionist. Which was foolish, Tom said.

"Don't let her get you down," he admonished one day. "Sure, she's outspoken. But underneath that blunt exterior is a heart of gold."

Heart of gold! Dola had never seen it.

ENVIRONMENT

Lovingly Susan wiped the perspiration that beaded Tim Partin's five-year-old brow. Then silently, like an Indian stalking game, she tiptoed to the hospital window and adjusted the shade to shut out the brightness of the offending street light.

They were land-bound mountain folk who hated tourist influx because their lives were little boxes with everything generations-intact. Newcomers! They could stay away.

CHARACTER TAGS (FOR QUICK AND/OR FREQUENT IDENTIFICATION)

Single tags:

freckles	red hair	a sigh
stuttering	optimism	staccato speech
a limp	pessimism	whistling

Compound tags:

agreeably snub-nosed (likable though snobbish)
gruff, yielding voice (gruff but kind)

solid-gold Scrooge (rich but miserly)
wistful, dependable migrant (hard-
    working but lonely)

NAMES OR NICKNAMES

Ilse—German	Snail—a lagger
Toni—Italian	Percival—a sissy
Fatso—obese	Happy—an optimist

Problem

Wherever you have people you have problems. Character and problems are as inseparable as a pianist and a piano. Neither produces music apart from the other. A problem suggests a specific person just as a person suggests a specific problem. Inherent in the physical, psychological, and social makeup of your focal character, the problem indicates the difficulty he faces in your story.

Note the characteristics of people of various ages found in the Appendix on pages 301, 302. Some problems are common to all ages. You could write a story about any one of these people as having been deprived of love. Each could, according to his age, struggle to overcome this lack in his life.

On the other hand, some problems are specifically related to particular ages. A teenager fights to achieve independence; a middle-aged man may be pressured by a company to get him to retire early on a reduced pension.

Whatever problem your lead character faces, be sure that it is *vitally* significant and that it grows *increasingly urgent*, perhaps also more complicated as your story unfolds. Plunge your lead character into conflict immediately. Under pressure, characters reveal their true natures—the characteristics you have given them. A person struggling with a significant problem gives your story its emotional impact. Recall the station-wagon incident on page 186? You weren't aroused emotionally as you read it, were you? No problem involved.

Always remember that a short story is a narrative with an emotional purpose (problem). If you think back you will realize that the stories you remember most vividly presented a problem or situation the solution of which aroused your interest emotionally. Guy de Maupassant said, "The public is composed of numerous groups who cry to us: 'Console me, amuse me, make me sad; make me sympathetic; make me dream; make me laugh; make me shudder. . . .' "

Joseph Conrad said, "Fiction, if it at all aspires to be art, appeals to the temperament"—i.e., to the feeling of the reader.

Many beginning writers ramble through two or three pages before they even hint at the story problem. They forget that it should come in as soon as possible in the beginning of a story.

Realize, too, that your story problem should be so well defined in your own mind that you can state it in a single sentence. In the Bible story about Abraham, the story problem may be stated: Will Abraham obey God rather than succumb to an overpowering desire to protect the son he loves? Assessing the story of Ruth, we may say the story problem is: Will Ruth be able to cope with the problems she will face in choosing to accompany her mother-in-law?

Place

Place, or setting, may not seem a vital, basic story ingredient. Yet a story must happen somewhere. This somewhere is the specific location of your tale—the seaside, a cotton plantation, a circus tent, an ocean liner, an airport, a school playground, an Indian reservation, a city ghetto. Your story setting should fit your central character just as well as the problem does, and indeed some settings almost produce the characters natural to them: the cowboy on a western ranch; a slow-spoken New England farmer with his deadpan humor.

Description of a locale isn't complete unless you include intimate details associated with it. In a ghetto setting you will speak of crumbling sidewalks, littered streets, broken windows, and related smells and sounds. These touches give the place its distinctive flavor and help establish the mood of a story.

But setting is still more inclusive. It takes in the particular era and general region in which the account unfolds. These may be a time and place with which you are familiar or some unfamiliar setting that interests you.

If you choose an unfamiliar locale, realize that your choice involves research. You may read about it or you may visit it. If you visit a particular area, carry a notebook with you. Note weather conditions during different seasons. Check the region's industries. Read local history. Jot down names of streets, parks, important buildings. Secure information about special festivals. Carry a camera with you, too. Take as many pictures as possible. They will prime memory's pump when you begin writing.

To familiarize yourself with unusual settings, you should also file newspaper clippings describing rodeo, tournament, flood, earthquake, tornado, fire, and air-crash scenes.

Some places are so full of mood that they become almost one with a person or a problem, or the premise of the story.

Perspective

When you have created your characters and are well aware of their problem and setting and ready to begin writing, you must choose a viewpoint character, usually the chief actor, to tell the story. You may use the third-person approach in which you refer to your viewpoint character as *he, him, his,* or his name. Or you may use the first person, the confession, the *I, me, my* approach.

An effective use of the *I* viewpoint involves a minor character who stands at the periphery of action and sees, summarizes, and evaluates what takes place.

Whichever you use you become that person. Nothing must happen in the story that he does not see, hear, or feel—that you do not see, hear, or feel. Since you are he, you have access to his personal thoughts, which in writing you disclose to your reader so that he, too, feels as if he is inside of the character whose outlook gives the story's perspective.

No doubt you have read stories written from an omniscient, all-seeing point of view, where you were aware of what everyone saw and thought. Since this is difficult to handle with steady perspective and smooth transitions, novices should shun its use.

For the most part you will retain a single viewpoint throughout your story. Change is seldom necessary, except in novels and novelettes. You will find deviations from this rule in published fiction; when you do, check to see who wrote the story. Most likely the author will be an expert in the field. Try this kind of thing when you have had a good deal of experience and have done considerable reading.

Note the change of viewpoint in the following illustration.

Entering the hotel lobby, Lew found Blenda lounging, eyes closed, head resting against the back of a corner chair. He looked at his watch. I'm early, he thought. He slipped behind her and whistled softly in her ear.

Startled, Blenda came to life. "Where did you come from?" she asked. She didn't wait for him to answer. It was enough that he had come. She stood up. When Lew took her in his arms, she felt her heart tap-dance excitedly. Today is our day, she thought, and no one is going to spoil it.

The change from Lew's viewpoint to Blenda's could have been avoided by saying:

She didn't wait for him to answer. Instead she jumped to her feet. When he took her in his arms he sensed the excitement that raced through her. Lew knew that she, too, was thinking, Today is our day and no one is going to spoil it.

Premise

Webster's International Dictionary defines a premise as "a proposition antecedently supposed or proved; a basis of argument."

In fiction the premise (as I use the word) is really the meaning of your story which subtly becomes the basis of argument for it. For a writer begins not only with a theme, but with his own conviction of the consequences or moral logic inherent in the problem of the story. His work will unfold not just the theme, but also *its outcome or value* as the writer has seen it from the beginning. Thus the premise permeates the entire story as dye permeates a swatch of cloth. We are all familiar with examples of this kind of penetration:

King Lear by Shakespeare (blind trust leads to destruction).
Ghosts by Ibsen (the sins of the father are visited on the children).
"The Diamond Necklace" by Maupassant (vanity may be the seed of bitter regret).
The Bible story of Joseph (integrity and faith overcome misfortune).

Blind trust is the *theme* of King Lear, but the disastrous result to which it will come is the *premise* of the play, vividly foreseen by the playwright. One can imagine the same general theme with other consequences: a poignant story, for instance, about blind trust—perhaps a child's—that ends up justified.

In choosing story themes and "premises" you will find that many affirm the moral standards by which you strive to live. This is as it ought to be. True Christianity sets forth the highest, most meaningful concepts about human life in the world. Scripture identifies many.

A soft answer turneth away wrath. (Prov. 15:1)
A man that hath friends must show himself friendly. (Prov. 18:24)
Where no wood is, there the fire goeth out. (Prov. 26:20)
He that loseth his life for my sake shall find it. (Matt. 10:39)
Whatsoever a man soweth, that shall he also reap. (Gal. 6:7)

Books of quotations, *Aesop's Fables,* and the *Thesaurus of Epigrams* also help in the choice of premise.

Moral indignation is jealousy wearing a halo. (H. G. Wells)
Patience is bitter, but its fruit is sweet. (Rousseau)
Pride that dines on vanity sups on contempt. (Franklin)

And some premises come from memory's storehouse.

Steel whets steel.
You can't sell the cow and keep the milk.
Many a pearl is still in the oyster.

Religious contention is the devil's harvest.
The present is down payment on the future.

When your characters begin to assume personalities of their own you will find they suggest premises, truths about which you should write. In the case of a penny-pincher pitted against a credit-abusing wife, your premise could be, "Compromise mends broken fences." When a perfectionist clashes with a careless subordinate, the premise, depending on the story's resolution, may be: "Compassion is better than perfection."

There will be times, of course, when a particular premise will suggest a story character.

Whichever way it comes, the premise pervades the story; it is its driving force, its direction and meaning.

People, problem, place, perspective, premise—these are the ingredients of good fiction, any one of which may suggest a short-story plot.

CHALLENGE ASSIGNMENT

1. Write a two-page in-depth character sketch of someone you would like to use in a story.

2. Choose a problem which fits the age and temperament of your character. State it in one sentence.

3. Create a world (a setting) where this person is most apt to have this problem.

4. List ten basic premises which you believe would make good story themes.

5. Select a published story that you enjoy. Underline all references to the lead character with a green-colored pencil, all references to setting in red.

6. From whose viewpoint is the story told?

7. State the story problem in one sentence.

8. State the story premise in one sentence.

24. *The Fiction Triad*

Having learned the identity and function of story ingredients, you are ready now to learn how to put them to work properly in a short story.

We call this work procedure *plotting*, a term which may bother some people. I can understand why. The danger is that we emphasize structure at the expense of story substance. When this is done, beginning writers may falsely assume that a story will be successful if it merely parades an array of writing techniques.

A plot is like a skeleton which unless fleshed out and given substance fails to achieve its purpose. Nevertheless, structure cannot be ignored. How can you put flesh on a skeleton if you don't know where the bones are?

To me a plot—a story plan—is as basic a requirement for a fiction writer as an architect's drawing for a builder. More stories fail because of inept plotting than for any other reason. No matter how relevant the premise, how fully realized the characters, how delightful the writing, unless these elements mesh in some viable kind of form the story invariably founders.

A plot may also be thought of as a cake or bread recipe. Because the basic mixing procedures seldom vary, you need to learn what they are. Once they become automatic, you can experiment with variations all you like.

A good plot presents a chief character, the leading actor, in a significant situation or dilemma which he alone must work through or resolve. After struggling with the complications of his situation, in the most basic type of story he faces a crisis in which he makes a decision, comes to realize some concept of life, or acts to resolve his difficulty.

Remember, as a fiction writer you are a creator. You fashion a world from scratch and people it with characters specifically adapted to the environment you have made. In relating their struggles or progress in that world, you write a story which has a beginning, a middle, and an ending—your first fiction triad.

The Story Beginning

The beginning, which should be placed in time as close to the ending as possible, is a dramatic episode which presents

1. The story problem—note that the beginning poses the story problem.
2. The setting, time, and mood of the story.
3. The principal characters with approximate ages.
4. Pointers and plants.

   Pointers are significant clues (traits, statements, actions) which, when the story is resolved, the reader recognizes in retrospect— and which make its development natural rather than sudden, jerky, or not quite believable.

   A casual mention of a boy's mechanical ability in the beginning of the story gives credence to his repairing a motor later in the story.

   Plants are usually physical objects which will be utilized as your story unfolds, of whose existence the reader must be made aware in advance. A letter, the contents of which are divulged in the latter part of the story, will have been mentioned, examined, or referred to in the beginning.

5. Antecedent information—background circumstances which caused the problem situation. Such information may be presented by means of a flashback immediately following the problem presentation; by dialogue in the beginning of the story; by interspersion, feeding this information as the tale is told.

The Story Middle

The middle of the story contains win-or-lose struggle *scenes* in which the chief character, the protagonist, attempts to achieve his goal.

Note the difference. The beginning is an *episode* or incident whose chief function is to present the problem situation. It does not attempt to solve it.

Think of the scenes of the story middle as acts of a play. They are showcase struggles in which action takes place. Each resembles a miniature story with a problem of its own, the solution of which either aids or impedes the protagonist's progress. Each scene is a single attempt on his part to achieve his goal. Use only as many scenes as you need to bring the situation to its crisis. The last scene of the middle dramatizes the crisis conflict, the most suspenseful moment—sometimes called the "black moment"—when the protagonist's goal appears to be doomed.

As miniature stories scenes contain

1. Purpose and setting of scene action.
2. Meeting of opposing forces.
3. *Action*—here is where you show the struggle of the chief character to achieve the scene's goal.
4. Resolution of the action. Win or lose?
5. The effect of the scene on the story resolution.

Step 5 deserves special consideration, for at this point the reader learns the status of the story problem. When step 5 has been presented, he should know whether the protagonist is closer to his goal or farther from it.

The Story Ending

The story ending presents the climax when the protagonist decides what he must do to resolve the story problem.

Think of your story parts as: problem situation (beginning); complications and crisis (middle); climax (ending).

Short stories should also be considered in terms of types: the *purpose* story; the *decision* story; the *theme* story—a second triad. Each of these story types has variations of its own.

The Purpose Story

Here the lead character struggles to achieve some goal, and here is where "situation, complications, crisis, and climax" may be adapted most effectively.

Variations of this type of tale are:

1. The *purpose-achieved* story. The protagonist wins his struggle. He may fail repeatedly, but—following a crisis scene when all seems lost —he makes a decision on which he acts to win.

In the story, "Long Live the Lion," by Barbara Rohde,[1] an unconventional, very creative man takes over the leadership of a group of Boy Scouts. In a departure from conventional procedures, he struggles to lead his group creatively and wins against the protests and contriving of those who oppose his efforts.

2. The *purpose-failed* story. In this version the protagonist fails to achieve his goal. The chief character may fail, win, fail, then in a crisis scene appear to win. Instead he fails. Or he may win repeatedly, then fail.

In "Devil to Pay," Viña Delmar tells how a beautiful woman, one of the devil's agents, tries to compromise the life of an honest, respected businessman and fails.[2] She wins, wins, wins—then fails.

In "The Lame Shall Enter First," Flannery O'Connor tells the story of a man who, in trying to rehabilitate a lame delinquent, neglects his own son.[3] In the end he loses his struggle with the delinquent and his son as well.

3. The *purpose-abandoned* story. Here the protagonist abandons his struggle. One such story tells how a child, a victim of divorce, attempts to get in touch with his father. After several attempts he gives up, realizing he has no choice but to stay with his mother.

A *Boys' Life* story describes a teenager's desire to become a parachute jumper like an older brother. After a hazardous though successful jump, he decides to abandon his goal—it really isn't what he wanted after all.

Some writers refer to this type of story as a wish-abandoned story. It is especially adapted to youth; the lead character may desperately wish to achieve a designated goal. When he learns he lacks certain qualities or aptitudes, he transfers his energies to helping someone more adept to reach the goal. The protagonist's action may win him an unanticipated reward, or it may cause him to consider new goals for himself. Such variations of the purpose-abandoned tale closely resemble the come-to-understand tale explained later.

The Decision Story

The decision story also embraces three variations:

1. The *decision-reversed* story. In this version the lead character makes a decision in the beginning of the story, which after a tug-of-war, pressure, or enticement struggle, he reverses.

"Teacher's Pay" by M. J. Chute, is this type of story.[4] In the beginning the protagonist, a high-school music teacher, decides to quit teaching and accept a more lucrative position. In the end, after a tug-of-war struggle with himself and others, he decides to continue teaching.

2. The *decision-faced* story. Here the entire account presents the struggle of a protagonist faced with a decision which he doesn't make until the end of the story.

An example of this is "The Children's Story" by James Clavell,[5] in which Johnny, a young elementary student in a school taken over by Communists, is confronted by the need for a decision regarding total capitulation to Marxist rule. After struggling through several enticement scenes, he decides to go along with the rest of the children who have already capitulated.

3. The *decision-affirmed* story. Here a decision made in the beginning of the story is more strongly affirmed in the end. I recall an example where a teenage girl made a decision which placed duty ahead of pleasure. She is pressured to reverse it, but in the end she more vigorously affirms her original decision.

The Theme Story

The theme story isn't so much a struggle or a decision as it is a situation which involves the lead character in drama which continually explores a basic premise of life. Here the story problem is more definitely visible as an extension of the story premise. The beginning sets the stage and introduces the premise; the scenes of the middle heighten and reiterate it. The ending clinches it so strongly the reader leaves the story, not as if he had read about a fight or a struggle, but as if he had read the dramatic presentation of a sermon.

Because this is true, we can think of the purpose and the decision stories as ascending in nature, with tension constantly rising. The theme story, on the other hand, may be said to be linear or episodic.

1. The *theme-exposure* story. Though most stories are written with a premise in mind, the chief purpose of this type of theme story is so to disclose it that the reader, on finishing, will say, "Aha! That's just the way life is."

In the serial, "The Stuff of Dreams," by Phyllis Reynolds Naylor,[6] a lonely teenage girl, who lives under trying circumstances in the home of a married sister following the death of her parents, turns to drugs. When she becomes hopelessly addicted, her pusher cuts off her narcotic supply. He suggests the only route left—prostitution.

An open-ended story, where the resolution isn't spelled out, it leaves the reader saying, "That's what life is like in that business. What other recourse does the girl have?" Note that in this instance it is the *reader* who comes to understand the basic premise the story expounds.

2. The *come-to-understand* story. This type of theme story presents a series of dramatic episodes relevant to the story premise. In evaluating them, the lead character comes to understand their meaning as it applies to his life. He then acts accordingly.

As a rule, an aggressive lead character will act positively when he understands the basic premise. A passive lead character does nothing. He accepts the premise as his fate. Open-ended, many so-called quality stories follow this pattern.

In "Edge of the Crowd" by Ethelyn Parkinson,[7] the group from whom the lead character seeks acceptance is friendly to her only when they want a favor. After a series of dramatic episodes, the girl comes to understand she has been used. She returns to the fellowship of her more trustworthy friends.

A misunderstanding between the protagonist and the antagonist in the beginning of the story may reveal a lack of understanding of the basic premise of the story. Then when personal differences are resolved in the end, the protagonist comes to understand the premise as it applies to his life and acts accordingly.

"The Night Song" by Ruth Moose exemplifies this type of story.[8] A new mother feels neglected and abused when she learns her husband left the hospital during her long night in labor. She misinterprets his action.

Later, in a dramatic scene, she discovers that he had really shown unusual concern during that interval. She comes to understand how much he loves her and that judgment should be withheld until all facts are known. She acts on this knowledge.

No doubt you have read many come-to-understand stories. If you are like most beginning writers, you may have said, "What a simple tale!"

Such stories may appear simple when read. The writing is another matter, however. The understanding the protagonist achieves must be triggered by one or more dramatic episodes. I cannot emphasize this fact too much. In a short-short story one significant episode may suffice to enlighten the lead character. In a longer one it may take several such experiences. Just be *sure* they are there. Remember, human beings do not change easily. Something must happen to make the protagonist arrive at understanding what you want him to.

A Parable

To further illustrate the three main short story categories, I refer you to the New Testament Prodigal Son parable. Here we have three stories in one: the father's, the prodigal's, and the elder brother's.

I believe the father's story is a purpose-achieved tale in the sense that he proves by his actions, in spite of conflict within

himself, and ridicule and pressures there may have been from
outside forces, that love has no limit. He has trusted his son with
his inheritance, we might assume, in the hope that when he is
on his own, with seasoning that comes from contacts in the
world, he will be able to find himself. Had the story indicated
that the father tried to find and persuade his son to come home
it would also be classified a purpose-achieved story. Then it
would have contained win and lose attempts to carry out this
purpose.

The story premise: Love knows no limit.

The story problem: Will the father with patience, retain his
trust in his son?

The prodigal son's tale is a *decision-reversed* story. The son
makes a decision in the beginning—to leave home—which, following events of a tug-of-war or enticement nature, he reverses.

The story premise: Repentance leads to happiness and joy.

The story problem: Will the prodigal succumb to the evils
around him or will he decide to return home?

The third story, the elder brother's story is a *theme-exposure*
story in which each scene exposes a basic premise of life.

The story premise: Self-righteousness leads to destruction.

The story problem: Will the elder brother learn that self-
righteousness destroys?

Note how the story problem becomes an extension of the
story premise in the latter story.

It is to our advantage that the same characters appear in all
three stories. Since we have already learned to give the
protagonist two-pronged dominant characteristics which war
with each other, we'll proceed on that basis now.

Adela Rogers St. Johns once described Damon Runyan as a
man who possessed an "impassive manner and expressionless
pan that were frozen over the biggest heart in the world."

One might describe the prodigal's father as a wise man (think
of the sense of values he expresses to the elder brother) whose

insistence on order and obedience fashioned a shell that encompassed the most compassionate heart in the world.

What are the dominant traits of the prodigal? Great respect for his father, set against a love of freedom and perhaps pleasure.

We could show the prodigal's respect for his father in an encounter with people from home who chance to meet him in a compromising situation in a distant city. He implores them not to tell his father. He can say, "It would break his heart—"

In another instance we could show him swinging along the narrow streets of Babylon or Alexandria whistling a merry tune. This might be the most natural thing he does. If this trait is used symbolically, he would cease whistling when he comes to the end of his resources. Once at home, a forgiven son of the family, he would begin whistling again.

The elder brother? We already know he is self-righteous. Since we are considering this a theme-exposure story, we need something to accentuate the trait. Why not make him jealous too?

Both the father's and the prodigal's tale could be told from the third-person (he, his, him) viewpoint, or in the first person (I, my, me).

In the elder brother's story, however, the first-person viewpoint should not be attempted. It could require more than a beginner's skill to expose through his own narrow words and thoughts, failure to come to understand that self-righteousness destroys. Yet well handled, this could be effective.

The first-person viewpoint could be used if a minor character, a servant, perhaps, were to tell the story. Let's suppose she loved the elder brother dearly and longs to see him change. At the periphery of action, she would see, summarize, and evaluate his self-righteousness and jealousy.

Our next focus involves the time when the narratives begin. We could open the father's story at home, showing him talking with his wife about the boy's departure; showing her disapproval and possibly that of the elder brother; revealing, introspectively, the father's love for the boy who is gone, his concern for his welfare—his own poignant knowledge of the risks he took—and his vulnerability.

The prodigal son's story might begin at a point where he has lost all his money, followed by a flashback informing the reader of how he originally came to be in such a plight. It might also show how he was enticed further and further from home disciplines.

I can imagine the elder brother's story beginning with the moment when the prodigal says good-bye. Disgruntled he will betray his feelings and immediately pinpoint the self-righteousness which will be exposed in each encounter the reader has with him.

We know the middle of the story contains scenes which attempt to solve the story problem. In the father's case these may show him receiving more and more disquieting news about the prodigal and feeling overwhelmingly (due partly to pressure from others) that he ought to find and persuade him to come home, yet knowing he must not. His wife might say, "It's your fault. You gave him the money. You should have made him stay at home."

And the father understanding the boy more fully, with great pain might remain firm in his insight and purpose and answer, "No, he had to go. Love isn't love if it's forced. I won't give up hope. I'm convinced he will find his own way."

The middle of the elder son's story will contain scenes that reveal his jealousy and self-righteousness despite family concern about his brother.

The story problem in each case is resolved quickly through the lead character, who responds to the black moment according to a dominant trait, skill, or tool he has been given.

You may never write a story using these Bible characters as your people. I challenge you, however, to write a modern story based on the themes and problems I have suggested. Loving fathers, prodigals, and elder brothers are everywhere.

Challenge Assignment

1. Study as many periodicals or story anthologies as necessary to locate each type of story described in this chapter—
The purpose story: achieved, failed, abandoned.
The decision story: reversed, faced, affirmed.
The theme story: theme-exposure; come-to-understand.
2. In one sentence state the premise of each story.
3. In one sentence state the problem of each story.
4. Outline each story. Tell what facts are included in the beginning of the story. Count the number of scenes in the middle of the story. What is the crisis scene? What skill, character trait, or device is used by the lead character to resolve the story and bring it to a satisfactory conclusion?
5. Write a modern parable (that is, a story) using one of the characters listed below.

THE FATHER	THE PRODIGAL	THE ELDER BROTHER
1. A father or mother whose child has run away from home	1. The son or daughter	1. A sibling
2. A wife or husband whose spouse has left home	2. The spouse who deserts the family	2. A relative
3. A church	3. A delinquent member	3. A self-righteous church member

25. *Learning from the Experts*

A writing-conference student once questioned a statement I made challenging beginning writers to study writing techniques.

"I just had a letter from _____ (she named a well-known author). She told me not to worry about study, just to go ahead and write. She said this is what she had done."

We conversed for a time, then the student explained that her correspondent had learned writing techniques through critical reading of the work of authors she admired. I smiled. "Isn't that study?" I asked.

It is. And it is the kind of study to which I direct you now. As you may well imagine, it requires some very purposeful reading.

According to Sir Francis Bacon we read "not to contradict and confute; not to believe and take for granted; not to find talk and discourse; but to weigh and consider." I believe we read for all these reasons, but as writers we should read primarily to weigh and consider how particular effects are achieved. Such reading is as valuable to a writer as repeated reworking of his own manuscripts.

In his book, *Professional Writing*, Walter Campbell advised would-be authors to read fiction backward, in the following manner:

1. Read just the beginning of a story.
2. Skip to the end and read the story ending.

3. Now backtrack. Begin with the last scene and work your way back from climax to crisis, through the scenes of the story middle, to the beginning problem situation.
4. Read the story again, this time more rapidly, from beginning to end.[1]

I suggest a fifth step. Read the story several additional times, slowly, stopping frequently to examine techniques which intrigue you. You know you must never plagiarize another author's work. You can, however, appropriate an interesting device by writing an original version of it. I clip and paste (using rubber cement), or write, an interesting device in my technique notebook. (Some writers use 3″ × 5″ cards.) Below I write my version of the device, adding an (o) to indicate it is original. Often I record only my version of a given device.

The only exception to this procedure occurs when I record brief emotion-relevant phrases or bits of jargon which, when used, bear no resemblance to another author's use.

I suggest that you record devices in a notebook or on 3″ × 5″ cards under the following subject headings:

Emotions		Transitions
Characterizations:	brief	Flashbacks
	compound	Settings
	tags	Beginnings
	group	Endings
Dialogue		Sentence plots
Names		

Emotions

Be alert to primary emotions. Some are positive: love, empathy, hope, faith, enthusiasm, peace, joy. Some are negative: fear, superstition, jealousy, hatred, revenge, greed, anger, disgust. Because men differ greatly in their thoughts, but far less in their emotions, a writer must constantly appraise his character's emotional response to every situation in a story. Note the emotional response in the following excerpts.

AGITATION

Fighting a civil war within himself he paced back and forth, his hands clasped tightly behind his back. He ignored the concern of those who watched him.

Her troubled eyes followed him. She winced. If only he'd listen to his son.

AFFECTION

Their eyes held, a sweet silence between them.
She opened her hand and laced her fingers in his.
The chubby twins hugged each other luxuriously.
She willed her pulse to behave.

ANGER

The knives were out.
spoke sharply, flaming with rage
She sent him a lethal look.
mad all over
made fists with his hands

SHAME

sting of shame
felt a stab . . . so sorry
conscience stung

Characterization

BRIEF CHARACTERIZATIONS

Often only a few words will sketch an individual significantly.

a man who always goes through the door first
his mouth hung open like that of a fish
doesn't know thunder from a drum
a yo-yo Christian
wrinkled, whiskered, and jovially autobiographical
rambunctiously tousled, a jean-tattered devotee of traps, fish, and swimming holes

You should be especially alert to the skill with which published authors feed in bits of characterization throughout a story. The following examples are taken from the book, *Greenwillow*, by B. J. Chute, a well-known writing expert.[2]

Micah talked incessantly.
tirelessly out-chirping the grasshoppers
silence burst its buttons
spilling news like a shower in drought
leaping, telling as he leaped
didn't believe one moment of silence should be linked with another
speaking for Sheby

COMPOUND-CONTRADICTORY CHARACTER TRAITS

"What's good about a fat salary if you insist on being a private welfare society?"
gracious, charming, but as stubborn as her father
chum-bummy
too smart always to be broadcasting her woes
A wry sense of humor lay behind his staid front.
Short, shaped like a silo, he waddled like a duck,
yet kids were drawn to him like steel shavingsto a magnet.

TAGS

You already know that tags help identify and characterize story people. In one story a woman's bangs helped describe her state of mind. Depending on her mood, throughout the story she patted them, blew them upward, or twisted them. Another person may

scratch his head or neck
clinch an argument by wringing his hands as if he were screwing a lid on a jar
clean his fingernails by running them along the front of his shirt
show derision by extending his lower lip and blowing air upward (phoof!)
removes glasses and scissors bows
play with coins in pants' pocket

close eyes while speaking contemplatively
hum a particular tune

GROUP CHARACTERIZATIONS

Occasionally you will need to characterize a group of people. Shirley Jackson's description of the mob in her story, "The Lottery," merits your scrutiny. Be sure to clip and file other examples. They will help you when you write your own.

The more conservative element of the town controlled the city council. There was Hank Barlow, broad, blustery *Times* editor, whose senate-page experience made him an authority on all issues of the day; Carlton Storm, a retired real-estate broker whose denunciations of "new-fangled-equipment" spending were broadcast near and far; Pete Paulson, white-haired bank director to whom Hank Barlow was heavily in debt; bald, hard-of-hearing Frank Johns, who, folks claimed, voted by sight, not by reason.

I just happened to be there when the policemen herded the robbery suspects into the patrol wagon. The tall, stringy-haired white boy swaggered to the van, head high, lips curled contemptuously. His broad-shouldered black companion aped his stance. The girl, wearing a sweatshirt and cut-off jeans, followed meekly. Long wisps of breeze-blown hair veiled a grimy, tear-stained face.

Dialogue

Make dialogue the wheels, not the brakes of your story. Pay special attention to an expert's use of dialogue to feed information, heighten conflict, characterize, and convey emotion.

Listen to people talk; note job jargon, geographical expressions, and especially the rhythm, and phrasing typical of a vivid personality or a region of the country. When you write your own stories give each character a speech pattern that fits him precisely. Literary English ought not be used unless it suits a specific character.

Be especially wary of current slang. By the time your story is published it may be out of date. This is especially true of teen talk. With care, the experts adapt the casual language teenagers use:

Love is a mushy game.	shove off
weird	It's creepy.
The freeze is on.	push around
blast off	clobber
muscle stuff	on the double
elementary	riding him
Want me to jump	parents call a summit
up and down?	meeting

How a man addresses his wife gives you a good clue to his status and character. Make a list of such terms from stories you read.

dearie	Mom	woman
good-looking	old lady	sweetie-pie
honey babe	Ma	Mother
darling	honey	my dear
Grandma	Jo	the missus

When you preface your dialogue by emotion and action you prepare your reader for what is going to be said. Examples:

He threw his words at Jim as if they were stones. "You're a liar!" he shouted.

Bart's voice rose in derision. "And I'm supposed to shoulder the blame?"

Mom sank into a chair. Her mouth dropped open. "You didn't! You couldn't."

Most dialogue is brief. Should your story require a lengthy speech, however, break it up. Note how published authors allow the speaker to move around the room, pick up a book, pace the floor, stop and look out of a window while he speaks. The expert dips into dialogue, leaves it, then returns to it again.

In your study of dialogue note how by overlapping it may serve to heighten conflict.

"I'm sorry . . . I . . ."

"You're sorry. That's not going to help you any. You're to blame, you know."

"I'm not to blame. His car hit mine."

"His? His car! Think my boy can't drive?"

Names

All of us have read stories in which we had difficulty keeping the names of characters straight. Most often the fault lay in the author's selection of names which either begin with the same letter (Madeline, Mary, Martha) or contain the same number of syllables (Ted, Tom, Matt, Pat), or in some other way are easily confused. Avoid these mistakes when you name your characters. Many authors, Phyllis Whitney among them, keep notebooks in which they record names they believe they may use at some future date. Too, they strive, as you should, to make the name fit the person for whom it is chosen. If the right name escapes you as you begin your story, you might try substituting a character trait for the name of the person concerned. Later you can give him his story name.

Mr. Storm	Gabby
Stuffed Shirt	Miss Fluff
Know-it-all	Mum
Suffering Sue	Tightwad

Transitions

Though transitions were considered in chapter 5, it is worth your time to note how they are made in fiction.

CHANGE OF PLACE

The stillness of the house suddenly oppressed her. She put on her shoes and went outside to see if the newspaper had come.

Once in the car, he broached the subject again.

CHANGE OF TIME

All that night while the children slept, Flora sat sewing in the den. By morning she had finished Sally's dress.

The night deepened, the rain went on, never stopping, coming down in torrents at times. At midnight Sue retired.

CHANGE OF MOOD

Cathy looked at the two trails. Confidence changed to panic.

His anger had subsided by the time he reached . . .

It was ridiculous to feel such sudden anger, she told herself as she turned from the phone.

CHANGE OF WEATHER

By night the rain had turned to sleet. It was cool, and it would get colder.

Her predictions were right. A world of white faced her in the morning.

ENTRANCE OF A NEW CHARACTER

Dave had been so engrossed in the discussion that he failed to see Lita enter the room.

"Hi, chum," she whispered as she touched his shoulder. Dave jumped to his feet. "Hi, yourself. Where did you come from?"

The insistent buzz of the telephone pulled her from her thoughts. She lifted the receiver. Carl? Oh, no!

Flashbacks

How do professional writers present antecedent information that is needed to make clear what has taken place before the story begins? Through dialogue in some instances. A story about an upset, rule-the-roost father began:

Sam Collins slammed the door as he strode into the kitchen where his wife Martha had begun to prepare dinner. He sent his briefcase skidding across the counter.

"I won't have it. Who does that stubborn son-in-law of mine think he is? Taking a job halfway around the world. Now we'll never see Sally and the baby. I've told him there's always a place for him in the business."

"He doesn't want handouts," Martha answered cautiously.

"Who said this is a handout? I need him. He's better than most."

"You're sure?" his wife asked meaningfully. "Well, perhaps he wants to run his own life from now on."

"What do you mean? Think I'm trying to run it?"

"How about the wedding cruise you insisted he and Sally accept? And the down payment for the house on Elm Court?"

"Too proud for his breeches, that's all. But he'll come around. He'll have to. I'll make him an offer he can't afford to turn down."

Antecedent information may also be supplied in a thumbnail background and character sketch:

Why was sophisticated, world-traveling Eleanor Simpson Carrey (magna cum laude), fifty-five, ex-wife of millionaire Henry Carrey III, mother of fifteen-year-old Sheryl Carrey and ten-year-old Paul Carrey, seated on the platform with the noted evangelist? The answer is simple. Eleanor isn't the woman she used to be.

Often antecedent information follows the presentation of the story problem and links the beginning to the middle of the story. In using this technique you introduce the flashback in the past perfect tense, then immediately shift to the past to make it seem as if it were happening in a *now* of its own.

Mary recalled the day Perry had told her the truth about Tim [past perfect tense]. "Mary," he said [past tense], "Dr. Blaine swears there is no hope. Tim can't live. It's leukemia."

"No!" she shouted. "It isn't true [end of flashback]." But now Mary knew it was true. Today she must . . . [transition back to the story].

At other times antecedent information is interspersed throughout the story. In one such instance the proprietor of a filling station keeps the secret of his past famous life from the wife with whom he lives in backwoods lake country. Quite by chance a newspaper reporter discovers the man and does a feature article about him.

The story begins one day when the lead character opens the morning paper and is confronted by the article. He lays the paper aside, realizing that he must face his wife with the truth when he gets home from work that evening.

During the day he goes about his business. At intervals he runs into people who have read the story. When he is alone driving his car on an errand, he relives his past life. The reader learns what it was like and why he became disillusioned with it.

The story would have been ruined had all the antecedent information been presented in a solid block of flashback.

Settings

When you read stories written by professionals, note how settings are presented in the story beginning. Identifying a locale, the setting is so intricately woven with character and problem, you are scarcely aware of it as a distinct element. Descriptions of settings are detail-specific. Skillful authors insert intimate detail sparingly with a quick, exact, memorable touch.

Ann stood in the spare white hospital consultation room and watched Dr. Blane's face warily as he spoke.

Though the white blizzard raged around him, Paul settled himself more comfortably in his cozy, warm automobile. He whistled softly, unmindful of the long line of igloo-shaped cars which blocked the road in front of him.

As with characteristics, setting is often interspersed throughout a story.

As the many-gabled hotel emptied on weekends, it soon filled with new arrivals—elderly men and women, often alone; young couples; families with two or three children.

Flower-framed balconies opened toward the sea.

The rising sun lay shimmering over the sea. Gentle waves lapped the pale ocean sand.

Sea gulls squawked overhead . . .

Fishing boats bobbed lazily against a distant pier.

Setting may also be introduced immediately to establish the mood of a story.

When her mother turned on the TV, Selena slammed her book shut and marched into the kitchen. She spread a slice of bread from the still open jar of peanut butter on the table. As she ate, she stood looking out the window at the apartment building facing theirs. Open windows, tattered curtains pulled back to let in a breath of air. Dingy sinks and cupboards. Dear God, why?

To heighten setting realism it is well to include career, job, and climate references. In a story about football players I included the following:

> Leave it to the kids to foul things up.
> clobbered him
> hit him like a four-ton tackle
> Don't count your field goals before they are scored.

A *Saturday Evening Post* logging story, "Bait for a Bachelor," by Frank A. Clarvoe,[3] used the following terms:

> He bulldozed through the door, . . .
> fish-lure earrings
> voice cracked like she had been poked in the throat with a peavey handle
> voice like water gurgling through the cracked plank in the pool dam.
> fitted her like bark on a tree, burls and all
> split-log effect

Story Beginnings

Though you have learned what should be included in a story beginning, it's a good idea to study and record beginnings which you will note serve specific purposes. A beginning may

CHARACTERIZE THE PROTAGONIST

Everyone liked Charley until they learned to know him well. He always had the best intentions, but somehow lacked the stability to stay at a task until it was finished. Then, when prodded, he became defensive and inevitably lost his job.

AROUSE INTEREST

He kissed his wife, tossed his small son into the air, hugged him briefly, and said good-bye.

"Jim, do you really have to go?" Marilyn asked, her lips a tight line of fear. "Couldn't someone else . . . no, I guess not . . . they trust you."

He turned the starter, shifted gears, and waved with more gaiety

than he felt. In his heart he knew this assignment might change everything for them.

INTRODUCE CONFLICT

Driving to church that night, clergyman Tripplet rehearsed what he
would say to the church board. The more he thought about it, the more
he realized there was no other action he could take.

This was his job and they'd have to accept his plan or he'd resign.
He had to prove to himself and to the world that Christianity isn't a
box.

SUGGEST MOOD

Paula dozed, not quite awake—not asleep either. Something moved
in the hallway. The cat? Cats don't make floors squeak. Carl? He
wouldn't be home until tomorrow.

Icy fear grabbed her. She lay still, waiting. . . .

SET THE STAGE

Maria glanced at the clock. A quarter to eleven—the yellow kitchen
timepiece told the truth. A little less than an hour and Bill would be
home for lunch. She'd never get used to a town where men came home
to eat at noon.

Story Endings

From published writers you will learn that endings, too, serve
specific purposes. An ending may

REVEAL CHARACTER CHANGE

He extended both hands. Melinda walked into his arms.

"I took a bad fall," he blurted, "and I couldn't get up. But I called
for help, didn't I? That's a start isn't it?"

She hushed him with a kiss. Strangely excited, she knew what he said
was true. It was a start, a very small start, but he'd go on, she knew she
could depend on that.

BRING STORY TO SATISFYING CONCLUSION

Susan blinked away the tears that filled her eyes. In the elevator the
full impact of their parting hit her. I've thrown away Mike's friendship,
she thought—I must be out of my mind.

The elevator door opened. For a moment she hesitated. Then resolutely she stepped out and made her way to the ward where little Tim Parten lay waiting.

The boy's eyes lit up like a Fourth of July celebration. He grabbed her hand. Susan stooped and kissed his brow. This was right. She knew it was. Maybe someday Mike would come back. Then again, maybe he wouldn't. If he didn't she supposed she would manage. One thing was sure, she knew she would always have to do what she believed was right.

REVEAL UNDERSTANDING OF BASIC PREMISE

"Of course I envied him."

"Then why so glum?"

"Well, it's like this. I never dreamed, not once, just how much he envied me."

INDICATE PURPOSE ACCOMPLISHED

"Please, Mother, I've made up my mind. We're going to be married right after the Sunday morning service. In the presence of all my fr . . . all my relatives. They are relatives, Mother, relatives in Christ.

"But, let's not talk about it now. Later. Okay?" She kissed her mother and turned to Matthew.

He closed his hand over hers, touching his grandmother's ring, the one thing she had wanted more than anything else.

RECAP TRAITS OF PRINCIPAL CHARACTERS

"Now Sarah," Charles soothed.

"Don't you stop me, Charles Cranston. Don't you say one word. Understand? No one, not even you, is going to tell me no."

Charles took her sun-bronzed face in his work-worn hands. He kissed her lightly on the lips.

Embarrassed, Sarah wiped her mouth with the back of her hand. Then she took his hand and together they trudged across the grassy knoll to their home.

Sentence Plots

You have learned that a plot represents the skeleton of a story. In this section you will learn how to locate that skeleton. Each time you read a story you especially like, write a brief synopsis of it. Then squeeze the synopsis into a sentence which then becomes the skeleton, the plot pattern of the story.

I can best illustrate this procedure by calling your attention to three different stories. The first is a *purpose-achieved* story titled "Jessamine," written by Harriet Frank, Jr.[4]

Story premise: A kind, willing heart is more to be desired than strong hands.

Story problem: Will Jessamine win a place for herself in Tom's home?

Synopsis

City-reared Jessamine, a petite, kind, willing individual, loves and marries Tom, a proud, strong, hard-working young farmer who takes her home to live with his family.

Father, mother, and an aged grandmother—also proud, strong, hard-working farm people—welcome Jessamine with reserve and suspicion. A bolt of yellow silk which she unpacks is belittled as impractical.

In a series of scenes, she willingly tries to adjust to the situation for which she is so poorly equipped. She blunders through tasks assigned her, chiefly because the women in the home refuse to help her. To make matters worse, when she shares lengths of the yellow silk, hoping to dispel some of the discouragement of two individuals in the community, she is rebuffed.

At a point of despair, Jessamine learns of the grandmother's imminent birthday. She dreams up a gift she believes will soften the aged woman's heart. While Tom sleeps she fashions a fancy silk sunbonnet for Grandmother.

"Up-itty! Unsuitable!" Grandmother snaps, refusing to try it on.

Now Jessamine knows she has reached the end of her resources. She has no choice but to leave (the crisis scene). The climax occurs when, at the very last moment, a remorseful Grandmother approaches Jessamine wearing the bonnet, which she admits she loves. She begs her to stay, promising that she herself and the family, whom she has already chastised, will help her as much as they can. Having won this much ground, Jessamine unpacks, believing final victory assured.

Now without referring to specific characters (Jessamine, Tom, and his family) or to the specific problem (winning a place in Tom's farm home), we can state this plot pattern in a single sentence.

Sentence plot: A kind, generous individual, placed in a position where she isn't wanted and for which (because of her background) she isn't qualified, makes several attempts to win acceptance and fails, deciding eventually to leave the situation; but when she learns that the one who rebuffed her most recent friendly gesture is ashamed and has gone to bat for her, she decides to continue her struggle, believing victory is possible.

The second example we'll consider is a *decision-reversed* story, my own, titled "No Blue Star."[5]

Story premise: Failure isn't measured by one defeat.
Story problem: Will Polly decide to try again?

Synopsis

Polly, a primary student, comes home from school discouraged because a particular paper didn't merit her usual blue-star award. She enters the kitchen where her mother is baking a cake; dejected, she doesn't stay to talk but hurries to her room.

Sensing a problem, the mother follows. In listening to Polly, who says she is *never* going back to school, she becomes so engrossed in her daughter's problem that she doesn't hear the stove buzzer and burns the cake. Mother and daughter examine the cake. The mother shakes her head and tells Polly solemnly she doesn't think she'll ever bake another cake.

Pondering this radical suggestion Polly compares the burnt cake with the many good ones her mother has made. She decides that one mistake doesn't mean a person shouldn't go on, and so reverses her decision and tells her mother she will go back to school.

Again without referring to specific people or a specific problem, we come up with the following *sentence plot:*

Having met defeat, a character decides to quit trying, but after weighing the defeats of one or more other persons against their former victories, she decides to try again.

A variation, somewhat more complicated, could be: *Having met defeat, a character decides to quit trying, but after weighing the fate of a person who refuses to try again against someone else's victory over a much greater defeat, she decides to make another effort.**

---

*In each of these three story synopses the masculine pronoun can replace the feminine and the plot be utilized in stories about men and boys.

You may use these sentence plots in writing similar stories at some future date. Your protagonist, a teenager, grandparent, teacher, minister, doctor—whoever—will face a fail/try-again problem situation specifically suited to him.

The third story, a simple *come-to-understand* theme story by Mary Lange Jones, titled "A Welcome Tomorrow,"[6] may not appeal to Women's Libbers. I chose it because it shows how two scenes in the middle determine the resolution of the story.

Story premise: Love discerns priority claims.

Story problem: Will Beth, who loves her husband and children, come to understand family priorities?

Synopsis

Beth, wife and mother, a competent, conscientious person, is pleased when given a holiday from family responsibilities by everyone's temporary absence. As she plans activities she had neglected when they were all at home, she wonders what it will be like when her children are on their own.

Two scenes follow in which Beth encounters acquaintances. In the first she meets a neighbor who, freed from the responsibility of children who have left home, completely ignores her husband. This woman invites Beth to join her in a selfish outing. When Beth declines, the woman chides her for being overly conscientious.

In the second scene Beth is shown with a friend who is so dedicated to her family that she smothers them, especially the children. From this woman she reluctantly accepts a kind, but gratuitous favor, which causes her to ponder further her responsibilities to her family.

In a crisis scene Beth is awakened and frightened by the noise of what she assumes is an intruder. When she finds her husband has returned on an emergency errand, she is delighted. Contemplating further, she comes to understand that, though present responsibilities encompass both children and husband, someday when her children have left home her husband will be her chief responsibility. This night, she thinks, is a "taste" of that tomorrow.

Sentence plot: A competent, conscientious person ponders two opposite views about life's priorities, and after encounters with individuals who represent extreme points of view on this matter, comes to understand what is right for her.

Since life frequently demands that we choose priorities this brief plot may be used repeatedly in a variety of situations.

Now you are on your own. Choose a published story, write a synopsis, squeeze it into a sentence plot, then discard the original story as well as the synopsis. In time you will forget the story. This is as it should be, for then, following the sentence plot you have recorded in your technique notebook, the story you create will be your own.

No matter how many stories you analyze, you will find the same basic plots repeated over and over again. That's because the same plots recur in so many different guises. Dig them out and use them creatively, incorporating all the techniques you learn from the experts who have proved their worth.

CHALLENGE ASSIGNMENT

1. Read a short story in a current magazine or in an anthology.
2. Make a list of emotional reactions you discover in the story.
3. Are the characters given compound-contradictory characteristics?
4. How is the antecedent information handled?
5. Describe the setting.
6. What kind of a story is it? State the problem and the premise in separate sentences.
7. Do you find any plants or pointers in the story opening?
8. Write a synopsis of the story.
9. Now write a sentence plot omitting specific details.

26. Writing from Experience

When you were first introduced to fiction you learned why a real-life incident may not be considered a short story. But now that you know how to assemble fiction ingredients properly by following specific plot patterns, you are ready to learn how to use experience in fiction. Hitherto you have looked outside yourself for devices to simplify your writing. Now you are asked to look inside.

At some time, recently or long ago, when you experienced something that moved you deeply, your subconscious commanded, "Hold onto this, bank it, keep it in reserve for some future need."

Without being aware of this direction, you obeyed. Now you are called upon to look back, look long, and dig deep so that you can draw upon this experience reserve. As much as anything, these poignant recollections will heighten the realism of your stories.

In time you will learn to trust these memories because you felt the original experience so keenly, and because you believe someone else will be able to feel them in the same way. To you they represent truth, truth that is joyful and exciting, as well as what is seemingly sad or intolerable.

It's at this point, however, that we who are Christians often fail our readers. We whitewash and water down tensions we have had or still have. We forget that in the long, mellowing process of becoming mature Christians we often face more problems than we leave behind. We make sacrifices we were never called upon to make before. Further, we suffer mental breakdowns—yes, we do—and we become discouraged, we are tempted, we fail!

It's from remembered experiences in such situations that we gain the quality of insight and the urgency of concern that enable us to help others in a similar plight. No matter how ugly or how much they hurt, these experiences demand that they be exposed. And fiction is as effective a way as any to reveal them.

Emotion is paramount, of course. The teacher from whom I learned most about fiction writing began her first class session by asking us to recall two or three particularly poignant emotional experiences from our youth. From memory's bank I withdrew several episodes involving a mongoloid sister whom we siblings loved with defensive devotion even though she often exasperated us. One memory was of a scene I had observed when she interrupted the sandbox play of two younger sisters and their neighbor friends. Objecting to her presence, one of the visiting youngsters called her "a crazy kid." Immediately incensed, my sisters rose to her defense. Shortly afterward the neighbor children picked up their toys and left. The memory of my sisters' conflict, torn between their love for the retarded child and their desire to play with their peers, never left me.

A few years passed before I used what I had written describing this scene. When I did use the experience it became an action scene in which my lead character, a senior high-school student, rose to the defense of his mongoloid sister. The scene introduced conflict and characterized the boy.

Craig knew the fellows didn't like playing when Sheryl was around. Something always happened. It would today, Craig knew it would.

He was right. They had pitched only a few balls when the explosion came. When Dan dropped a ball, Sheryl ran and picked it up. She decided to keep it.

Bristling, Dan grabbed it away from her. "Go back to your swing," he told her, adding irritably, "Say, Craig, do we always have to have this kid around when we play?"

Before Craig could answer, a furious Sheryl scooped a fistful of sand and hurled it at Dan.

"Why you . . . you crazy kid!" he sputtered. "That's what you are, a crazy kid." He shook his head vigorously, brushing his hair to rid it of sand. His lips curled contemptuously. "Just like everyone says."

Craig hurried to Sheryl's side. He put a restraining hand on her shoulder. He felt her relax. Much as he hated her interference, he came to her defense. He couldn't help himself.

"Listen, Dan, you know very well Sheryl isn't crazy. She just wants to play."

"Sure, sure, but does she know how? Of course not. That's because she hasn't got any brains, that's why."

Craig pulled Sheryl closer to him. "You'd better leave," he told Dan.[1]

The recollection of a real-life experience never begins on paper. It begins in your mind. You go back, way back. You check your reserve of encounters, settings, and conversations you once felt most keenly. Jot these recollections in your idea notebook. You can never be sure just when you will use them. An experience which may seem useless at the moment you recall it may prove vitally important at some future time.

The strange thing about this memory bank arrangement is that any number of associations may be combined with your original experiences, and when they come up in life may cause you to withdraw a memory you deposited long ago but have seldom—perhaps never—thought of since. Or the reminder may powerfully evoke it every time. Let me suggest a few such associations:

SMELLS

forest fire	flowers
paper mill	hospital
fresh bread	new-mown hay
heavy perfume	fish

SOUNDS

musical instrument	sobbing
foghorn	baby crying
church bells	ambulance siren

PERSONAL EXPERIENCES

dreams	special birthdays
Christmas	a broken promise
a valentine	a family gathering
a family secret	a relative's visit

ENCOUNTERS WITH PEOPLE

friends	a doctor
employers	schoolmates
a teacher	business associates
a student	fellow travelers

Stored for future withdrawal is a devastating practice-teaching experience when I, a nonsinger, was asked to teach seventh-grade music.

CONVERSATIONS

opinions	jargon
dialects	arguments
idioms	expressions of devotion

One day I heard an older minister chide a young seminary graduate about his easy life compared to the hardships of a generation ago. My thoughts went back to the depression-difficult days when my clergyman husband and I served our first parish. Here's a story, I told myself. Thinking about the circumstances I came to realize that, in certain situations, a young clergyman might prove to be every bit as plucky as I like to believe we were. I titled my story, "Pup Clergyman."[2] Its premise: "It's well to withhold judgment until all the facts are known."

EMOTIONS

loneliness	love	weariness
disgust	desperation	admiration
joy	depression	concern
anger	disappointment	sympathy
hope	fear	jealousy

Recollections are most meaningful when they are recorded in the heat of a particular emotional experience, as the following two examples were. In the first I responded to some gossip I heard.

Little by little disgust inched through me. I bit my lip, inwardly clapping a restraining hand across my mouth. I clenched my teeth until my gums ached.

The whole thing was so utterly, ridiculously untrue, yet I wasn't permitted to reveal what I knew. This only intensified my anguish. I felt like a pressure cooker ready to explode.

In the second instance I recalled how I felt one day following back surgery when, as I sat relaxing momentarily in a living-room chair, friends came to call and stayed too long.

"Please go home . . . please!" my mind pleaded. But I was the only one who heard.

I murmured pleasantries; forced my lips to shape responsive smiles, then set the muscles of my face to hold them in place. Conversation buzzed around me like the distant drone of a dozen airplanes. My body ached from weakness and fatigue. If only I could snap my fingers and, like some genie, disappear.

I thought of my sunny bedroom where my rented hospital bed beckoned. There on the white spread, rays from the afternoon sun played tag with shadows made by rustling leaves outside my window. These things were magnets pulling me from my friends.

"Please, please go home!"

SETTINGS

a lake	a schoolroom
a mine	a home
a forest	a church
a cave	a mountain peak

I recorded the following experience after listening to my son speak in a slum mission.

I was totally unprepared for his relaxed, easy pulpit manner. His voice was low, well-modulated, persuasive.

My son? A year ago, little concern. But tonight—a slum pulpit.

The room was bleak; the podium, a battered lectern. Shaggy, unkempt heads lifted bleary eyes. Except for an occasional cough and some shifting of feet, the place seemed uncannily quiet. The odor of unwashed clothes and bodies engulfed me. I wished someone would open a window.

But he was getting through to these men. I felt it as tangibly as I felt the hard back of the bench against my shoulders. Then suddenly, as if compelled by some great sorrow, the man in front of me buried his face in his hands and wept bitterly.

MAJOR EVENTS

a flood	a forest fire
a death	a court trial
a birth	a funeral
a wedding	an accident

THE PRINTED PAGE (THE WORLD'S THOUGHT AND EXPERIENCE)

poems	magazine articles
short stories	novels
profiles	biographies
science	scripture quotations
news reports	hymns
billboard messages	

ART AND MUSIC

These may involve amateurish productions as well as work of the masters.

a seascape	a favorite hymn
a folk song	an old quilt
a lullaby	a piece of sculpture

DRAMA

Some incident in a play may cause you to remember something similar in your own life.

When amended and altered, real life experiences may be used to—

1. Characterize (remember the brother and his mongoloid sister?).
2. Introduce a story problem.

The recollection of an almost hopeless search for a part-time job when I was a college student during depression days became the problem of a short story about an engineer's search for work following the loss of his job due to air-force cutbacks.

3. Influence a decision.

A lead character may face seemingly impossible alternatives which he resolves because you remember how you, or someone else, handled a similar decision.

4. Present antecedent information.

Your lead character may be given a past with which you are familiar.

5. Authenticate.

A story of mine titled "Shoes Are for Walking"[3] grew from the seeds of two vivid recollections: one personal (difficult back surgery), the other a friend's (her husband presented her with a pair of utilitarian oxfords while she was in the hospital for some minor ailment).

In my story the lead character, who suffered pain as I did, believed she would never walk again (not my experience). On her birthday her husband presented her with an expensive pair of alligator shoes (note alteration), which though they incensed her at first, made her realize he really believed she would walk. She determined she would.

So though a real life experience cannot be made literally into a short story, it is one of the fiction writer's most valuable tools. Because you or an acquaintance have solved a crucial problem, your story characters may be able to solve theirs. In a given situation your fictional people will experience the same intense emotion you yourself felt so keenly, at the time you obeyed your subconscious mind's command to hold onto the experience—to bank it, keep it in reserve for some future need.

CHALLENGE ASSIGNMENT

1. Dig deep in your memory and locate three poignant emotional experiences. Describe them in detail.
2. Mull over these experiences. Which one do you believe

could be used in a story, if with suitable changes it becomes a problem, a characterization, a resolution—whatever?

3. Plan a story. Choose the type of story, characters, problem, setting, premise.

4. Write your story using no more than 1700–2000 words.

27. *Evaluate Your Story*

"Cool it!" You have heard this direction before. Pay special attention to it now. For if you are like most beginning writers, you may not realize that when you write the last words of a story, you really haven't finished it. Revisions are in order.

Revisions should not be made immediately, however. At the time you complete your story you are too close to your brain child. Put it in cold storage for several days or a week or two. Immediately begin work on another, and another. Then when you have several stacked in a pile, pull out the first and take a good look at it again. Read it aloud. You'll find flaws you never dreamed were there.

Some dialogue will sound stilted and unnatural; a particular scene may stand out as irrelevant; the beginning may not grab you as it did when you wrote it.

Be especially alert to your handling of transitions. Check to see if they move the story smoothly from place to place, from time to time, from mood to mood. Change those that don't.

Eliminate superfluous words. With the aid of a thesaurus, substitute the meaningful word for the blah. Check emotion. Does one really *feel* the emotions your lead character is supposed to experience? Do you need to heighten emotion?

And what about length? Does your story fit the length requirements of the publication for which you intend it?

Further, is your story honest—plausible in the best sense? Mary, a child who stretches the truth beyond imagination's validity, doesn't suddenly stop telling lies because she attends Sunday school once or twice. Nor should Johnny's story problem be resolved in thin air just because he prays. He may pray for wisdom in solving his problem, but in the actual resolution he does "his thing" to solve it.

Honesty involves caution in oversimplifying temptations and problems alike. It also carries with it psychological implications.

I recall reading a story in a weekly church-school paper which recounted an experience of the narrator. A very sick dog came to her house. She took it in and nursed it lovingly. In spite of her care, the dog died, and she buried it in a beautiful spot overlooking a river.

On her way home, a small boy stopped her and asked if she had seen his dog. When he described it, she realized that the dog she had buried was his. He repeated his question, "Have you seen my dog?"

Apparently believing that what the boy didn't know wouldn't hurt him, she answered, "No, I haven't seen your dog."

I don't recall the resolution of the story. Perhaps at a later date the narrator helped the boy find another dog. I only remember I was terribly annoyed because the narrator told a lie. I was annoyed, too, because of her lack of psychological perception. This could have been a beautiful story had the child been told of the dog's death, been permitted to grieve—even perhaps to have a part in burying the pet (possible in fiction, where you can arrange sequence to fit your story). Psychologists tell us we ought not deprive children of valid grief experiences. They are part of life. What they don't know *can* hurt them.

Now let's get back to your story. Are you as excited about it as you were when you wrote it? You should be.

A last admonition. Take your story and examine it again carefully. Check it against the following questions and suggestions.

1. Is it really a story? Does it have a plot, a story plan? Did you write that plan in a single sentence?
2. Does the story have a beginning, a middle, and an end?
3. Does the beginning present a believable character who faces a

vital problem he is capable of solving? Does the problem fit the character's age and temperament?

4. Can you state the problem in a single sentence? Is it one with which your reader will identify?

5. Does the story beginning
   a. present the problem quickly?
   b. indicate the mood of the story?
   c. give the place and time of it?
   d. characterize the protagonist?
   e. present and characterize the antagonist? In what ways does he differ from the protagonist?
   f. provide plants, tools, and skills which will be used in the solution of the story?

6. At what point does the story beginning end? Remember, the beginning presents the story problem. All attempts made by the lead character to solve it occur in the middle of the story.

7. How many scenes are there in the middle of the story? Have you included only those that are necessary to solve the problem?

8. Do these scenes sustain interest?

9. From whose viewpoint is the story told? Is this consistent throughout the story?

10. Do your story people always speak and act in character?

11. Is the dialogue natural? Does it move the story?

12. Have you avoided trite phrases and situations?

13. How have you handled antecedent material? Was a flashback necessary?

14. What is the emotional impact of the story? Is it impressive and vivid?

15. Does the story make you feel *this is life, this is real?*

16. What is the premise of your story? State it in a single sentence.

17. Is the crisis black enough?

18. How does the lead character, through his own efforts, solve the story problem? (Chance may not be used to help the lead character, though it may be used to hinder him.)

19. By what special tool, skill, or character trait does the protagonist solve the story problem?

20. Is the story ending convincingly satisfying? It need not be an "all's well" finish, but it must be satisfying to the reader even if it is a "that's too bad" ending.

CHALLENGE ASSIGNMENT

1. You are ready now to revise one of the stories you have written. Test it against the suggestions given in this chapter. Then send it to your chosen market.

2. Offer to judge some other writer's short story. Give him one of yours. Then get together and talk about what you have learned.

8

Books

28. *Nonfiction Books*

Moving from the writing of an article to the writing of a non-fiction book isn't as difficult as moving from the short story to the novel form. If you have successfully marketed a number of articles I assume you have already established professional writing habits. You know how to evaluate and brainstorm an idea, how to do necessary research and, as important, how to present a clear, concise, logical product to an editor.

In your book preparation it isn't enough to latch onto an idea, however. You must decide if the idea can be researched and expanded beyond article requirements to the extent that it feels big enough to be handled in a book. You also must be prepared to work hard for a considerable length of time—at a minimum, a large portion of a year.

Because so much time and work are involved in writing a book it is wise to submit a book proposal before you mail the complete manuscript. Such a proposal should include:

1. A statement telling the publisher why you feel qualified to write the book. A list of credits—articles and books, fiction and nonfiction, you have had published.
2. Why you believe the proposed book is significant and timely.
3. Who the intended readers for the book are.
4. A suggestion of promotional possibilities.
5. A synopsis and a table of contents with a paragraph or two describing each chapter.
6. Two or three completed chapters to give the publisher an opportunity to evaluate your writing ability.

If an editor is interested you will receive a letter indicating so. Changes, rearrangement of material, a writing deadline, additional research sources or any other suggestions may be made then.

It's at this time some editors offer a contract which may or may not promise an "advance" on royalties. Others prefer seeing the completed manuscript before offering a contract. Be aware that the responsibility for acceptance of a book manuscript does not fall to one person. The managing editor, readers, consultants, and sales people are involved in the decision. All must agree on the book's credibility and sales potential.

You will, of course, continue to brainstorm your idea, to saturate yourself with facts, statistics, quotations, anecdotes about the subject, organize, and write while you wait for a reply to your book proposal.

Before you begin you will want to file all material in some manner. Many authors use manila folders, one for each chapter. Make sure that you indicate the source of each resource item you file.

When you feel you are ready to do a first draft you should proceed logically, chapter by chapter. Choose and discard just as you do when you write an article. Pay particular attention to chapter transitions. Well done, they give continuity and flow to your material. Often the concluding words, sentence, or thought at the end of one chapter may be used in some manner to begin the next.

In my book *Looking Ahead—The Realities of Aging: Face Them with Faith,*[1] chapter 4, entitled "Hobbies and Second Careers," ended with these words: "Make the most of your assets. After all, it is you who make retirement boring or full of promise." Chapter 5, entitled "Helping Yourself by Helping Others," began: "Though hobbies and second careers do add interest and significance to one's life, they can be overdone. An added ingredient is needed—meaningful involvement in other people's lives, as the following story aptly illustrates. . . ."

I can cite another example from my book *Louise,*[2] a story of a family's escape from Russia via Siberia and China, which is told through the eyes of the fifteen-year-old daughter. Although it is not a work of fiction, the principle is the same. The first chapter began with a frightening experience that had occurred in Siberia after the girl's father died. I knew that the following chapters had to inform readers about what had happened up to that point. They also needed to know a bit of Mennonite history. Chapter 1 ended with Louise asking her mother why, if God loved them, He allowed such things to happen.

"Mother answered, 'God is love. It is men who are evil. We must trust God and be true to Him always as our forefathers did.' She hesitated, suddenly in a reflective mood. 'You want I should tell you about my people?'

"'Yes, Mama,' I answered, longing to be reminded of the good times we enjoyed before my father died. 'And tell me again how Papa found you.'"

The second chapter picks up the "telling" theme: "While I was interested in the immediate past, Mother often spoke of long ago events, as they pertained to our people—even when I was young, though I failed to understand much of what she said at the time. She, like other parents, constantly declared we were Hollanders, not Germans or Russians. Yet, we spoke German as well as Dutch and we lived in Russia.

"'Our ancestors were born in Holland,' she told me. 'Like us, they believed . . .'"

With that Mama tells past history, with Louise interacting from time to time. Toward the end of the chapter she tells how her husband courted her.

When you have finished your book, set it aside for a time. Later begin to groom it. Check spelling and punctuation, compare reference numbers to source notes, verify the accuracy of names and date credits, etc. Note, particularly, paragraph transitions. Read the book again, this time aloud. Listen! Do you detect a pleasing cadence? If you stumble over certain sections you can be sure they need revision. It's a good idea to have someone else, someone whose ability you trust, read your book. He or she may point out errors you missed.

The next step is the final typing, another proofreading, followed by the actual mailing of the manuscript. Package your material carefully—in a box, if possible. Always enclose return postage.

If the book requires an index this is the time to begin working on it. There is no standard procedure that everyone follows. But I know what works best for me. I retain a copy of the manuscript and go through it carefully, circling every indexable word and its possible cross reference. In the margin I indicate if the word should be a main entry or a sub-entry. I constantly ask myself, "What would I want listed? Which words would I like to locate?"

The circled words are then transferred to a set of 3" × 5" cards and filed alphabetically in a card file. On each card I pencil the number of the page or pages on which the word appears in the manuscript. Though these numbers will differ from the numbers on the proof pages, they will approximate them. When the proof pages (or galley sheets) arrive for final checking, time is at a premium. I must work quickly. I consult the numbered index cards, then seek the exact location of each word in the text. Next, I replace the penciled number with the correct book page number on the index cards.

When I have done this, I am ready to type the index pages as they will appear in the book. Fortunately they have already been alphabetized.

If you have never prepared an index, I suggest you study how it is done, noting particularly how related material refers back to the main subject entry. A good resource is *A Manual of Style* (The University of Chicago Press).

Here is a brief idea of the types of books being sought by publishers.

Biographies

The biography, a written history of a person's life, presents a challenging, as well as a difficult, opportunity to a writer. A biographer chooses a subject because he or she is interesting, an achiever, or a person who is well known. The subject may be living or dead. To successfully write such a book, the author should apply all the techniques of the novelist, as well as those of a nonfiction writer. Because so many people read biographies, they enjoy an appeal denied some of the best novels.

If you are interested in writing a biography, your first step is to select your subject. Walter S. Campbell once suggested a subject is chosen because:

1. Such exposure is timely. The country, a denomination, or an organization may be contemplating a celebraton of the anniversary of the birth or death of the subject, or of some great achievement accomplished. Some writers check future calendars in the hope they can take advantage of such events.
2. The subject, though formerly unknown, has suddenly become famous.
3. Present biographies of the subject need updating.
4. The subject has gained prominence in his or her field of work.
5. Simply, the subject is striking.

For the most part publishers are looking for biographies of people who will prove interesting to a great many people.

Few types of writing require as much research as a biography. It is only after the author has gathered, appraised, and sifted all that can be found on the subject that he or she is able to write realistically about that person. Mere facts are useless, however, without an interpretation of them. An author needs to step into the shoes of the subject and react as he or she would.

A biographer must scrounge for every possible bit of information about the subject. Often such research takes years. The biographer must understand race, country, customs—everything that fashioned the book's subject.

This gathering of the material involves travel, correspondence, phone calls, and reading—of journals, newspapers, letters, and comments made by the subject or persons close to the subject. All facts must be verified.

Usually this data is recorded on cards, then classified under subject divisions. Many biographers use a large ledger with numbered pages on which they record the events that occur each year of the subject's life.

A biographer needs to be even-handed. He or she must not cheat by failing to include the faults and failures as well as the virtues and accomplishments of the subject.

Walter S. Campbell suggested that once the data has been

collected and evaluated, it is wise to write, at top speed, a 15,000-word synopsis of the subject's life—without reference to research notes. This brief version will capture the high spots and help simplify the revision of the book's outline.

When my friend Margaret Troutt wrote the biography of Evangeline Booth (to commemorate the centennial anniversary of the Salvation Army's work in America), she traveled throughout the United States, Canada, Great Britain, and Sweden. In all these places she read documents, journals, letters, and news items about Booth and her achievements. When Troutt returned to her home she was forced to cope with hundreds of cards filled with research information and a vast number of tapes on which she had recorded interviews with persons who knew Booth intimately. The time expended in research and writing took close to three years.

In attempting your biography you will *accumulate*, *assimilate*, *articulate*, and *activate* your research material—in that order.

A few examples of published biographies are *No Greater Love* (on Anna Cara Moss) by Mildred Tengbom and *The General Was A Lady* (on Evangeline Booth) by Margaret Troutt.

Devotional Books

This type of book is intended to inform and to inspire. It is different from the daily devotional book in that it is longer and usually speaks of the personal experiences of the author and of other people. The purpose is to exalt the Lord Jesus Christ and to explore God's love, His guidance, and care.

A few examples:

Beyond Ourselves by Catharine Marshall

Either Way I Win by Lois Walfrid Johnson

A Slow and Certain Light by Elisabeth Elliot

A Shepherd Looks at Psalm 23 by Phillip Keller

Song of Ascents by E. Stanley Jones

A Call to Commitment and *A Search for Silence* by Elizabeth O'Connor

Afterglow by Sherwood Wirt

Educational Books

These are books written to teach. Here we may list text-books—and this book, for instance. Books about books of the Bible used in adult teaching situations and books that are considered how-to's are also included. They may address the matter of church officers' responsibilities, the organization of a home Bible study group, visitation and evangelism techniques. Information about a particular organization or group, the purpose of which is to inform readers of its work, falls into the area of education.

A few examples:

What the Bible Is All About by Henrietta C. Mears

The Evangelism Explosion by James Kennedy

How to Cope with Conflict, Crisis and Change by Lloyd Ahlem

Careers in Religious Journalism by Roland Wolseley

James: Wisdom That Works by David A. Hubbard

Mark the Day of All Nations by Willard M. Swartley

Creative Procedure for Adult Groups, Harold D. Minor, editor

Why Doesn't Someone Do Something? by Daisy Hepburn

Good Times with Old Times: How to Write Your Memoirs by Katie Funk Wiebe

Experiential Books

These books relate the experiences of an individual or a group of people. They are written because the author and publisher believe they contain a "spiritual-takeaway" impact. It is hoped the reader will become a better person for having read the book.

Sometimes persons selected for this type of exposure cannot articulate their experiences well enough in writing to prepare a book. This is why many experiential books carry not only the subject's name but a by-line that includes the writer's name, usually with the phrase "as told to" or "with."

The writing of such books greatly resembles the writing of a novel, except that the events are true. Characterization, plot, dialogue, descriptions, and theme should be skillfully rendered to approximate that of fiction. Here, as in the writing of a biography, the author needs to step into the shoes of the subject.

As in a biography, the experiential book requires a great deal of research. In preparing to write *Louise* I studied new and old maps of Russia, China, and Japan so that I could pinpoint the exact route taken by the escapees. I read other experiential books and novels about similar escapes. I also read several volumes of Mennonite history before I felt qualified to condense the past into the page limit I had assigned it. I interviewed persons who had taken the same escape route. I spent a great many hours with Louise's mother, as she recounted intimate details of her family's life. I located and interviewed the guide who led the family to safety across the Amur River. It was necessary, too, that I know what had happened politically in Russia at the time.

A few examples:

The Hiding Place by John and Elizabeth Sherrill

Born Again by Charles W. Colson

The Down Way Up by Carol Gift Page

The Unhurried Chase by Betty Carlson

Heartaches by Ceil McLeod

Historical Books

Nonfiction historical books can be written about any period of history. Histories of missionary organizations, denominations, and institutions have been preserved in this manner.

A few examples:

The Light and the Glory by Peter Marshall

By One Spirit by Karl A. Olsson

The Wit and Wisdom of Our Fathers by Herbert E. Palmquist

Issue- and Problem-Oriented Books

This type of book provides unlimited opportunities to writers. People are constantly bombarded by issues and problems they must face. Because the content for this type of book is precisely defined they are not too difficult to write once necessary research has been done. They present a danger, however. Authors too often write superficially from limited knowledge instead of probing into every resource to substantiate what they write.

If you contemplate writing such a book, you will need to read widely on the subject you choose—secular treatises as well as those in the religious field. Make use of the *Reader's Guide to Periodical Literature* to learn what has been written in periodicals about the subject. Constantly ask, "What can I add that is new and meaningful about the subject?"

A few examples:

Where Is God When It Hurts? by Philip Yancey

God's Psychiatry by Charles Allen

After I've Said I Do by Dwight Henry Small

The Recovery of Family Life by Elton and Pauline Trueblood

Your Aging Parents: When and How to Help by Margaret J. Anderson

Missionary Books

A missionary book may be an account of the experiences of one person or a group of people. It is experiential in nature, written in the first- or third-person viewpoint.

Again, a vast amount of research is required. Personal involvement can prove a great asset. Often writers who have not been involved in the story visit the area where it occurs to gain insight and experience that adds authenticity needed to make the book come alive.

A few examples:

Angel at My Shoulder by Kenneth Wilson

Peace Child and *Eternity in Their Hearts* by David Richardson

Kidnapped by Karl and Debbie Doritzbach

Through Gates of Splendor by Elisabeth Elliot

The Night the Giant Rolled Over by Jerry Jenkins

Theological Books

Written to convey theological truth, to provide greater understanding of the Scriptures, and to inspire, these books are often more erudite than other Christian books. However, the trend is toward a more popular presentation.

A few examples:

The Waiting Father by Helmut Thielicke

Called to Maturity by Myron S. Augsburger

A Mind Awake: An Anthology of C.S. Lewis compiled by Clyde S. Kilby

Psychology, Religion, and Healing by Leslie D. Weatherhead

Purity of Heart by Søren Kierkegaard

Ring of Truth by J. B. Phillips

These lists are far from complete. Bookstore shelves underscore the fact that many other types of books are marketable: anthologies, cookbooks, books of quotations, books of prayers, books for specific people (writers, clergymen, Sunday school teachers, women, men, executives, singles, the elderly . . .), and many others.

If you feel qualified to undertake a nonfiction book, whatever the category, write to the publishers you believe may be interested. Ask for their book catalogs. By doing so you will learn what is being published and where your proposal may find acceptance. Also check *Books in Print* at your public library or at local bookstores.

CHALLENGE ASSIGNMENT

1. Choose a subject about which you feel compelled to write a book. Ask yourself: Is the subject timely? What age group would be most interested? Can I expand and add new light to the subject? Are resources available? Do I have sufficient skill to write the book?

2. Check *Books in Print* to learn how many, if any, books have

been published on the same subject.

3. Now do the necessary research. Read periodicals and books on the subject. Interview people knowledgeable on the subject.

4. Write a book proposal and send it to the publishing house you believe will be most receptive to your submission.

5. Add to the list of books I have mentioned a list of those you have found helpful under the various types.

29.   *Adult Novels*

If you are a short story writer you may have wondered whether you could be successful writing book-length fiction. Many novelists admit to having written a great many short stories before attempting the novel. This was true of many of the authors who wrote the great Russian classics. And yet others, Mary O'Hara, of *My Friend Flicka* and *Thunderhead* fame, for instance, began writing novels without previous experience in the short story field.

You need to be aware that a novel differs greatly from a short story. A short story is what it claims to be—a story that is short. It must be contained in a limited time frame in which the lead character resolves a particular problem, makes a significant decision, or comes to understand some basic premise about life. Unlike the novel, the short story allows no time to develop dimensional characters. It appropriates a tight dramatic plot that leads, scene by scene, to a threatening or perplexing climax that is resolved in a logical and satisfying manner.

A novel is not an extended short story. Nor is it a series of short stories strung together. Concept and theme take precedence over problem in the preliminary structuring process. Yet, of necessity, the novel explores a number of problems and decisions that are resolved as the story progresses. In a novel we can take more time. We are concerned about the basis and the cause of problems. It's a matter of cause and effect . . . cause and effect. . . .

Be aware that a novel is fiction—a fabrication, an exaggerated interpretation of life. Characters need to be intriguing and the plot suspenseful so that they compel the reader to keep turning pages to learn how the story is resolved.

Most novelists compile extensive dossiers about their novel characters. They include information about childhood, education, parental influences, problems, disappointments, phobias, physical descriptions—anything and everything that will make story characters come alive.

In the planning stage, a conscientious novelist will also make and file notes about places, time, descriptions, dialogue, philosophies, frailties, political events, etc. Again—anything and everything pertaining to the overall development of the novel.

Chapters may be thought of as acts of a play made up of scenes that dramatize its action. The first chapter will establish viewpoint, place, primary characters, time, and mood. This will help to set the scene, hint at the theme, and establish the story problem. Flashbacks can be presented in chapter segments or they may be fed in bits and pieces in several chapters.

The last chapter resolves the story problem, and ties all loose ends together in a valid, satisfying conclusion.

Novelists differ in the manner in which they approach their writing. A recurring theme, an intriguing character, a setting, a remembered experience, a quote from literature, music, or a chance remark may set the wheels of their mind turning to the point where they say, "I have the makings of a novel."

Some authors claim that characters, once they have come alive, set the stage and determine the story plot. Others may look to the theme or the concept to establish the story line. Thus some novelists never plot their novels in detail, while others plot extensively before they begin writing, even though they realize changes and rearrangement of material may be necessary as they proceed.

I like to think of the general plot of a novel as the *hub*, on which the story turns, and from which the *character spokes* extend (develop and interact) to the *rim*, where the theme reveals itself in repeated contact with the story's world.

The consensus of opinion among novelists is that a book-length fiction writer must:

1. Continually experience life—be aware, observant, feel emotionally, probe the "whys" of situations and character behavior.

2. Read published novels. Other authors can be a writer's best teachers. Read modern work as well as the classics and secular as well as religious novels. In studying the work of other authors, take their novels apart as a watchmaker takes a watch apart, not to find out what is wrong with it as much as to discover how it was put together.

3. Get under the skin of the novel's characters to the extent that all facets of their lives are revealed and understood. Insight is important.

4. Choose a familiar setting (one that is experienced or well researched).

5. Feel a burning compulsion to undertake the writing of a novel.

6. Understand that persistence and commitment are involved in the time and energy required in writing this kind of book.

Allegory, Fantasy, and Science Fiction

An allegory is a story that expands and explores a particular truth or concept by means of symbolic fictional characters and settings. In *Pilgrim's Progress* John Bunyan wrote allegorically about the trials, temptations and victories the character called Christian experienced as he traveled to his eternal home. In his allegory *The Holy War* Diabolus (Satan) fights and subdues the city of Mansoul. Corruption follows. Eventually the city is recaptured by an army led by Emmanuel. As in *Pilgrim's Progress* good wins over evil.

Fantasy and science fiction authors take people, animals, and occasionally inanimate objects and create a story that, though it logically couldn't happen, appears to be possible.

Author Phyllis Whitney once said it takes a knowledge of story techniques, a keenly logical mind and, most of all, a touch of genius to write this type of story. Certainly C. S. Lewis in his *Chronicles of Narnia* and J. R. R. Tolkien in *The Hobbit* and *The Lord of the Rings* evidence this touch of genius.

According to Webster's dictionary science fiction deals primarily with the impact of actual or imagined science upon society or individuals. Madeleine L'Engle's *A Wrinkle of Time*, *A Wind at the Door* and *A Swiftly Tilting Planet* are excellent examples of this type of writing.

Biblical Novels

Biblical novels are written about Biblical characters and events. In many instances a great deal of liberty is taken with characterization and interaction, though basic Bible truths should be kept intact. One who writes this type of novel must thoroughly research customs, culture, clothing, political events, and geographical settings to give authenticity to the period of time in which the story takes place.

A few examples:

Prince of Egypt by Dorothy Clark Wilson
Two from Galilee by Marjorie Holmes
Song of Deborah by Bette Ross
David and Bathsheba by Roberta Kella Dorr

Though research is apparent in all of these novels, I was impressed by the firsthand knowledge evident in Dorr's description of terrain, architecture, culture, and customs as they related to the Philistines as well as the Israelites. Her portrayal of sin, punishment, and forgiveness will lead readers to empathize with Bathsheba and to understand David's despair as he sought God's forgiveness for his sins.

Concept Novels

Any religious novel that attempts to establish a particular concept which affects a Christian's behavior may be called a concept novel.

A few examples:

Tell No Man by Adela Rogers St. Johns
In His Steps by Charles Sheldon
Cry, the Beloved Country by Alan Paton

Detective and Mystery Novels

This type of story presents a character or characters who strive to expose one who has committed a crime, or to clarify a mystery of some sort. Popular with young people, they also find a ready market with adults.

A few examples:

The Kilbourne Connection by Gaylord Larson

Code Name Sebastian by James Johnson

Margo by Jerry Jenkins

Both Johnson and Jenkins have written a series of books utilizing characters in the books listed above.

Historical Novels

Demanding as much skill and research as Biblical fiction, historical novels may be written about any period of history.

A few examples:

Uncle Tom's Cabin by Harriet Beecher Stowe

Unto a Good Land and *The Emigrants* by Vilhelm Moberg

The Gulag Archipelago by Aleksandr Solzhenitsyn

Romance and Love Stories

A few examples:

Christy by Catharine Marshall

The St. Simon's Island Novels by Eugenia Price

Kara by Carol Gift Page

Some Christian publishers now accept novels that closely resemble the romance novels made popular by secular publishers. A "Christian romance" should present spiritual values, however. They should not be tacked on, but inherent in the makeup of the characters and the plot.

Plot patterns for this novel seldom vary, though the setting may be in any country and in any historical period. The heroine, a young, beautiful, often adventurous woman meets a handsome, eligible man to whom she is immediately attracted. Conflicts arise immediately. There may be other suitors. There is almost always another woman who is a threat to the heroine. It isn't until the last chapter, often the last page, that the heroine and "her man" declare their love for each other.

Though the purpose of this chapter is primarily to inspire and to categorize, techniques need to be considered.

In her book *Novel in the Making*,[1] Mary O'Hara describes the struggles she went through in writing *The Son of Adam Wingate*. She researched, wrote, revised, and finally discarded several nearly completed versions before she gained the direction that caused her to write her publisher and exclaim, "This is it. This is my book."

When I asked Jerry Jenkins where he obtained his ideas for his *Margo*[2] mysteries, an adult series for women, he facetiously answered in the words of another novelist, "I make them up."

Does he start with character or plot?

Depends. If I see a photograph of a young woman somewhere (usually in a woman's magazine) and if her eyes and the corner of her mouth suggest something's happening, I begin to wonder: "What problem does she face?" "Does she have a secret dilemma a detective could solve?"

If I already know the dilemma, I search earnestly for a face to fit it. "Who might have that problem?" I ask. When I find the right person, I clip her photo and pin it to the wall where I can see it while I type. Very soon the picture becomes a real person who acts her part in the novel plot.

So sometimes it's a germ of a plot: a woman judge trying a man for a murder she commited. Other times it's a haunting picture: a flight attendant who is being followed around the country.

Deadlines? Jenkins says deadlines force him to sit and make things fit together. "It's rarely easy, but there's no greater challenge, no greater fun."

In interviewing Carol Gift Page, an up-and-coming novelist, I asked her to explain how she approached the writing of her novel *Kara*.[3]

She told me she could have begun in a number of ways—with an idea (a single unifying premise), with a particular character (through whom the theme would be revealed), or with a particular plot (story action).

Eventually all elements must be interwoven to create a novel.

For this particular mystery-romance novel, I began with a character—a former college roommate. By the time I began writing, however, my main character bore little resemblance to this girl.

For weeks I pondered over bits and pieces of ideas until an appropriate plot and theme evolved out of my character's needs and motivations.

Once Page had the story line in mind she sat at her typewriter for a six-hour nonstop marathon and typed a 9,000-word synopsis.

As rapidly as possible I put down thoughts, developed subplots, fleshed out scenes, and recorded whole sections of dialogue. Later I divided the synopsis into chapters and made a folder for each one. Into these chapters I stored accumulated information regarding characters, local history, customs, story issues, and trends.

Then Page wrote detailed dossiers about primary and secondary characters, including physical and emotional characteristics, backgrounds, strengths, habits, and goals. She also referred to magazine photographs she felt best depicted her characters. This helped her remember a character's color of hair and eyes as well as other physical features. To add authenticity to her story she researched drug abuse and visited a hospital burn unit.

During the book's nine-month gestation, I tried to write a chapter at each sitting. I gave Kara significant problems worthy of her wholehearted concentration. After her father dies mysteriously and her mother is severely burned, Kara discovers the long-kept family secret: her maiden aunt is her real mother. Kara's search for her natural father propels her into danger, romance, a brush with death, a test of faith, and an encounter with a family she never knew she had.

If you have established yourself as a competent novelist, you will be able to approach an editor with an idea. He or she will know that you can complete your work if a go-ahead is forthcoming.

If you have never written a novel, chances are strong that an editor will want to see a good portion of your book before a go-ahead is given. You may write a book proposal enclosing three or more chapters, thus proving your writing ability and exposing your writing style.

Personally, I can think of nothing more rewarding than to write a novel that will entertain and influence a vast number of readers.

CHALLENGE ASSIGNMENT

1 Select a novel you have enjoyed reading. In one sentence state its basic appeal to you.

2. On a sheet of paper, answer the following questions about the book:

   a. How would you classify the book as to novel type?

   b. What is the predominant theme of the book?

   c. Study the first chapter. Name the main characters and tell what appear to be their roles in the book.

   d. Examine a chapter you especially enjoyed. Number the scenes. What is the chapter's problem? Is it resolved? If so, how? Does it lead into the next chapter?

   e. Choose another chapter and note its emotional appeal. Read the dialogue aloud. Note how successfully the author used intimate detail. (For further study, dip into some of the novels of Pulitzer-prize-winning novelist Wallace Stegner, a master at this type of writing.)

   f. Evaluate the novel's Christian influence. Is it inherent in the text without being preachy?

3. Write a one- or two-page dossier of the lead character. List in detail his or her description, background, habits, weaknesses, strengths, religious persuasions, pet peeves, choice of music or art, sports involvement, and so on.

4. Select an age group for whom you would like to write and plot a novel. Write a synopsis of the book, then divide it into chapters. Research thoroughly.

5. Now write your novel. Rewrite until you feel it is ready for market.

30. Children's Books

"Think ahead," children's book editors advise. "Don't assume the type of book that has found acceptance one year will be salable the next."

When these editors were asked what will happen in the next ten years in nonreligious book publishing, they said writers can anticipate:

1. An increase in the number of children of junior high school age who will demand books to supply their needs.
2. More original paperbacks and increased simultaneous publication of hardbound and paperback editions.
3. Fewer full-color picture books.
4. More emphasis on the reading interests of the eleven- to thirteen-year-old youngsters.
5. An increase of high interest/simple vocabulary books.
6. Increased subsidiary purchases for audio and film use.
7. Greater demands by libraries for quality writing and illustrations.

Whether these predictions materialize remains to be seen. Nevertheless, we who write for the religious market ought to consider them seriously. I say that because I believe this market is not closed to us. Editors still look for honest, moral (not preachy), idealistic manuscripts that are skillfully written.

Appraising religious book publishing, Patricia C. McKissak, children's book editor for Concordia Publishing House, points to the steady growth in the development and sales of all kinds of material for children in recent years. She believes there has never been a more opportune time for those of us who want to write religious material for children. Her reasons:

Increased parochial school attendance

Increased Sunday school attendance in many areas

A greater number of church libraries

A growing concern by parents for the spiritual growth and nurture of their children.

More qualified writers who will attempt this specialized type of writing.[1]

Note, she said qualified writers.

Of primary importance is the spiritual stance of the writer. Certainly this person should be well grounded in the Christian faith and in the Bible. He or she must like children and understand fully the personality traits of the age groups who will become readers of the published material.

To learn about the children in a particular age group, a writer should read articles and books that describe the psychological and physical nature of these children. It is necessary, too, that one study books written for them. Editors suggest authors read hundreds of children's books before attempting to write one.

Before you begin to write you should also talk to city and church librarians. Ask:

What type of books are circulated most often?
How popular are nature, fantasy, biographical, and history books?
Which picture books do you recommend? Why?
At what age do older children do the most reading?

Examine *The Book Finder*, volumes 1 and 2, and *A Guide to Children's Literature: About the Needs and Problems of Youth, Ages 2–15* by Sharon Spredman Dreyer. Also check the *Reader's Guide to Periodical Literature* to locate children's book articles published in the *Writer* and the *Writer's Digest*. And consult *Children's Books in Print* at your local library.

You also might ask children to name favorite books and why they enjoy them. Note spring and fall supplements that review children's books in both local and major newspapers. Read *How to Grow a Reader* by John and Kay Lindskoog,[2] and *Honey in a Child's Heart* by Gladys Hunt.[3] You also might offer to review children's books for your Sunday school or your church newsletter. Attending a Children's Literature Conference in the area where you live might be helpful, as would reading college textbooks that deal with children's books.

Visit your local Christian bookstore for information regarding the sale of children's books in your area.

In your study of books you will discover that children of all ages have basic needs. Some are common to a particular age, while others are common to all ages. Children are interested in:

Themselves	Sounds	Home	Friends
Play	Surprises	School	Water (ocean/lake)
Pets	Birthdays	Family	Fishing (other sports)
Machines	Toys	Music	Fire engines
Nature	Cars	Mystery	Vacations
Science	Adventure	Church	Other countries

In addition, your study will lead you to sense the needs of children:

to know acceptance as a person

to love

to feel loved

to be liked by others

to like others

to feel secure

to be successful

to know and understand

to grow

to express thoughts and feelings

to feel, see, smell, taste and hear.

Since editors constantly stress the last need listed, that of seeing, feeling, smelling, tasting, and hearing, I recommend Jacqueline Jackson's book *Turn Not Pale, Beloved Snail*. The book is valuable not only to writers but to teachers of small children. In it Jackson describes how she taught her own children to "sense" life, a lesson all authors need to learn.

No study of children is complete without considering the *problems* they face. The following list is a result of a brainstorming session at a Mount Hermon, California, Writer's Conference:

Peer esteem	Physical problems
Loneliness	Alcoholism
Shyness	Absent parent(s)
Speech impediment	Poverty
Fear of a bully	Affluence
Stature (too short	Inability to read
or too tall)	Hyperactivism
Sibling rivalry	Death of a parent
Mental deficiency	Death of a sibling
Mental superiority	Death of a friend
Quarreling parents	Lack of affection
Language barriers	Physical abuse
Temper	City boredom
Fears (height)	An incurable disease
Shoplifting	A physical handicap
Lying	Moving to a new location
Drugs	Accepting a step-parent or a step-sibling
Moral issues	

In reading children's books, notice the viewpoint that appears most acceptable for each age group. Study story settings, intimate detail, emotions, and dialogue.

Most subjects covered by nonreligious publishers can be handled in the religious press. However, there are areas that only religious writers may feel competent to handle.

Devotionals and Prayers

Examples are *Lord, I Want to Tell You Something* by Chris Jones and *Just a Minute, Lord* by Lois Johnson. These are books of prayers for the early teens, written in unrhymed verse. A similar book is *Lord, I've Been Thinking: Prayer Thoughts for*

High School Boys by Ron Klug.

I have written *Happy Moments with God* and *Let's Talk About God*, devotionals for families with young children, which have sold consistently for several years. The first book has been translated into Spanish and German, and the second into Norwegian.

The Authentic Bible Story

Though the Bible tells its own stories best, its language is often difficult for young children to understand. That's why retold Bible stories written in easy-to-understand language are so popular. They prepare children for reading and studying the Bible at a later date.

A few examples:

Egermeir's Bible Story Book
Taylor's Bible Story Book
My Good Shepherd Bible Story Book
Stories About Jesus, the Friend of Children

Bible-Based Books

Basic Bible facts are kept intact in this type of book. Editors may agree to the inclusion of characters not mentioned in the Bible, however. Often a fictional character becomes the person through whom the facts of the Bible are revealed in story form. Other editors allow the inclusion of fictional events that are not recorded but may have happened to Bible characters. I treasure my copy of Dorothy Clark Wilson's book *The Gifts* (now out of print). In this book the author dramatizes events that occurred when Jesus was a child. She imagines how Jesus, who believed the wise men's gifts belonged to him, disposed of them as he felt he should—to persons with specific needs. Authenticity is inherent in the gifts, in Jesus' compassionate nature, and in the customs and culture of the people who lived in Nazareth. Wilson allows Jesus to be a child, though a perceptive one—who frequently forgot to follow the precise, confining traditions of his people.

Seasonal Books

An appealing authentic Bible book, *The Story of Christmas for Children*, was written by Catharine Brandt. She does not stray from the original text in her delightful account of the birth of Jesus.

Marion Chapman Gremmel's *The Cat Knew the Meaning of Christmas* is the story of a cat who believed Jesus should be placed in the same manger where she placed her kittens. The seasonal instruction book *My Christmas ABC Book* by Ron and Lyn Klug is also worthy of attention.

Activity Books

How-to books and activity books tell and show how to make or do something. The *Make and Tell* series published by Harold Shaw Publishers and intended for home use are good examples of this type of writing. Other books may be prepared for children's use in Sunday school or vacation Bible school. You will find similar books advertised in book catalogs of several publishing firms.

Having assessed children's books according to subject matter, we turn now to books categorized according to age levels.

Preschool Picture Books

Though these books may be treasured by all children, they are written primarily for preschool children. Their success depends as much upon illustrations as upon text. Often more space is allotted to illustrations than to text.

The picture book has twenty-eight to thirty-six pages, including front, title page, copyright page, etc. Some are done in full-color, others combine color with black and white. In most instances the author and the artist receive an equal share of a book's royalties. Be aware, however, that publishers discourage the submission of art work with the text. They prefer hiring their own illustrators from a stable of artists whose work they rely upon.

Though picture books usually tell stories that entertain, they may describe adventure, instruct, or lead to a decision or understanding of some concept.

A *House of Her Own* by Beatrice de Rengier helps children understand everyone needs a place for privacy. In reading *The Little Engine That Could* children learn it pays to be persistent when confronted by a difficult task.

Kindergarten and Primary Books 5–7

Books for this age group are usually about 64 pages. Utilizing fewer pictures than preschool books, they can be read to children who usually progress to the point where they can read them themselves. An example is *The Christian Family Bedtime Reading Book*, compiled by Ron and Lyn Klug—a collection of stories written by many authors.

Books in this category are similar to preschool books, though instruction and concept are usually more advanced. Preschool children will no doubt be able to enjoy the *Concept* books published by Concordia Publishing House. However, kindergarten and primary children may get the most out of them. The series includes: *If You Should Live, If You Should Die, You and Me* (on friendship), and *God Loved a Muddle* (on creation).

A picture book that is destined to instruct as well as entertain kindergarten and primary children, as well as preschool youngsters, is *Pillar of Pepper and Other Nursery Rhymes* written by John Knapp II and illustrated by Dianne Turner Deckert. The book's humorous verse has a lilting, delightful cadence children are bound to enjoy.

About the writing of this book, author John Knapp II says:

I really care about what goes into books for the children. A child's book should be much more than a "good lesson" set off by daubs of color. Life's best lessons are usually not labelled as such. With born-again creativity we must go beyond "whipping up" stories and poems that merely make a statement of faith.

I come to children's literature as a father, Sunday school teacher, former elementary and secondary school teacher, and, lastly, as an associate professor of English at a state university.

My adult experience convinced me of the power of Mother Goose as a language builder for children who collect and recall a great deal more of what they hear than what they read.

Surprised at how few Bible facts children retain, I wondered if I could stuff bits and pieces of Biblical information into the spry skin of children's rhyme and if I could do so without making a fool of myself.

A *Pillar of Pepper* echoes the rhythm and meter of Mother Goose without appropriating traditional content. Though I let myself become adventurous with vocabulary, not a child has batted an eye over any of the words.

I wrote and recited my verse to my wife, my children, and my colleagues. Then I revised again and again, completing 75 of the 85 poems in fifteen months.

Intermediate Books 8–10

These are usually 10,000–18,000 words and we could call them middler books. Children are at a transitory, often stormy, questioning period at this age. Because they dislike being preached to, lively, exciting novels appeal to them most. Ethelyn Parkinson's *Brookfield School* series, which features a lively, fun-loving gang of boys in various adventures, has enjoyed a ready market.

The structure of novels for this age group and for older children needs to have the same elements as an adult novel, though they are, obviously, not as involved. Characters should be well delineated. Books should provide suspense and deal with relevant subjects. A few good examples are *Street Boy* by Fletch Brown and *Treasure of Squaw Mountain* by Marjorie Zimmerman.

The Incredible Journey by Sheila Burnford has not lost its appeal. A good book to read to young children, it can be enjoyed by all ages. It is the story of the trek of three animals, a Siamese cat, an aged bull terrier, and a Labrador retriever, as they make their way through 250 miles of Canadian wilderness to the family who owns them.

Juvenile Books 11–13

Books for this age group are usually 18,000–25,000 words. Youngsters in this preteen age have many of the characteristics of the intermediate group. Girls for the most part are more sophisticated, and boys are more willing to put up with girls. Romance begins to raise its head. Yet, these youngsters are questioning and pondering the world around them. They enjoy sports, science fiction, and mystery books, among other things.

In this category are the *Danny Orliss* series by Bernard Palmer and the *Sarah* series by Margaret Epp.

Some eleven- to thirteen-year-old children, especially those interested in science fiction, enjoy *A Wrinkle in Time*, *A Wind at the Door*, and *A Swiftly Tilting Planet* by Madeleine L'Engle. A young friend of mine read the *Chronicles of Narnia* by C. S. Lewis three times by the time he was eleven.

For some time publishers have preached the need to present realism in books. The problem, however, is the manner in which it is presented. Good morals are as realistic as bad morals. I wouldn't want any child to read some of the so-called realistic books about death. On the other hand, I recommend *Bridge to Terabithia* by Katherine Paterson without hesitation. *Never Miss a Sunset* by Jeanette Gilge dramatizes realistically pioneer life through the viewpoint of the oldest daughter of Wisconsin homesteaders. In this book the author utilizes a thread of guilt to maintain suspense.

We have reason to lament some of the explicit handling of sex in some teen and preteen secular books. We can be grateful, however, that religious publishers are able to present a Christian viewpoint of these subjects. *Heather's Choice* by Carol Gift Page handles premarital sex with dignity. Of the writing of this warm, skillfully fleshed-out, and realistic book, Page says:

To avoid bombarding my young readers with a dreary adult lecture, I selected the novel format with fictional characters confronting problems teens face today. Before writing a word, I read a dozen teen books, talked with my daughter to sense "where she was coming from." I also scanned newspaper and magazine articles on teenage pregnancy, abortion, and teen fads and trends. The more I read the more I became convinced of the need for a book that would reach young people before they began forming their dating standards.

More important than the message was that my book be captivating. A good story. Otherwise, who would read it? In creating Heather, my main character, I borrowed the vulnerability I felt at age 12, the spunkiness of my younger sister, and the easy comradery of my brother. Desiring to capture the wistfulness and timeless magic of Thornton Wilder's *Our Town*, I involved my characters in a school production of the popular play.

Young Heather emulates the heroine Emily. In subtle ways the events of *Our Town* parallel the incidents in Heather's life, symbolizing the pathos and fragility of young love. The plotline traces Heather's quixotic, sometimes joyous, sometimes problematic journey into adolescence. As her world expands to embrace grownup feelings and problems, including her teenage sister's unwanted pregnancy, Heather comes to realize the importance of making right choices—for her life.

Teens 14–17

Books for this age group can run 25,000–40,000 words. Idealistic, more mature physically and perceptively than preteens, youth in this age group consider themselves only a step away from adulthood. They may become impatient and demand options not meant for them—a car, unlimited freedom, etc. This is the time of deepening friendships, both with others of the same sex and those of the opposite sex. Busy in school and extracurricular activities, they sometimes have little time to read. Nevertheless, an attractive, exciting book will catch their interest.

These young people enjoy romances, biographies, detective and mystery stories, science fiction, sports. . . . They resent being written down to and can begin to appreciate books written for adults.

Realism? Yes, if written from a Christian viewpoint.

Another sensitive book about premarital sex, though shorter and more casual in style than *Heather's Choice*, is *Just Like Ice Cream* by Lissa Halls Johnson. Here the book's central character experiences the trials and heartache of having an unwanted child and giving it up for adoption.

In referring to the preteen and teen categories, I've stressed fiction above other types of writing. Do realize, however, that nonfiction may be written for this age group too.

Writing for children, whatever their age or type of book, demands as much dedication, knowledge of writing techniques, creativity, and understanding of current and timeless needs as any other type of writing. The market is there. It's up to us to satisfy it.

CHALLENGE ASSIGNMENT

1. Visit your public library. Examine *The Book Finder*, volumes 1 and 2. Make a list of the needs and problems described, and then make a list of the published books listed that deal with these needs and problems.

2. Check out and read several of the children's books that interest you.

3. Visit Christian bookstores. Ask which books are most popular.

4. Choose the type of book you wish to write. Determine age level. Then research, write, and send a book proposal to an editor you believe might be interested.

9

Drama

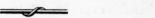

31. Writing Church Plays

Persons who write short stories or novels are better qualified to write drama than persons who write nonfiction. They are accustomed to dramatizing life in scenes. They've learned how effectively dialogue characterizes, imparts information, conveys emotion, and heightens conflict. When a play's theme is chosen, characters must be developed who can act out and prove the validity of the theme.

Fully developed, realistic characters will more or less dictate how and what they say. Dialogue in drama is brief, purposeful—it does not ramble. Each word serves a specific purpose. Most dramatists believe that dialogue is the most important ingredient of a play. It speaks the language of the audience. When the curtain goes up, two or more actors are on stage. They must speak. The play is on! One playwright claims dialogue is to the dramatist what paint is to the artist, clay to the sculptor.

Drama is alive and immediate. Where the novel may encompass a lifetime or an entire era, drama presents relationships and action at the moment. A novel or short story is meant to be read, pondered, and possibly reread, but a play is meant to be experienced.

Drama magic depends upon immediate identification and response. What happens in a play is not so much the message that is conveyed to the viewer, as how he or she reacts to it. Drama is more than a manipulative tool. One writer says it is a "corrective lens" that enables members of the audience to see themselves not as they would like to be, but as they are. Drama by itself does not change people. It exposes. But, as with the gospel message, the individual involved must respond in some manner to the message. That is why drama is a legitimate activity of the church.

The trend has been set. Rarely has there been such a demand among churches for plays that carry a message, as well as entertain. Such plays may involve families, young people or children. Others are directed to men, to the aged, to women, or any special group.

Several years ago Baker House Books published some one-act plays for young people by Daniel Seagren. The intent was to spark audience discussion.

Some similar one-act plays that revolve around the Christian family were prepared by Vivian H. Randle for an annual meeting of the National Council of American Baptist Women. When published, they included a number of possible discussion questions for each play.

One of Randle's plays dealt with a family whose father had just received a job offer from a large distillery. Wonderful! This would place him in a much higher income bracket. After his wife, daughter, and son had oohed and aahed about all the things they would be able to afford, the father suggested he would be able to give a great deal more to projects contemplated by their church.

Yet, there was a certain amount of hesitation. After a rather extended pro and con discussion, the family is forced to consider the moral implications of such a move.

Drama for the church may involve Biblical subjects, missionary work, historical events, character portrayals, etc. Alberta Hawse has written a great many Biblical plays. Many of them, like her Biblically based short stories, involved characters that may have been present at Biblical events.

One Sunday a ten-year-old, handicapped boy confronted Mrs. Hawse with the question: "Why don't you write a play about a handicapped boy, so I can be in it?"

"That's a good idea," Hawse answered. "I'll do that. On several occasions God used handicapped people in Bible times to honor Him."

In Midst of Violence, performed by her church drama group, placed the boy in a family torn by conflict between Christianity and paganism at the time the apostle Paul preached in Ephesus.

Mrs. Hawse's proficiency is reflected in the comment made by one of the actors: "Bertie writes plays so that the dialogue is as easy to say as 'pass the butter.'"

When I asked Mrs. Hawse about the marketing of her plays, she said, "I never try to place a play until it has been tested in a performance in my own or some other church. It's when one sees a play in action that the 'bugs' show up.

"When I'm satisfied I've worked out all of the problems I type and mail my manuscript to a publisher."

Though some churches include a stage in their building plans, many do not. Churches may make use of a portable stage or convert the sanctuary platform into a stage when a play is performed. Space enough for a living room setting that can be converted into other settings is adequate for most church plays that include five or six actors. Props should be kept at a minimum.

The one-act play customarily has three or more dramatic scenes. The number of scenes in longer plays usually vary.

A one-act Christmas play, *Dust in the Road*, by Kenneth Spencer Goodman, has been produced thousands of times over a period of years. Its dramatic conflict involves the spirit of Judas Iscariot, returned to life in the form of a tramp, who tries to persuade a man not to betray a friend.

The play utilizes five scenes for the resolution of its conflict.

Introductory statement:

Long ago Peter Steele and his wife, Prudence, were asked by a soldier friend to hold three thousand dollars in trust until the man's son reached maturity. In the meantime, Peter, a thrifty, church vestryman, invested the money to the extent it increased considerably. Tomorrow, Christmas Day, it is meant to be repaid. Having become very greedy, Peter and his wife wonder why they should give the money back. Only one person, a dependent uncle who lives with them, knows about the money. The boy doesn't know. There is no public record to give them away.

Scene 1: On Christmas Eve Prudence turns a shabby, lame beggar away from their door in spite of her uncle's protests and his reminder that he knows about the money. They argue and she rebukes him soundly.

Scene 2: Immediately a tramp appears. Terrified, Prudence at first mistakes him for a thief. The tramp calms her fears, and then shows her 30 pieces of silver stained with blood and tells her he is a friend of the beggar. When Peter is heard approaching the house the tramp disappears.

Scene 3: Peter returns from a vestry meeting at the church troubled about the money he owes his friend's son, but determined to keep it. Hysterically Prudence tells him about the tramp's visit. He scolds her for dreaming, then makes her promise she won't go back on her promise to stand by his decision to keep the money. He tells her to go to bed.

Scene 4: The tramp reappears, this time to Peter. Angry, Peter tries to force him out of the house. The tramp resists and a fight ensues, which the tramp wins. Now Peter believes he is a traveling preacher bent on interfering. The tramp reveals himself as the spirit of Judas, one who knows all the details regarding the money and Peter's betrayal of his friend. He warns Peter about the dire results of such action and leaves.

Scene 5: Unable to sleep because of a troubled conscience, Prudence returns to find Peter in a repentant mood. Both confess their guilt and find peace of mind and soul. They resolve to pay the boy the full amount. The play ends with Peter leaving the house in search of the beggar whom he and Prudence have decided to ask to join them for Christmas morning breakfast.

Note that only one room is needed for this play and that characters are limited to five.

Play writing involves more than characters and setting. One must know how to present the play professionally—where to place action, dialogue and directions in the manuscript.

Customarily a play will begin by describing the setting and the names and descriptions of the person or persons on stage when the curtain rises. This information is set off by parentheses.

You may use either of two formats. Names of the actors speaking, dialogue, directions, and music fade-ins and fade-outs may be placed so they begin at the left-hand margin or, as is most common in America, placed in the center of the page.

The best way to learn proper format is to study published plays. They can be obtained from Christian education leaders, libraries, bookstores, or firms that publish them. A few you might write to are: Friendship Press, New York, NY; Standard Publishing House, Cincinnati, OH; Moody Press, Chicago, IL; The Christian Education Press, Philadelphia, PA; Samuel French, Inc., New York, NY; Baker House Books, Grand Rapids, MI.

If you attempt writing plays you will need to synchronize time with action and dialogue. Determine how long it takes to walk across a room—a few seconds, perhaps. That's all. To change clothing—seven minutes. Be aware that these minutes must be filled by dialogue.

When you believe your play is ready to be mailed to a publisher—don't. Do as Alberta Hawse did—test it in a live performance. You may direct it yourself or ask someone who understands directing to do so. Having someone else direct enables you to see mistakes more easily.

Many churches have drama groups where one of the members handles directing. Others assume responsibilities for scenery, advertising, programs. etc. Whoever directs the play should, when distributing it to the cast, show a ground plan of the setting and explain the general movement and grouping, and describe the timing, tempo, and rhythm of the play.

One author suggests there be at least sixty hours of rehearsal for a long play, fifteen hours for a one-act play.

When you feel confident you have worked all of the bugs out of the play, then type it properly and mail it to your publisher.

CHALLENGE ASSIGNMENT

1. Locate several plays similar to the type you wish to write.
2. Study their form.
3. Try to determine length of time needed for each scene.
4. Write a play of your own.
5. Seek out a group who will be willing to give it a trial run.
6. When you have rewritten and feel satisfied with the play, mail it to a firm that publishes religious plays.

10

The Business End of Writing

32. Rights and Privileges

There are rights about which writers have little to say. Yet in personal contact with editors we shouldn't be afraid to bring up the subject of hoped-for rights.

Basic Courtesies

1. *Reasonably prompt consideration of manuscripts.* If a manuscripts isn't returned within two to six weeks, write a tactful letter to the editor asking if it has been received.

2. *Reason for rejection.* Editors don't have time to enter into long discussions about the merits of a piece of writing. We may hope, however, that they will make some comment when returning the manuscript.

Some editors include a sheet on which they have checked one of many reasons for rejection: too late for consideration—does not conform to doctrinal beliefs—not slanted to age level—not documented well enough—trite—we have covered this idea recently—good material, try someone else—too long—too verbose.

3. *Careful handling.* There are times when a manuscript comes back badly mutilated. I especially dislike having a manuscript returned with its pages stapled or clipped together. A writer has a right to tell an editor this is being done in his or her office.

I once had pictures returned without their cardboard protectors. Now I always enclose the cardboard protector in the return envelope where it isn't likely to be misplaced.

4. *Assignment for reprint rights.* Most secular publications buy only "first American serial rights" and release to the author

reprint rights after publication. With the new copyright law in effect, religious publications will adopt this policy. I believe a good manuscript should have as wide a distribution as possible.

5. *Some notification of needs.* A few editors send their regular writers a list of monthly themes they will be considering during a given year. As a beginning writer you have the right to ask for these lists.

OK OF MANUSCRIPT CHANGES

The right to see major changes in a manuscript before it is published, though often disregarded, does in fact belong to the author. The editor has the prerogative to ask for any changes he or she feels are necessary and may wish to make them in the office. Some editors simply go ahead and do it, possibly feeling that an author's changes might not be satisfactory.

I like to make my own revisions or to see the editor's revision if it involves a great deal of change. Many editors grant this right. Once an editor wrote me saying he would like to use a shortened version of a personality article I had sent him. Since time was at a premium, he included his version for me to check. Pleased with what he had done, I approved the alteration.

If an editor lets you know that he or she plans to make major changes you *do have a right* to ask to see them before the manuscript goes to press. As in most business relations, the value of this right to you may influence the degree and tone of your insistence on it—a matter of integrity to authors. A quiet, courteous assertion of it, within reasonable limits, can be helpful to all.

Established Rights

COPYRIGHT

Copyright is a form of protection provided by the United States government to authors of original literary, dramatic, musical, artistic, and other creative works.

The Copyright Act of January 1, 1978, the first revision since 1906, made important changes in copyright procedures. Of chief importance is the copyright protection that takes effect the moment a work is fixed in tangible form. For an author this means a piece of writing belongs to him or her the moment it is written. Only the owner or those deriving rights *granted by the author* can rightly claim copyright.

Section 106 of the Copyright Act generally grants exclusive rights to the copyright holder to:

1. To reproduce the copyrighted work in phonograph records.
2. To prepare works derived from the copyrighted work.
3. To distribute copies, or phonograph records, of the copyrighted work to the public for sale, or other transfer of ownership, or by lending, rental, or lease.
4. To perform the copyrighted material (literary, musical, dramatic, choreographic, pantomime, motion picture or any other audio-visual material).
5. To display the copyrighted work publicly.

There are exceptions, however. Titles, ideas, procedures, processes, concepts, systems, methods of approach, and discoveries not yet complete cannot be copyrighted.

Because the copyright of any submission to a periodical or any other collective work is vested with the author, publishers can no longer say, "We automatically buy all rights to submissions."

For a work-for-hire, however, the employer, and not the author, may claim copyright. A work-for-hire (in the publishing field) is a manuscript prepared by an employee within the scope of his or her employment, or a work especially ordered or commissioned for use as a contribution to a collective work—such as a motion picture, a compilation, an instructional text, an encyclopedia, or an atlas—*if* both parties agree and sign a written contract indicating the work is considered a work-for-hire.

One author dubs work-for-hire, "work for ire."

The American Society of Journalists and Authors (ASJA) came up with a statement that, when boiled down, says the use of works-for-hire and all-right transferences as a condition of sale is unethical and writers should not sign such agreements. One ASJA member says, "Under the new law the federal government recognizes that you own the copyright to your manuscript as soon as you write the work. By attaching the copyright notice to the manuscript you are announcing that you own the piece. You are demonstrating that you understand the new law and that you take it seriously."[1]

A compromise, of sorts, is often reached with periodical submissions. Because the procedure to contract for each periodical submission has proved costly to publishing firms, many now accept one-use right to submissions, thus acknowledging the author's ownership of copyright.

Increasingly, professional writers urge authors to be firm in insisting they retain the copyright to their work.

Because the advantages and disadvantages vary greatly in any matter dealing with rights it is very important to discuss the matter thoroughly with any potential publisher.

When a work is published a notice of copyright must be placed on all distributed copies. Example: © *year, your name.*

Though a copyright notice need not appear on an unpublished manuscript (nor is it necessary that an unpublished manuscript be copyrighted) it is wise to affix such a notice prior to submission. It can be placed in the upper left-hand corner of the first page, with the author's name, address, and social security number, or at the bottom of the first page.

There are times when it is to the author's advantage to register copyright of his or her work. Registration establishes a public record of the copyright, and it is needed in most infringement suits. If registration is made within three months after publication of the work, or prior to an infringement of the work, statutory damages and any attorney's fees will be available to the copyright owner in court actions. Otherwise, only an award of actual damages and profits will be paid.

If you choose to register your work, an application can be obtained from the Register of Copyrights, Copyright Office, Washington, D.C. 20559. They will eventually require, along with the completed application form, a $10 fee for each application and two copies of the published work.

Registration can be made at any time during the life of the copyright. When an unpublished copyright is registered it is not necessary to make another registration when the work is published, although the author may do so if desired.

Prior to the new Copyright Act of January 1, 1978, work was protected for 28 years, plus an additional 28-year renewal period. Today a copyright protects a work for the life of the author plus an additional 50 years after the author's death. In the case of works-for-hire, or anonymous works, protection remains in effect 75 years after publication or 100 years from year of creation, whichever expires first. Works that were created prior to January 1, 1978, were automatically brought under the statute and given federal protection in the same manner as new works—life plus 50 years.

Further information about copyrights may be secured from the U.S. Copyright Office, or from periodicals that have published comprehensive articles relative to the copyright law. Check the *Reader's Guide to Periodical Literature* for such information.

PERMISSIONS AGREEMENT

In preparing a manuscript, periodical or book, you may quote a reasonable amount from another work under what is called "fair use." Although the number of words has not been specified, according to *The Chicago Manual of Style* "fair use" means use of a quote that will in no way diminish the influence or value of the source. The proportion of the quote to the original work, along with the purpose of the use and the nature of the work, is more important than actual length.

Ordinarily authors must write for permission to use poetry or musical compositions. Churches and individuals are often guilty of using material of this type without first asking permission to do so. Normally a publisher grants the use of songs and choruses for duplicated song sheets if a credit line is affixed to them.

If at any time you question what constitutes fair use, write the permission editor (at the firm that published the original work) and ask if you may use the material you wish to quote. Indicate exact portion as explained in the following agreement form, which you may modify and duplicate for use in various situations. Send two copies so that one may be retained for the publisher's files and one used for your reply.

Dear Permission Editor:

I am working on (type of work), which has been assigned by (or which I contemplate marketing with) (publishing firm).

May I have permission to quote the following material from (title of work) by (author)? I have enclosed a copy of the material I would like to use.

I am enclosing a duplicate of this letter and a stamped self-addressed envelope for the convenience of your reply.

BOOK CONTRACTS

Ordinarily a book publisher sends an author a contract when the manuscript (partial or complete) has been approved by consultants, editors, and sales personnel.

Read the contract carefully before you sign it. Be sure you understand what it says. If you have questions ask your editor to explain them, or seek the counsel of someone who understands book contracts. Realize that this is the time to indicate in whose name the copyright will appear and what changes should be made in the terms of the contract.

Note the section where the publisher asks for the first option on your next book. Some authors feel this is a pretentious request. I do not, especially if you are a beginning writer. Be aware, however, that asking to look at a second book doesn't guarantee its acceptance. It may be a book the publisher doesn't want to handle or they may have a similar manuscript under consideration. If, all things considered, you do not feel that the option clause is to your advantage, ask to have it deleted. Make sure the contract spells out specifically the amount of royalty agreed upon. And note the section about subsidiary rights.

In some instances publishers offer an advance on royalties. This means you receive a specific amount of money when the contract is consummated. Do realize, however, that this sum will be deducted from your royalty earnings. As a rule, the purpose of an advance on royalties is to provide income while working on a project and waiting for the book to be published.

PERIODICAL CONTRACTS

If you are asked to give up all rights to a manuscript, you will be required to date and sign some type of contract to that effect. Remember, you have an option—you are not obligated to sell all rights. Such contracts will vary from one periodical to another. Some will be complicated, others very simple. Be certain you understand the intent of the agreement.

AS-TOLD-TO AGREEMENT

After you have established a name for yourself in the publishing field you may be asked to write someone else's book, be it a how-to, a personal experience, an autobiography, or the history of an organization.

After you have evaluated costs involved, research, and writing time, and come to a specific agreement with the person or organization for whom or about whom you are writing, you should document the agreement in writing. Cover all areas you feel might be challenged. An example:

I, _____ , agree to write (and research, if required)
   (author)

_____ for _____ who will supply me with
(type of writing)   (subject)

any necessary information within _____ .
                                  (time limit)

It is agreed that neither party will make any commitment regarding the publication or marketing of the manuscript without first consulting the other.

It is also agreed that _____ will appear un-
                        (type of writing or title)

der the byline _____ as told to (or with) _____ .
                 (subject)   (name of author)

I, _____ , agree to pay a fee of _____
   (subject)   (sum of money)

to _____ and to agree to a contract for a 50/50 royalty
   (author)

arrangement.

Date _____   Signature _____
                                            (subject)

                             Signature _____
                                            (author)

Most organizations pay a specific sum of money to have a book written about their history or work. A portion may be paid at the commencement of the writing; the rest on the completion of the project.

I strongly advise mini-contracts when you, the author, work with a nonwriter. Many authors who failed to take this precaution have suffered embarrassment, stress and, in many instances, have been subject to unfair assumptions regarding the work.

Some publishers insist a book (usually one involving a celebrity) be published with only the subject's name appearing on the cover. I, for one, feel such a procedure short-changes the author and I question the ethics of such arrangements.

Customarily, if you write a periodical article for or about someone, it is understood that you, the author, receive total payment for the piece.

CHALLENGE ASSIGNMENT

1. Write to the Copyright Office, Washington, D.C., 20559, for further information on the Copyright Act. Circular R–1 can be very helpful.

2. Ask a published book author if you may examine one of his or her book contracts to learn for yourself what it included.

3. Before you write an as-told-to book, ask persons who have been involved in such arrangements about their experiences.

33. Equipment, Files, and Records

As a freelance writer you should consider your work a business. You are the business—the president, office manager, secretary, accountant, research specialist, and mailroom processor.

In fulfilling these roles you will need an office. It may be nothing more than a corner of your dining room or den. As business expands, however, you will require more space and a variety of equipment—an adequate desk with at least one drawer file large enough to hold manuscript-size folders, a chair, a tape recorder, a typewriter, and additional files and storage shelves. If you watch advertisements you may be able to locate second-hand equipment at a greatly reduced price. Check the equipment thoroughly, however, to learn if it is in good condition or can be reconditioned at little cost.

Typewriters

You may be able to get along without some of the equipment listed above, but you won't be able to operate without a typewriter. Though some writers may find manual typewriters serve them well, increasingly the majority have turned to electric models. I purchased my IBM Selectric II from a legal secretary who, after buying all sorts of equipment so she could do freelance office work in her home, decided to return to her former job. The typewriter had been used only six months. I was fortunate. Many second-hand typewriters may have had the life beaten out of them in typing classes or by extensive office use.

Manufacturers, we find, are continually upgrading typewriters. From manual models they moved to electric, then to correcting typewriters on which you need only backspace to the error and strike a correction key.

Today we are confronted with electronic typewriters, often called "smart typewriters," still further advanced in operating skills. Costing $1200 to $1600, the simpler models provide such features as one-line memory systems for the correcting, automatic centering, and underscoring of copy. More advanced models, ranging in price from $1600 to $2500, allow for storage of paragraphs and phrases that can be recalled when needed. With such a machine it is possible to type a letter and recall it again and again in multiple copies.

The very sophisticated electronic typewriters can store up to 100 pages. Often called memory typewriters, they center, underline, return the carriage, and insert paper automatically. Some models are built with a one-line viewing screen.

The Word Processor

A mystery to many of us, word processors can make authors and editors drool. They are actually typewriter-computers. With their exceptionally high electronic IQ, they will in time revolutionize writing and editing. Some publishing firms have begun editing manuscripts on them. A few years ago we would have considered word processors science-fiction gadgets. Now, as we become more familiar with them, we have to accept them as wonderful tools and marvel at their capabilities.

WHAT A WORD PROCESSOR CAN DO FOR A WRITER

It allows you to:

a. Store a form letter in one section of the computer memory with names and addresses in another section.
b. Merge this information and type individual letters to each name that has been programmed. A great help in submitting multiple queries.
c. Prepare and maintain a computer file of books and magazine articles you wish to retain.
d. Research by phone hookup with other computers, "data bases" that research and stockpile information they can provide in a

matter of minutes.

Word processors are most utilitarian when it comes to the actual writing of a manuscript. They make corrections electronically—without correction tapes or fluids. You do not need to strike a button for a carriage return. The word processor handles that chore. The computer provides automatic centering, tabulates and positions material in columns, automatically hyphenates, and numbers manuscript pages.

Some word processors are able to use a "vocabulary program" that compares words of the text with a dictionary stored in the program and highlights on the screen any misspelled words.

This program also provides room for special-word dictionaries needed in scientific, medical or legal writing.

MECHANICAL APPARATUS

Primarily a text-editing machine, the word processor utilizes

a. A *display station*—the television-like screen that allows an operator to view documents.

b. A *keyboard*—like any standard typewriter keyboard, though it has additional keys.

c. *Diskettes*—floppy disks of magnetic material protected by a square paper jacket similar to one used to protect a 45 stereo record.

d. *Hard disks*—larger, more substantial magnetic disks with far greater storage capabilities than the floppy diskettes.

e. *Diskette drives*—that read and update information on the diskettes. Two disk drives allow an operator to transfer information from one diskette to the other or from the diskette to the printer.

f. A *pitch element*—that, when inserted into the printer, determines the size of the type. This daisy-wheel element is made of plastic or metal with radiating spokes tipped with embossed characters.

g. A *printer device*—that types the finished product onto paper.

SELECTION OF A WORD PROCESSOR

I knew very little about word processors when I was asked to include information about them in this book. I began my research by reading magazine articles and books that described them. I attended a word processing workshop. I studied manufacturers' brochures. Before long I discovered I had learned a new language—computer jargon. I now know that CRT refers to *Cathode Ray Tube* (or Terminal); I also know that RAM means *Random Access Memory* and that the greater the RAM the greater the computer's ability to handle complex problems.

In investigating the value of a word processor to writers I also asked for demonstrations—not from clerks in electronic stores, but from company-trained technicians and from persons who use the computer on a daily basis.

Though I am now convinced that the word processor is the best tool invented for writers, I'm also well aware that it cannot, obviously, on its own, produce well-written, marketable books, articles, or short stories. If I write poorly the computer will display and print out poor copy. Content excellence is my responsibility, not the computer's.

If you are planning to purchase a word processor, learn all you can about it. Ask for demonstrations so you can compare a variety of models. Ask salespeople and persons who own them about purchase, upkeep price, lease and rental agreements.

I am indebted to Lyndee Riley-Black, IBM systems engineer, for supplying additional questions you should ask manufacturer's representatives:

1. How recently was the product manufactured?
2. Is equipment tax credit passed on to purchaser?
3. Are all hardware components from the same vendor?
4. Can you provide a list of satisfied customers?
5. Are instruction and training provided?
6. Does history prove the product has good trade-in value?
7. Is a variety of software (programs) available?
8. Is software available from several vendors?
9. Does software carry a warranty?
10. Will updates be available when needed?
11. Are claims documented in writing?
12. Is marketing support available locally?
13. Are systems engineers available locally?

14. Are service and repair components locally available?
15. Is the service (parts, labor, travel) contract complete?

One author, Robin Perry, justifies his purchase of a word processor by comparing it to the purchase of a truck by an electrician or a plumber. In a *Writer's Digest* article he spoke of the volume of writing he had done in a ten-year period. "Enough," he said, "to warrant a word processor purchase even when prices were higher...."[1] If the volume of writing and your financial status justify such a purchase, chances are good your "business" will be enhanced greatly.

Records and Files

I doubt any writer has developed a foolproof filing and record-keeping system. Some use a $3'' \times 5''$ card arrangement. One file holds manuscript cards, each of which records a single manuscript's history: date submitted to an editor, rejections, editor's comments, date of sale, and amount of payment. Another file holds cards filed in special sections, divided according to age group: adult, youth, and children. On each card is recorded the name of a specific publisher or publication, its address, name of editor, type of material used, rights purchased, taboos, special interests.

When a manuscript is sent to a publisher, you, the writer, pull the manuscript card and the market card, clip them together, and put them in the OUT section of a third file, the circulation file.

When a manuscript sells, a notation of this fact is made on both cards, and they are returned to their original file locations. If the manuscript is rejected, a notation of this fact is made on both cards. Hold the manuscript card, but return the market card to its original file location. Now pick another market card, with name and address of the publisher or publication you intend to send it to next. Clip this to the manuscript card with its rejection notation. File them in the OUT section of your circulation file.

One writer who uses this system claims it works very well for her. No doubt this is because she writes more or less as a hobby.

Where a greater manuscript volume is involved I prefer the method which utilizes

1. A DAY-BY-DAY RECORD

For this I use a standard $5'' \times 8''$ ledger. The daily record appears on facing pages, and each month may use up one or more such pairs of pages (since some entries fill several lines).

The record of outgoing manuscripts is listed on the left-hand page, the OUT page. Here I record the date I mailed the manuscript, the title, the publisher or publication to which it was sent, and word count.

If a manuscript is returned I draw a line through that particular submission. Then when I send it out again I enter the title and relevant information on the OUT page on the date it was resubmitted. Some writers also record on the OUT page expenses connected with each submission. I prefer listing all tax-deductible expenses in a separate notebook.

On the IN page, opposite, I record manuscript sales, to whom sold, date of payment, amount of payment.

2. ACTIVE CARBON FILES

I also write the OUT and IN ledger record of a manuscript's status on the back of the carbon copy, which is placed in an OUT folder of a regular drawer file. Manuscripts returned go into an IN folder in the same file. This folder holds carbon copies of manuscripts I can submit to another publisher. Just as I draw a line through the ledger's submission record when manuscripts are returned, I draw a line through the entry on the back of the carbon to indicate its rejection. When a rejected manuscript is placed in the mail again, I record this date on the carbon below the information I crossed out when it was returned.

3. PAST-SUBMISSION RECORD

a. All past-submission carbons (i.e., of work no longer in the market) are numbered and filed in empty typing-paper boxes labeled SHORT STORY, PERSONALITY, NARRATIVE, DE-VOTIONAL, REPORTORIAL-EXPLANATORY, HOW-TO,

PROBLEM SOLUTION, PUZZLES AND QUIZZES, MIS-CELLANEOUS. Carbons are filed in the order in which they were written, so that the 1, 2, 3s are at the bottom of the box and the most recent manuscripts at the top.

b. Past-submission titles, with their proper numbers, are recorded on separate alphabetically arranged pages of a loose-leaf notebook, with a page for each title. Indexed sections of this notebook are labeled to correspond to the box categories. This cross-reference record facilitates the location of a given manuscript carbon.

I make entries in the manuscript notebook once a year, at the end of the year. This is not as tedious a task as it may seem, for I merely transfer information I have previously recorded in my day-by-day ledger.

Should an editor ask to use a manuscript he or she has seen published elsewhere, I can locate the carbon quickly by referring to its number listed in the manuscript notebook.

4. PROJECT IDEA FILE

There are few writers who do not have a backlog of clippings on subjects in which they are vitally interested and about which they plan to write someday. Some merely toss all clippings into a project idea box. The more meticulous writer files these clippings in folders under specific categories which, depending on interest, might include

archeology	Holy Spirit
Bible	narcotics
Christians in government	the occult
divorce	personalities
ecology	smoking
holidays	Women's Lib

5. PROOF-TEXT FILE

Because I frequently speak and teach as well as write, I also maintain a proof-text file. Material which I garner from my reading, from speeches, from conversations—whatever—is typed or pasted on 3″ × 5″ cards under a wide variety of subject headings.

When I find something for which I don't have a card division, I stop and make one. These are all filed in regular 3″ × 5″ card files.

6. TAX-DEDUCTIBLE EXPENSE RECORD

You should understand precisely which writing expenses are tax-deductible. If in doubt, check with the Internal Revenue Service in your area. Keep all receipts and checks to verify expenditures. List daily cash outlay in some kind of a notebook.

Deductible expenses include:

books and magazines
carbon paper and carbon tapes
cassette tapes
envelopes
office equipment (desk, typewriter, files, tape recorders, which
    must be depreciated over a period of years)
office space rental fee
postage
professional fees
research fees
safety deposit box rental fee
stationery
telephone expense connected with writing
travel expenses (travel, lodging, parking fees connected with
    writing assignments or research)
typing fees
Xerox copy expense

All this attention to detail may sound terribly complicated. Yet it is necessary, and once you get into the habit of keeping up-to-date records you'll find your job as a freelance writer greatly simplified. For one thing, you'll never have the experience I had before I began to keep accurate records. Upon opening a letter accompanying a rejected manuscript, I read: "I thought this sounded familiar. It wasn't until I began to edit it that I realized we published this article a year ago."

CHALLENGE ASSIGNMENT

Set up the kind of record and file system you feel best suits you.

11

The Challenge

34.   Now Write

"Swoosh!"

Like an avalanche, the daily mail cascades through the letter slot onto the floor. I stoop to retrieve it. How many mailing lists am I on, anyway? I sputter as I begin to separate the wheat from the chaff.

Much of the mail *is* chaff even though my name, in one form or another, appears on the envelope, in the salutation, and at intervals throughout many of the letters.

Knowing that computer-programmed machines feed thousands of names from deviously obtained mailing lists into prechosen slots, I am not impressed. A letter isn't personal just because it is addressed to me and contains pertinent facts about me, the recipient, the reader of the letter. A letter is personal only when the author proves he is genuinely concerned about me.

This is true of all types of writing. To project the personal concern you wish to convey to your reader, you, the writer, will have to put yourself into your writing. It's then and only then that you communicate adequately. Communication, someone has said, is causing to happen in someone's life what is extremely important to you.

And how do you accomplish this feat? By making sure that something important has happened to you. Writing that does not convey faith, hope, and love may be called chaff. Certainly it is not wheat that nourishes another's soul.

It's in this discrimination that we discover the Christian writer's imperative—an imperative which suggests some very important challenge objectives.

1. *Always do your best.* Excellence ought to be the norm, not the exception, for the Christian writer. I once heard a speaker claim that one well-known author "never wrote anything she would be ashamed to show God."

Such quality writing demands dedication and hard work. It is not true, as some beginning writers believe, that you must have pull—that you need to know an editor personally to achieve publication. An editor doesn't accept a manuscript on the basis of friendship. If a story or article is unsuitable no editor will publish it.

Doing your best requires that you practice perseverance. You don't sit down at your typewriter and wait for the right mood or inspiration to seize you before you begin to write. After proper planning and research, you prayerfully tackle the task at hand and complete it as well and as promptly as possible.

Excellence also demands that you write regularly. Set aside a slot of time and a specific place where you can write every weekday with no time off for leisurely cups of coffee, telephone chats, or shopping tours. Inform your family and friends that the time you set aside for writing is inviolate. You are not to be disturbed. Then write even if the only time you can spare is an hour in the morning before you leave for work or an hour after you arrive home at night.

Doing your best also implies that you constantly set higher goals for yourself. These goals should approximate those of the professional. In a sense you are like a pole-vaulter. No doubt you have studied some, practiced some, and attained commendable success. Your next step is to raise your standard a notch higher. Then don't just stand there and look at it. With all the energy you can muster, throw yourself up and over it. Immediately go on to higher goals—new techniques, more competitive markets, more challenging subjects. What you hope to achieve is what you will achieve. Your writing is worth exactly what you are willing to put into it.

2. *Be willing to accept criticism.* A good coach praises excellence, but he also points our flaws and criticizes craftsmanship.

He insists on an athlete's rectifying, through practice, the weaknesses he needs to overcome.

Every writer needs a good coach, someone more knowledgeable than he, someone who has earned the right to criticize another's work. Such persons are hard to come by. A good teacher may serve in this capacity. So may a writer who has earned his publishing salt. Remember, however, that writers are busy people. Nevertheless, there are a few authors who recall their own early struggles and will, for a fee, take a look at your writing. I would caution you to be particularly wary of persons who advertise this service. Rather seek the help of a qualified critic you or some other writer know personally. Above all, don't rely on your family and friends for reliable criticism. Most likely you wear a writing halo as far as they are concerned. Or possibly they think too little of your efforts.

If and when you do find a good critic, treat him with care. Listen to what he says. If he tears your work apart, realize he isn't tearing you apart. He's trying to help you blaze a trail marked *writing skill*.

One man who sought my help didn't understand this. In a letter requesting my assistance he outlined the following terms. "I have an article that I wrote, I am a little rusty on punctuation so I need your services. I wouldn't want one word changed, left out, or some other words added. I want it just like I wrote it. If you are interested please let me hear from you, what you would charge for a fee, if you charge one."

3. *Extend your field of influence.* We live in a nation where the government protects an author's right to speak about his faith. Yet we restrict ourselves by our narrow understanding of what it means to obey God's command to go and tell. We sit back and criticize newspapers, secular magazines, and college tabloids because they are filled with evil propaganda: immorality, the occult, oriental fads, radical philosophies of all kinds. Yet we do little to train for and seek positions where the Christian viewpoint could be presented to people segregated from its influence.

A group of Christian college students asked a well-known journalist to speak to their organization. During a give-and-take question-and-answer period the students spoke of the staggering amount of filth in college publications. The speaker asked for a show of hands identifying members of the group who had written to counteract this influence, persons who had written boldly of *their* faith. Not a single hand was raised. Then the man challenged, "Why don't *you* study journalism? Why don't *you* learn to write with such excellence that *you* can convincingly present the faith *you* believe through any media you choose?"

John McCandlish Phillips, the *New York Times* reporter and feature writer, often speaks to this issue. At the twenty-third convention of the Evangelical Press Association he said, "The mass media which have daily access to the public consciousness are not something wisely to be left entirely in the hands of unbelievers. Why do we not have in America some major newspapers and magazines owned and operated and chiefly edited by believers?" (Here Mr. Phillips speaks from an evangelical Christian stance. On the other hand, the *Christian Science Monitor*, owned, operated, and chiefly edited by persons of that faith, is a newspaper of such excellence it ranks with the best.)

Commenting on the desperate longing of believers in communist countries to share their faith through writing, Mr. Phillips added, "We do have that freedom, with nothing to stop us but the limits we have allowed to be put upon us. The result is that our freedom is no more effective than their bondage. The only difference: They cannot. We do not. Either way, the devil has it his way."

One means by which we can extend our outreach is by writing for the secular market articles about Christians respected in their fields. Readers, impressed by such a person's accomplishments, will accept without criticism information supplied regarding his faith.

In a piece titled "Not by Bread Alone," which appeared in *tic*, a national dental magazine, I asked my subject about his involvement in the church. He detailed activities, adding, "To be a well-rounded person, I believe a man must enjoy a personal relationship with God." The statement appeared intact in the printed article.

In sharing your faith avoid the sledge-hammer approach. I've said this before; I say it again. A well-written article or short story should resemble a cake or a particular type of bread where the flavor permeates the whole.

Speaking of this spiritual flavor which should be evidenced in writing, one author claims that God shows up in her writing whether she plans for him or not.

4. *Strive for creativity.* Train yourself to react creatively to life around you. A child speaks of bumper-to-bumper clouds. How do you describe them? When you hear thunder do you imagine, as one child did, that the sky is clearing its throat? Be a child again—experience life as he does.

Be inquisitive. Hunt for the story behind the story. Read between the lines. Try to discover motives for your character's actions. If you aren't able to come up with a solution to a problem, turn it over to your subconscious mind. In time, if you are patient, the solution will be handed back to you.

Be courageous. Dare to experiment with techniques you have learned.

Don't procrastinate. A creative person feels compelled to record a creative idea the moment it becomes a reality to him. Keep paper and pen on your bedside table. Indulge in creative writing sessions, too. Comment on the social implications of the children's poem, "Humpty, Dumpty," for instance. Write your interpretation of your pastor's Sunday morning sermon text. Explain how we can effectively help the person who faces death.

5. *Be alert to the fringe benefits writing provides.* Knowing that one has reached and touched the hearts of desperate, lonely, frightened, despondent individuals is a writer's greatest reward. Listen to the following testimonials from people whose lives have been affected by what they read. The first is from a Japanese friend, professor of literature in a university in Japan —a man who translated one of my books into Japanese.

I want you to know the chapter, "An Odd Way to Get Even," of the book you sent me changed my life.[1] I've been miserable. I've tried to convince myself that to forget means to stifle, to hide a grudge, but you taught me that to forgive meant to forget. Thank you.

For years I struggled with an unstable faith, desperately hungry for the assurance that God was real and that he loved me [a young businessman confided]. Then I read Sherwood E. Wirt's book, *Not Me, God*.[2]

Not me? The book was about me. Reading it was like having someone take my hand and hearing him say, "Come, let me show you the way."

A sixteen-year-old intellectual who scoffed at the church and all it stood for was introduced to Harold Myra's book, *No Man in Eden*,[3] by a friend. In a letter to the author she described what the book had done for her.

No Man in Eden brought me to Christ. I read it on a dare. In spite of myself, something clicked. I came to the same realization that Christ was the Son of God that David did in your book.

The whole thing is so revolutionary, so awe-inspiring, I can only say *thank you* to God and to you for writing the book.

"Thank you for writing about the death of your eighteen-year-old son," a woman wrote to Joseph Bayly after she had read his book, *Psalms of My Life*. "It's good to find someone who understands. Your poems are a great comfort to me."

A soldier in Vietnam read an article of mine about a businessman who gives half his income to the Lord. The man's faith and commitment prompted this response: "The article came when I was experiencing a spiritual low. It kept me from sin which would have ruined my life. It led me to a new commitment to Christ."

Many young people have written to authors saying that a particular article, short story, or book has made them consider a pastoral or missionary career. Adults say that writers have inspired them to support worthy institutions and organizations because their needs and merit were presented in an honest, carefully documented article.

That's what I mean by fringe benefits. There are others: meaningful friendships with editors and writers; invitations to speak to college journalism classes and at writers' conferences; intellectual and spiritual growth.

All of which should cause us to approach our task, not merely as an occupation or a craft we have learned, but also as a "calling" from God. For writing is a personal stewardship of aptitudes and training—a glad, ready response to God's claim on our lives.

Appendix

Age Characteristics That Determine Problems About Which to Write*

1. *Pre-school, 3–5:* Active, restless, curious; love repetition and rhthym; evidence great imagination (imaginary friends); like to touch, taste, smell, look, and listen; have brief attention span; no sense of ownership; are parent-dependent.
2. *Primary, 6–9:* Active, restless, inquisitive, imaginative; easily moved to tears; like ritual; may fear the dark, cats, and dogs; are somewhat selfish; tease younger children; rivalry is strong; enjoy new experiences—school and corporate play.
3. *Junior, 9–12:* Active, restless, inquisitive (want facts); are imaginative; tend toward hero worship; not interested in sex (boys as a rule can't stand girls); are interested in other boys, especially their peers; love adventure; gang spirit takes over.
4. *Young teens, 12–15:* Boys don't mature as fast as girls; some may grow more rapidly; are awkward (voices change); begin to mature sexually (sex shyness and curiosity replaces repulsion); strive for independence; age of truancy; choose buddies and special friends; can be very emotional; age when most decisions for Christ are made; begin to feel pressures of a relaxed moral stance; begin to be aware of career choice.
5. *Older teens, 15–18:* Idealistic; critical of establishment: parents school, and church; this is the period of budding romance; social consciousness aroused (want to belong); can't stand being different; physical height achieved; are more graceful; live in the future; extremely unselfish; crave honors and awards; feel pressures of prevalent moral lapse; think more seriously of career choice; may be more deeply involved in school activities (school paper, choirs, sports, and band); may have part-time jobs.

*Note: age groups overlap chiefly because problems of the various ages overlap (there can be no strict cut-off).

6. *Young people, 18–25:* Physical maturity is reached; health usually good; are idealistic but becoming more practical; college years; work; permanent friendships are being established; parental ties are broken; religion rational rather than emotional; face courtship and marriage experiences; worry about vocation; look for meaning and purpose in life.

7. *Adults, 25–45:* These are the years of prime physical health; these people establish stable social patterns; home becomes more important; children are reared; success is sought; grave danger of losing religious zeal; here strong will is evident; reading interest heightened; attendance at lectures and concerts; habits become fixed; friendships are sifted. These are the productive years.

8. *Middlers, 45–65:* Strength may begin to decline; increasing incidence of cancer, heart disease, and arthritis; changes in weight occur; judgment is usually reliable; mind at its best; reading is continued; occasionally become slaves to old habits, resent change; conversion less likely; occasional moral lapse; may be discouraged because of unfulfilled life goals; children leave home; concerned about retirement.

9. *Oldsters, 65–:* Begin to loose muscle control; experience fatigue and/or memory lapse; may become childish and irritable; some live largely in the past; find it hard to adjust to new environments; fear being crowded out (family, church, business); face loss of spouse and friends; face reduced income; may dislike the seeming "youth worship" in our society; can't cope with leisure time.

There's another side to the coin, however. Free from former responsibilities these people may enjoy new hobbies, travel, and educational opportunities. Many do volunteer work—often connected with their less fortunate peers. Mobile-home living in vogue for some. Some adapt nicely to new retirement environments. Many continue working past 65.

Notes*

Chapter 1. On Your Mark

1. Pamela Frankau, *Pen to Paper* (Garden City, N.Y.: Doubleday & Co., 1962), pp. 194, 196.

2. William H. Gentz and Elaine Wright Colvin, *The Religious Writer's Marketplace* (Philadelphia: Running Press, 1980).

Chapter 2. Finders, Keepers

1. Lawrence E. Nelson, "Acres of Articles," in Browne, Benjamin P., ed. and comp., *Techniques of Christian Writing* (Philadelphia: The Judson Press, 1960), pp. 99–105.

2. Margaret J. Anderson, "If Senility Strikes," *Together*, February 1965.

3. Elizabeth Yates, *Rainbow Round the World* (New York: Bobbs-Merrill Co., 1954).

Chapter 3. Sales Incentive

1. John M. Allen, "Writing for Reader's Digest," *The Writer*, November 1972.

Chapter 5. Disciplines of Style

1. "Kris and the Birthday Cake," *Sunday Digest,* May 10, 1964.

2. "Public Servant, Agent for Christ," *Covenant Youth Today,* October 12, 1962.

3. "Genetic Control of Life," *Power for Living*, November 9, 1969.

4. "Right On with Billy Graham, *The EVANGEL*, August 26, 1973.

5. "Toppled Plans," *Hi Call*, October 1, 1971.

Chapter 6. Writer Interaction

1. Lajos Egri, *The Art of Dramatic Writing* (New York: Simon and Schuster, 1960).

*All material without author credit is by Margaret J. Anderson.

Chapter 7. Bits and Pieces

1. "Up-to-Date; Down-to-Earth," *It's Your Business, Teenager* (Chicago: Moody Press, 1960), pp. 31–34

2. Ibid.

3. "The Love Chapter Revised," *Christian Herald*, 1961.

4. "Like the Body of Christ," *Covenant Youth Today*, February 22, 1959.

Chapter 8. The Devotional Meditation

1. "Torch Relay," *War Cry*, September 26, 1964.

2. "United We Serve," *Gospel Messenger*, February 10, 1962.

3. "Antagonism Toward Jesus," *The Quiet Hour*, January 13, 1969.

4. "The Friend of Sinners," *The Quiet Hour*, January 14, 1969.

5. "Jimmy Hit Me," *Happy Moments with God* (Minneapolis: Bethany Fellowship Press, 1962), pp. 48–49.

Chapter 9. Poetry, Light Verse, and Greeting Cards

1. Joseph Bayly, "A Psalm on the death of an 18-year-old son," *Psalms of My Life* (Wheaton, Ill.: Tyndale House Publishers, 1969), pp. 39–40.

2. Helga Skogsbergh, "The Home-going," *Songs of Pilgrimage* (Chicago: Covenant Press, 1962), p. 3.

3. Charles A. Waugaman, "Give Me a Drum," *Decision*, December, 1967, p. 2.

4. Ruth Cox Anderson, "Puddles," *Story Friend*, June 10, 1973, p. 4.

5. Edith Lovejoy Pierce, "The Wall," *Arrows to the Sun* (published by author), p. 29.

6. "My Legacy," *Covenant Companion*, May 9, 1958, p. 3.

7. Joan Truitt, "The Prodigal's Father," *Presbyterian Life*, August 15, 1962, p. 9.

8. Lois Leurgans, "Haiku," *On the Line*, June 3, 1973, p. 1.

9. Morris Anderson, "Film Take," *Decision*, February 1971, p. 2.

10. Judson Jerome, "*POETRY*, How and Why," *Writer's Digest*, May 1972, p. 10.

11. Sharon Harris, "My Son," *Rainbow Ministries* (Fresno, CA: Fresno Bible House).

Chapter 11. Groundwork

1. "They Buried the Cigarette Habit," *The EVANGEL*, February 21, 1971.

2. "Annie Vallotton: Shorthand Artist," *Church Herald*, December 11, 1970.

3. "Someone Who Cares," *Good Housekeeping*, September 1969.

Chapter 12. Article Segments

1. Daily Meditation, *Covenant Home Altar* (Chicago: Covenant Press), September 16, 1959.

2. Ibid., August 23, 1965.

3. "No Bias," *Today*, October 17, 1971.

4. "Young Minneapolis Artist Projecting the Christian Faith," *Minneapolis Tribune, Sunday Feature Magazine*, December 25, 1966.

5. "It Really Takes Years," *Christmas, An American Annual of Christmas Literature*, vol. 27 (Minneapolis: Augsburg Publishing House, 1957), pp. 35–37.

6. "A Salute to Uncle Sam," *Sunday Digest*, June 28, 1970.

7. "Teenagers!" *Teenways*, December 10, 1962.

8. "Everything's Different Now," *Vista*, February 4, 1973.

9. "Practice What You'd Reach," *Teens Today*, February 6, 1966.

10. "Her Year of Grace," *The EVANGEL*, June 6, 1972.

11. Clarence D. Anderson, "The Shirt Off Our Back," *War Cry*, July 5, 1969.

12. "Not By Bread Alone," *tic*, January 1958.

13. "Is Your Latchstring Out?" *Contact*, March 9, 1969.

14. "You Can Do It," *The EVANGEL*, June 2, 1957.

15. "Someone Who Cares," *Good Housekeeping*, September 1969.

16. "He'd Ban the Can," *Power for Living*, April 16, 1972.

17. "When Dedication Lives," *Young Soldier*, September 18, 1971.

18. "Genetic Control of Life," *Power for Living*, November 9, 1969.

19. "Lasting Gifts," *Minnesota Farmer*, September 1965.

20. "Mr. Turlock," *Sunday Digest*, August 20, 1972.

21. "The Voice of the Arctic," *Moody Monthly*, December 1963.

22. "There's Potential in Those Years," *Eternity*, February 1972.

23. "They Buried the Cigarette Habit," *The EVANGEL*, February 21, 1971.

24. "Genetic Control of Life," *Power for Living*, November 9, 1969.

25. "There's Potential in Those Years," *Eternity*, February 1972.

26. "Young Minneapolis Artist Projecting the Christian Faith," *Minneapolis Tribune, Sunday Feature Magazine*, December 25, 1966.

27. "It Really Takes Years," *Christmas*, pp. 35–37.

Chapter 14. The Reportorial-Explanatory Article

1. Walter S. Campbell, *Writing Non-Ficton* (Boston: The Writer Inc., 1944), p. 49.

2. "The Voice of the Arctic," *Moody Monthly*, December 1963.

Chapter 15. The Narrative Article

1. Bernard Palmer, "My Son, My Son," *Christian Life*, March 1968.

2. "If Senility Strikes," *Together*, February 1965.

Chapter 16. The Personality Sketch

1. "Not By Bread Alone," *tic*, January 1958.

2. "Her Life a Ladder," *Covenant Youth Today*, May 13, 1962.

Chapter 17. The Problem-Solution Article

1. Carl T. Rowan and Daniel M. Mazie, "Let's Fight the Bad-Driver Menace," *Reader's Digest*, October 1971.

2. William Schulz, "California Cleans Up Its Welfare Mess," *Reader's Digest*, August 1973.

3. "There's Potential in Those Years," *Eternity*, February 1972.

4. "Bringing Time to Terms," *Covenant Youth Today*, September 27, 1959.

Chapter 18. The How-to Article

1. "Candle Lights Without Fire," *Christian Life*, December 1951.

Chapter 19. Article Variations

1. "Right On with Billy Graham," *The EVANGEL*, August 26, 1973.

2. Jerry Engh, "Sailing on Ice," *Teen Time*, January 5, 1969.

3. "Fun with a New Telephone," *Hand in Hand*, May 1963.

Chapter 21. Writing to Teach

1. Robert Meyers, "Pleasures and Pitfalls of a Lesson Writer," *Interlit*, 1974.

2. Wesley Tracy, "Outlines for Success in the Religious Market," *Writer's Digest*, 1981.

Chapter 22. Brochures and Newsletters

1. Ed Elsner, "How to Design Pictorially," *Interlit*, September 1982.

Chapter 24. The Fiction Triad

1. Barbara Rhode, "Long Live the Lion," *Redbook*, June 1970.

2. Viña Delmar, "Devil to Pay," *Good Housekeeping*, February 1962.

3. Flannery O'Connor, "The Lame Shall Enter First,," in her *Everything That Rises Must Converge* (New York: Noonday Press, 1965), pp. 143–190.

4. M. J. Chute, "Teacher's Pay," *Saturday Evening Post*, May 16, 1959.

5. James Clavell, "The Children's Story," *Ladies Home Journal*, October 1963.

6. Phyllis Reynolds Naylor, "The Stuff of Dreams," *Teen Time*, May 1–May 29 issues, 1966.

7. Ethelyn M. Parkinson, "Edge of the Crowd," *Young People*, © by W. L. Johnson, 1953.

8. Ruth Moose, "The Night Song," *Good Housekeeping*, September 1972.

Chapter 25. Learning from the Experts

1. Walter Campbell, *Professional Writing* (New York: The Macmillan Co., 1938) pp. 121–131.

2. B. J. Chute, *Greenwillow* (New York: E. P. Dutton Co., 1956).

3. Frank A. Clarvoe, "Bait for a Bachelor," *Saturday Evening Post*, March 1, 1958.

4. Harriet Frank, Jr., "Jessamine," *Good Housekeeping*, November 1961.

5. "No Blue Star," *My Sunday Reader*, May 2, 1965.

6. Mary Lange Jones, "A Welcome Tomorrow," *Redbook*, April 1961.

Chapter 26. Writing from Experience

1. "The Reason," *Challenge*, November 14, 1965.

2. "Pup Clergyman," *Sunday Digest*, March 25, 1962.

3. "Shoes are for Walking," *Sunday Digest*, April 2, 1962.

Chapter 28. Nonfiction Books

1. *Looking Ahead, the Realities of Aging: Face Them With Faith*, (St. Louis, Mo: Concordia Publishing House, 1978).

2. *Louise* (Wheaton, Ill: Harold Shaw Publishers, 1978).

Chapter 29. Adult Novels

1. Mary O'Hara, *Novel in the Making* (New York: David McKay, Inc., 1950).

2. Jerry Jenkins, *Margo* (Chicago: Moody Press, 1978).

3. Carol Gift Page, *Kara* (Minneapolis: Bethany House Publishers, 1981).

Chapter 30. Children's Books

1. Patricia McKissak, *Writing to Inspire*, edited by William Gentz, (Cincinnati: Writer's Digest Books, 1981), p. 193.

2. John and Kay Lindskoog, *How to Grow a Reader* (Elgin, Ill: David C. Cook Publishing House, 1978).

3. Gladys Hunt, *Honey in a Child's Heart* (Grand Rapids, Mich.: Zondervan, 1969, 1978).

Chapter 32. Rights and Privileges

1. Norman Schreiber, "The Copyright War," *Writer's Digest*, January 1979, p. 20.

Chapter 33. Equipment, Files, and Records

1. Robin Perry, "A Writer's Guide to Word Processors," *Writer's Digest*, September 1981, p. 23.

Chapter 34. Now Write

1. "An Odd Way to Get Even," in my volume *It's Your Business, Teenager* (Chicago: Moody Press, 1960).

2. Sherwood E. Wirt, *Not Me, God* (New York: Harper & Row, 1966).

3. Harold Myra, *No Man in Eden* (Waco, Tex.: Word Books, 1969).

Bibliography

Armour, Richard. *Light Armour.* New York, Toronto: McGraw-Hill Book Co., 1954.

Bernstein, Theodore M. *The Careful Writer: A Modern Guide to English Usage.* New York: Atheneum, 1965.

Block, Lawrence. *Writing the Novel from Plot to Print.* Cincinnati, Ohio: *Writer's Digest Books,* 1979.

Browne, Benjamin P., ed. and comp. *Christian Journalism Today.* (Addresses delivered at the Christian Writers and Editors Conference, Green Lake, Wis.) Philadelphia: The Judson Press, 1952.

————, ed. and comp. *Techniques of Christian Writing.* Philadelphia: The Judson Press, 1960.

————, ed. and comp. *The Writers' Conference Comes to You.* Philadelphia: The Judson Press, 1956.

Burack, A. S., ed. *The Writer's Handbook.* Boston: The Writer, Inc., 1982.

————, ed. *Writing and Selling Fillers and Short Humor.* Boston: The Writer, Inc., 1963.

Campbell, Walter S. [Stanley Vestal, pseudonym]. *Writing: Advice and Devices.* Garden City: Doubleday & Co., 1950.

————. *Writing Magazine Fiction.* New York: Odyssey Press by arrangement with Doubleday, Doran & Co., 1940.

————. *Writing Non-Fiction.* Boston: The Writer, Inc., 1944.

Curry, Peggy Simpson. *Creating Fiction from Experience.* Boston: The Writer, Inc., 1964.

Dreyer, Sharon Spredman, M. E. *A Guide to Children's Literature: About the Needs and Problems of Youth, Ages 2–15.* Circle Pines, Minnesota: American Guidance Service, 1981.

Egoff, Sheila; Stubs, G. T.; and Ashley, L. F., editors. *Only Connect—Readings in Children's Literature.* Toronto, New York: Oxford University Press, 1929.

Egri, Lajos. *The Art of Dramatic Writing.* New York: Simon & Schuster, 1960.

Elbow, Peters. *Writing with Power*. New York: Oxford University Press, 1981.

Erdman, Laura Grace. *A Time to Write*. New York: Dodd, Mead & Co., 1969.

Evans, Bergen, and Evans, Cornelia. *A Dictionary of Contemporary American Usage*. New York: Random House, 1957.

Fitz-Randolph, Jane. *Writing for the Juvenile and Teenage Market*. New York: Funk & Wagnalls, 1969.

Flesch, Rudolph. *The Art of Readable Writing*. New York: Harper & Brothers, 1949.

Foster-Harris, William. *The Basic Formulas of Fiction*. Norman, Okla.: University of Oklahoma Press, 1944.

Frankau, Pamela. *Pen to Paper*. Garden City: Doubleday & Co., 1962.

Gentz, William, ed. *Writing to Inspire*. Cincinnati, Ohio: Writer's Digest Books, 1981.

Gunning, Robert. *How to Take the Fog out of Writing*. Chicago: Dartnell Corporation, 1964.

———. *The Technique of Clear Writing*. New York: McGraw-Hill Book Co., 1964.

Hamilton, Ann. *How to Revise Your Own Poems*. Boston: The Writer, Inc., 1946.

Jackson, Jacqueline. *Turn Not Pale, Beloved Snail*. Boston: Little, Brown and Company, 1974.

Jacobs, Hayes B. *Writing and Selling Non-Fiction*. Cincinnati: Writer's Digest, 1967.

Kearney, Paul W. *Free-lance Writing for a Living*. New York: David McKay, 1953.

Kilby, Clyde S. *Poetry and Life: An Introduction to Poetry*. New York: Odyssey Press, 1953.

Lewis, Claudia. *Writing for Young Children*. New York: Simon & Schuster, 1954.

McCleary, Dorothy. *Creative Fiction Writing*. Boston: The Writer, Inc., 1947.

MacDougall, Curtis D. *Interpretative Reporting*. New York: The Macmillan Co., 1958.

Meredith, Robert C., and Fitzgerald, John D. *Structuring Your Novel: From Basic Idea to Finished Manuscript*. New York: Barnes and Noble Books.

Meredith, Robert C., and Fitzgerald, John D. *The Professional Story*

Writer and His Art. New York: Thomas Y. Crowell Co., 1963.

Newcomb, Duane. *How to Make Big Money Free-Lance Writing.* West Nyack, N. Y.: Parker Publishing Co., 1970.

Nichols, Sue. *Words on Target.* Richmond, Va.: John Knox Press, 1963.

O'Hara, Mary. *Novel in the Making,* New York: Van Rees Press, 1950.

Perrine, Laurence. *Sound and Sense.* New York: Harcourt, Brace & World, 1969.

———. *Story and Structure.* New York: Harcourt, Brace & World, 1950.

Publicity Handbook. Cincinnati: Sperry and Hutchinson Co., 1965.

Ryken, Leland. *Triumph of Imagination.* Downers Grove, Ill: Intervarsity Press, 1979.

Sayers, Dorothy. *The Mind of the Maker.* New York: Harper & Row Publishers, Inc., 1970.

Scott, Jack Denton. *How to Write and Sell for the Out of Doors.* New York: The Macmillan Co., 1962.

Smith, Helen Reagan. *Basic Story Techniques.* Norman, Okla.: University of Oklahoma Press, 1964.

Stauffer, Donald A. *The Nature of Poetry.* New York: W. W. Norton & Co., 1946.

St. Johns, Adela Rogers. *How to Write a Story and Sell It.* New York: Doubleday & Co., 1956.

Strunk, William, Jr. *The Elements of Style.* (With revisions, introduction, and a new chapter by E. B. White.) New York: The Macmillan Co., 1962.

Taylor, Howard B., and Scher, Jacob. *Copy Reading and News Editing.* Englewood Cliffs, N.J.: Prentice-Hall, 1951.

Untermeyer, Louis. *The Pursuit of Poetry.* New York: Simon & Schuster, 1969.

Wenninger, J. C. "Church Editors' Views on Publicity Release." (A survey conducted by J. C. Wenninger in 1950.) Unpublished.

Whitney, Phyllis A. *Writing Juvenile Fiction.* Boston: The Writer, Inc., 1960.

Wyndham, Lee. *Writing for Children and Teenagers.* Cincinnati: Writer's Digest, 1968.

Zinsser, William. *On Writing Well.* New York: Harper & Row Publishers, Inc., 1976.

Index